ROUTLEDGE LIBRARY EDITIONS: THE ECONOMY OF THE MIDDLE EAST

Volume 1

THE ARAB ECONOMY IN ISRAEL

THE ARAB ECONOMY IN ISRAEL
The Dynamics of a Region's Development

RAJA KHALIDI

LONDON AND NEW YORK

First published in 1988

This edition first published in 2015
by Routledge
2 Park Square, Milton Park, Abingdon, Oxon, OX14 4RN

and by Routledge
711 Third Avenue, New York, NY 10017

Routledge is an imprint of the Taylor & Francis Group, an informa business

© 1988 R.K. Khalidi

All rights reserved. No part of this book may be reprinted or reproduced or utilised in any form or by any electronic, mechanical, or other means, now known or hereafter invented, including photocopying and recording, or in any information storage or retrieval system, without permission in writing from the publishers.

Trademark notice: Product or corporate names may be trademarks or registered trademarks, and are used only for identification and explanation without intent to infringe.

British Library Cataloguing in Publication Data
A catalogue record for this book is available from the British Library

ISBN: 978-1-138-78710-0 (Set)
ISBN: 978-1-138-81188-1 (Volume 1)
Pb ISBN: 978-1-138-81577-3 (Volume 1)

Publisher's Note
The publisher has gone to great lengths to ensure the quality of this reprint but points out that some imperfections in the original copies may be apparent.

Disclaimer
The publisher has made every effort to trace copyright holders and would welcome correspondence from those they have been unable to trace.

THE ARAB ECONOMY IN ISRAEL

THE DYNAMICS OF A REGION'S DEVELOPMENT

RAJA KHALIDI

CROOM HELM
London • Sydney • New York

© 1988 R.K. Khalidi
Croom Helm Ltd, Provident House, Burrell Row,
Beckenham, Kent, BR3 1AT
Croom Helm Australia, 44-50 Waterloo Road,
North Ryde, 2113, New South Wales

British Library Cataloguing in Publication Data
Khalidi, Raja
   The Arab economy in Israel: the dynamics
of a region's development.
   1. Arabs — Israel — Economic conditions
   I. Title
   330.95694′089927   HC415.25
   ISBN 0-7099-1583-7

Published in the USA by
Croom Helm
in association with Methuen, Inc.
29 West 35th Street
New York, NY 10001

Published in Arabic by
Samed Publishing House

Library of Congress Cataloging-in-Publication Data
Khalidi, Raja
   The Arab economy in Israel: the dynamics of a region's development.
   Raja Khalidi.
      p. cm.
   Bibliography: p.
   Includes index.
   ISBN 0-7099-1583-7: £19.95 (est.)
   1. Israel — Economic policy. 2. Palestinian Arabs — Israel —
Economic conditions. 3. Palestinian Arabs — Employment — Israel.
4. Palestinian Arabs — Government policy — Israel. 5. Israel — Ethnic
relations. I. Title.
HC415.25.K53   1988
338.95694 — dc19   87-30089
                                                              CIP

Printed and bound in Great Britain by Mackays of Chatham Ltd, Kent

CONTENTS

LIST OF TABLES
PREFACE
ACKNOWLEDGEMENTS

Introduction
THE PLACE OF THE PALESTINIAN ARABS IN ISRAEL   1

One.
PREVALENT ANALYSES OF THE
ARAB ECONOMY IN ISRAEL.   7
    THE ZIONIST POLITICAL ECONOMY OF
    ARAB MODERNISATION   8
    NON-ZIONIST POLITICAL ECONOMY:
    PROLETARIANISATION, INTERNAL
    COLONIALISM AND CONTROL SYSTEMS   15
    ALTERNATIVE FRAMEWORKS   23

Two.
HISTORY, POLICY, PEOPLE AND SOCIETY:
THE DETERMINANTS OF THE ARAB REGION   30
    THE DUAL ECONOMY OF MANDATORY PALESTINE   31
    THE EVOLUTION OF POLICY SINCE 1948   34
    THE RANGE OF POLICIES, PAST AND PRESENT   41
    REGIONAL DEVELOPMENT POLICY IN ISRAEL   43
    REGIONAL EFFECTS OF
    NATIONAL ECONOMIC ACTIVITY   46
    THE GEO-DEMOGRAPHIC
    FRAMEWORK OF THE ARAB REGION   49
    SOCIAL STRUCTURE IN THE ARAB REGION   56

Three.
AGRICULTURE: A RESERVE
FOR REGIONAL GROWTH   64
    ARAB AGRICULTURE IN ISRAEL:
    THE HISTORICAL LEGACY   65
    FACTORS AND ORGANISATION OF PRODUCTION:
    LAND, THE REGION'S INHERITANCE   72
    WATER AND IRRIGATION, THE REGION'S HANDICAP 76
    CAPITAL, TECHNOLOGY AND REGIONAL ISOLATION   79

LABOUR, THE REGION'S COMPARATIVE ADVANTAGE	84
SHIFTS IN PRODUCTION PATTERNS: THE REGION SURVIVING	91
PRICING, PROCESSING AND MARKETING: REGIONAL FRAGMENTATION	99
REGIONAL AGRICULTURE IN THE NATIONAL ECONOMY: SPECIALISATION AND PRODUCTIVITY DIFFERENTIALS	103

Four.
ARAB LABOUR IN ISRAEL:
THE REGION SUBSERVIENT ... 113
   LOW ARAB PARTICIPATION IN LABOUR FORCE ... 115
   ARAB UNEMPLOYMENT CUSHIONS ISRAELI RECESSION ... 118
   SECTORAL STRUCTURE: AGRICULTURE GIVES WAY TO CONSTRUCTION AND INDUSTRY ... 119
   OCCUPATIONAL RIGIDITIES AND THE DE-SKILLING PROCESS ... 125
   INCOME DISTRIBUTION AND HOUSEHOLD EXPENDITURE ... 133
   ARAB LABOUR MOBILITY: THE REGION'S 'NATIONAL SERVICE' ... 141
   ARAB LABOUR AND THE NATIONAL ECONOMY: A REGIONAL ECONOMIC ANALYSIS ... 146

Five.
ARAB INDUSTRY AND COMMERCE IN ISRAEL:
WORKSHOP ECONOMY AND ENTREPRENEURSHIP ... 155
   THE LEGACY OF THE ARAB WORKSHOP ECONOMY ... 156
   ISRAELI INDUSTRIAL DEVELOPMENT POLICY ... 162
   NATIONAL CAPITAL PENETRATION OF THE REGION ... 166
   INDUSTRIAL STRUCTURE: SCALE, MIX, EMPLOYMENT, LOCATION ... 171
   ARAB INDUSTRIAL AND BUSINESS OUTLOOK AND PRACTICE ... 179
   ARAB FINANCIAL RESOURCES ... 182
   ARAB PRIVATE ENTREPRENEURIAL FORMATION ... 184
   LOCAL AND REGIONAL INSTITUTIONAL INITIATIVE ... 187
   THE NEW ARAB BUSINESS SECTOR IN ISRAEL ... 191

Six.
REGIONAL GROWTH PATTERNS AND THE
FUTURE OF THE ARAB ECONOMY IN ISRAEL ... 200
   DEVELOPMENT, IMPROVEMENT OR STAGNATION OF THE ARAB ECONOMY? ... 200

WHAT ROLE FOR REGIONAL ANALYSIS?	201
ALTERNATIVE DIRECTIONS	203
GROWTH MODELS FOR ARAB REGIONAL DEVELOPMENT	205
HARNESSING ARAB PRIVATE BUSINESS GOALS TO REGIONAL DEVELOPMENT	208
FROM SELF RELIANCE TO PARTICIPATORY DEVELOPMENT	211
PARTICIPATORY DEVELOPMENT IN REGIONAL STRATEGIES	213
COMBINING POLICIES AND MECHANISMS TO BRIDGE THE ARAB/JEWISH DEVELOPMENT GAP IN ISRAEL	215

Appendix 1.
FIELD SURVEY METHODOLOGY   220

Appendix 2.
ARAB LOCALITIES IN ISRAEL, BY DISTRICT, LOCAL
AUTHORITY STATUS AND DEVELOPMENT ZONE   227

REFERENCES   232

INDEX   240

TABLES

2.1	Population in Israel, by District, Sub-District and Population Group, Selected Years	50
2.2	Population in Israel, by Type of Locality and Population Group, Selected Years	51
2.3	Households in Israel, by Size of Household, and Head of Household's Population Group, 1985	53
2.4	Sources of Population Increase in Israel, Selected Years	54
2.5	Population in Israel, by Religion, Selected Years	55
3.1	Input and Output in Agriculture - Selected Data, 1981	84
3.2	Comparative Ratios of Labour Input in Arab and Jewish Agriculture, 1981	91
3.3	Arab and Total Cultivated Area in Israel, by Branch and Selected Crops, Selected Years	96
3.4	Growers and Value Added, Change Indices 1971-81	106
3.5	Value of Arab Agricultural Production in Israel, Selected Crops, Selected Years	107
3.6.	Volume of Arab Agricultural Production in Israel, Selected Crops, Selected Years	108
4.1	Arab Civilian Labour Force Characteristics in Israel,	116
4.2	Arab Employed Persons Aged 25 and Over in Annual Labour Force Who Worked in Israel in 1978 and 1983 By Sector, 4 VI 1983	124
4.3	Employed Arab Labour Force in Israel, by Occupational Characteristics and Status at Work, Selected Years	128
4.4	Arab Employed Persons Aged 25 and Over in Annual Labour Force Who Worked in Israel in 1978 and 1983, By Occupation, 4 VI 1983	132
4.5	Average Annual Net Income Per Urban Employees' Household, By Size of Household, And By Head of Household's Occupation and Years of Schooling, 1982	135
4.6	Households in Israel, By Income Groups, 1982	136
4.7	Index of Gross Annual Money Income Per Urban Employees' Household, Selected Years	136
4.8	Source of Income of Households - 1982	137

4.9	Income, Expenditure and Savings Per Urban Household in Israel, 1979/80	140
4.10	Mix and Share Analysis of Arab Employment in Israel, 1974-84	147
4.11	Location Quotient Analysis of Arab Employment in Israel, 1974-84	149
4.12	Economic Base Analysis of Arab Employment in Israel, 1984	151
5.1	Histadrut Economic Projects in Galilee, Arab and Jewish Sectors, 1982	170
5.2	Features of Industrial Enterprises in Arab Localities in Israel, 1983	173
5.3	Industry in Nazareth and Umm al-Fahm, 1983 and 1984	176

PREFACE

Dr. Rodney Wilson
Pro-Director, Centre for Middle
Eastern and Islamic Studies,
University of Durham

There have been numerous studies of the economies of the West Bank and Gaza in recent years, but the position of the Palestinian Arabs within Israel has been largely neglected by economists. Indeed, some would deny that there is a distinct Arab economy within Israel, or that Israeli Arabs need to be considered separately from other Israelis. Unlike their compatriots on the West Bank or in Gaza, they have Israeli passports and can vote in Israeli elections. They have been living under Israeli rule for almost twice as long as the inhabitants of the occupied territories, and in legal and political terms are not considered to be under "occupation". In these circumstances assimilation into the economy of Israel might be expected, and any differences in economic status should be in the process of being eliminated.

Raja Khalidi demonstrates that despite the linkage between the Israeli Jewish economy and the Arabs living in Israel, economic integration has not occurred. Indeed it is possible to identify a separate Arab economy within Israel, with its own structures and development momentum. There is, of course, much trade and financial interaction with the majority Jewish population, but this has not brought about economic convergence; in many respects, the Jewish economy in Israel is moving further away from the Arab economy.

The major question which of course arises is why economic assimilation has not occurred. Was the major factor Arab resistance, or were the institutions and policies of the state not geared to Arab economic need? The former would be understandable given the situation of the Israeli Arabs. Less excusable is the latter: if the state of Israel really did aim to serve both the interests of the Jewish majority and the Arab minority, rather than merely the former, then more attention should have been paid to the economic aspirations of the Arab population. In practice there was a reluctance to recognise that the Arab minority had separate needs, perhaps because of the fundamental implications perceived for the state itself. Yet the admission of plural needs does not have to be interpreted as a sign of weakness or division. If successive Israeli governments were really serious about bridging the gap between the Jewish and Arab economies, then a prerequisite was recognition of the latter, followed by policies of positive discrimination in the economic sphere.

In terms of economic analysis, a specific framework is clearly needed to assess the progress and identify the constraints which the Arab economy in Israel faces. Raja Khalidi believes regional analysis can provide such a framework. Although the Arab population does not live in a geographically contiguous area, there is sufficient economic interdependence, similarity of structure, and differentiation from the rest of the Israeli economy, that the Arab economy can be considered a separate regional entity. This approach certainly provides useful economic insights and a context in which policies can be formulated.

Methodologically the approach is interesting, as it could also be applied to the economies of minority groups in the West who continue to maintain separate identities. Parallels are often drawn between Israel and South Africa in terms of apartheid economies, but from the point of view of Arabs in Israel, a more useful comparison might be the situation of religious minorities in the United Kingdom. The Muslim populations of English conurbations or the Catholics of Northern Ireland are entitled to full British passports and enjoy comparable political rights to the Arabs in Israel. Yet they wish to maintain a separate social and cultural identity, and are hindered by government policies designed to suit minority interests. Economic advance is difficult, and there is a clear disparity in status between them and the majority population.

Raja Khalidi's study deserves to be brought to the attention of a wide readership and not merely Middle Eastern specialists, or those concerned with Arab-Israeli relations. I have provided academic supervision for the study for three years, and have been impressed by the diligence and thoroughness of both Raja Khalidi and his colleague, Zuhair Sabbagh. Both have been to Durham, Raja Khalidi on many separate occasions, and have been actively involved with the University's Centre for Middle Eastern and Islamic Studies. The approach to the research has been scholarly and objective throughout.

One interesting finding of the study is that although the Arab economy in Israel has suffered greatly as a result of being subject to centralised and inappropriate economic policies, it is those businessmen who have enjoyed some degree of success that have been hindered the most. Entrepreneurship has been inhibited rather than encouraged in spite of the fact that Israel's economic system is often regarded as liberal, and the climate conducive to free enterprise. If Arab entrepreneurs were given freer reign, then there would undoubtedly be spin-off effects for the regional economy. Raja Khalidi is careful, however, to avoid oversimplification of the issues and their policy implications. The main need is for a separate Arab identity to be recognised within Israel, and economic policies designed to ensure that this is taken into account.

ACKNOWLEDGEMENTS

This study is the result of a research project undertaken in 1984 and 1985. In addition to the various statistical and published sources used, information was gathered and cross-checked at field level. The essential field work was made possible thanks to the assistance of Zuhair Sabbagh. His early encouragement and dedication to this research were crucial to its initiation and implementation. His close involvement in the design, elaboration and in supervising field surveying (described in Appendix 1) in difficult circumstances, and his participation in other stages of data collection and analysis were invaluable to the success of the project. It is to him, first and foremost, that my deepest appreciation and gratitude is due.

This work could not have been completed without the advice, help, support and encouragement of many colleagues and friends. Rodney Wilson provided regular and incisive comments at every stage in the process of the research and writing. I was especially fortunate to benefit from the support and valuable comments on earlier drafts offered by Basim Abdelfattah, George Abed, Maher el-Kurd, Khalil Nakhleh and Yusef Sayegh. John Richardson's careful reading of the text was especially helpful in improving its flow and consistency and in providing further insights. Jane Sell spent many hours carefully computerising statistical and qualitative data.

A number of others also offered advice, data and research assistance that was important to the success of this book, including the American Palestine Educational Fund, Hanna Abu Hanna, Hussein Agha, Kate Baillie, the Centre for Middle East and Islamic Studies (Durham), Ibrahim Dakkak, Aziz Hayder, Fatma Hreash, Faisal Husseini, Jaffa Documentation and Media Services, Najwa Makhoul, Muhammed Miari, the Middle East Centre (Oxford), Elfi Pallis, Alex Pollock, Nadim Rouhana, Samed Institution, Selim Tamari, Salem Khalidi, the Welfare Association and Amnon Zichroni.

A special note of thanks is also due to Yoram Ben-Porath and Henry Rosenfeld, of the Hebrew University and University of Haifa respectively, whose early encouragement to 'search out the identity of the Arab economy' helped to provide an important focus for the eventual research. The patience and encouragement shown from the outset by Emtiaz, and others - family, friends and colleagues - helped to ease me through the research and writing of this book. Needless to say, while expressing my gratitude to the above, I alone bear responsibility for this book and the views expressed in it.

Last, and by no means least, I wish to express my special appreciation to two Palestinian Arab scholars in Israel, pioneers of socio-economic research about their people, the late Bakir Abu Kishk and Sami Mar'i of Bir Zeit University and the University of Haifa respectively. I had the privilege of enjoying their friendship and benefitting from their advice and encouragement during early stages of this project. Until their untimely deaths in 1986, they had devoted themselves and their work to the pressing problems and needs of their society. Their warmth, dedication, experience and wisdom will be sorely missed by their family, friends, colleagues and students alike.

**This book is dedicated to the memory of
Bakir Abu Kishk and Sami Mar'i.**

Introduction

THE PLACE OF THE PALESTINIAN ARABS IN ISRAEL

Almost 40 years after falling under Israeli rule, Palestinian Arabs[1] in Israel today occupy a position of increasing influence and strength. Scattered through the Middle East by the wars of 1948 and 1967, Palestinians are now minorities in most states of the region. Since the establishment of the state of Israel in 1948, the fate of those Palestinian Arabs isolated within Israel's borders has attracted growing attention from different quarters. Politically, the community's role in the Israeli-Palestinian conflict has grown appreciably and its unique position within the Jewish state has been the subject of an abundance of sociological, political, geographic and economic studies, especially since the 1970s.

In certain fields, such as education and political status, this research has produced clear and definitive results, and a certain degree of consensus among those working in the area. However the extensive research related to social and economic change and status has been largely inconclusive. Different ideological and methodological approaches have yielded contradictory hypotheses and conclusions and no lasting or comprehensive view of the issues has emerged.

Discussion of the Arab economy in Israel is a case in point. Perspectives have been developed mainly in the context of other disciplines failing to properly deal with the subject itself. Sociologists, anthropologists and political scientists have taken the lead in analysing the economic position of Arabs in Israel from their respective disciplinary standpoints. Attempting to fill this research vacuum with a study of the Arab economy serves first and foremost a worthwhile academic and reference function.

I do not wish to argue for a narrow 'economistic' approach to what is not a clearcut 'economic' issue. I would contend, however, that a comprehensive study of the Arab economy in

The Place of the Palestinian Arabs in Israel

Israel within the terms of the discipline itself should precede analysis of economic issues from other viewpoints. Further, a rigorous economic analysis can provide a fruitful starting point in the process of elaborating a more comprehensive and relevant analysis of the overall position of Arabs in Israel.

This methodological approach is all the more necessary in light of the fact that most existing theoretical (and terminological) characterisations of the Arab economy in Israel are identified with, or effectively support, definite political or ideological interests. Though unavoidable and perhaps desirable in much socio-economic research, it is unacceptable when research becomes more concerned with justifying or proving ideological positions, than with accurately and honestly describing and explaining the issues being investigated.

The significance of the economic development of Arabs in Israel, and the importance of studying the related issues, can be understood to lie within three dimensions: their relevance to other Palestinian communities, especially those under occupation; their role and position within Israel; the wider development context of their experience.

PALESTINIAN ARABS IN ISRAEL AND THE PALESTINIAN PEOPLE

The Palestinian experience in Israel since 1948 bears certain striking similarities to that of Palestinians under occupation in the West Bank and Gaza Strip since 1967. Though legally and politically, this is not a case of military occupation, the processes and effects of domination by Israeli Jewish society, economy and political system of Palestinian Arabs corresponds in these two cases too closely to be disregarded.

The 617,000 Arabs in Israel in 1985 (excluding annexed East Jerusalem and the Golan Heights populations) constituted just under 30 percent of Palestinians living under Israeli rule (calculated from Israel 1986: 45; 49; 683).[2] If we include the 130,000 inhabitants of Arab Jerusalem in the figure for the Arab population in Israel (as Israeli law and official statistics do), the number rises to 749,000, or some 36 percent of the Palestinians still living inside the borders of historic Palestine.

There are a number of obvious themes in the Palestinian experience in Israel which have also characterised the situation in the 1967 occupied territories:
* land expropriation, witnessed especially in the 1950s, but continuing intermittently until today in Arab areas in Israel;
* the associated problems of access to natural resources, notably cultivable land and water, faced by Arabs in Israel;

The Place of the Palestinian Arabs in Israel

* the difficulties of undeveloped Arab industrial potential in reaching levels where it can compete with a highly capitalised and aggressive Jewish industrial sector;
* the intervention in, and acquisition of, external trade markets of the Arab economy by Israeli Jewish private and public sector institutions and the simultaneous exclusion of Arabs from them and from the enjoyment of most of the accruing benefits;
* the utilisation of a large, unskilled, mobile and manual labour force in specific tasks in construction, agriculture and industry;
* the experience of military rule which, though replaced inside Israel in 1966, left a specific imprint on the popular conception of the state's interests *vis a vis* the Arab population.

It is not my purpose here to develop a comparative study, but rather to affirm how, in terms of its size and experience common to other Palestinians, the Arab population in Israel occupies a position of special relevance. In 1983, there were some 4.5 million Palestinians;[3] the Arabs in Israel constituted about 15 percent of that total. The Arab experience in Israel has much to offer the Palestinian people as a whole, because of the important political and 'developmental' lessons acquired through some 35 years of regular contact with the Israeli regime and economy. Equally significant is the relatively recent crystallisation of national sentiment and identity in a community which in the 1960s had been given up as a lost cause by most of their compatriots. They were long referred to as 'Israel's Arabs' even by many of their fellow Palestinians (see, e.g. Lustick 1980: Chapter Seven; Tessler 1980: 13-24; Nakhleh 1980: 3-9).

There are, of course, a number of significant differences between the situation of Palestinians in Israel and that of other Palestinians. Most obvious is that Palestinians in Israel are full citizens of the State of Israel, entitled in principle to all benefits, rights and obligations which derive from that. As shall become clearer below, this is not often the case in practice, since various legal and extra-legal factors mitigate against the equal distribution of resources and opportunities between the Arab and Jewish communities in Israel.

Nonetheless, Palestinians in Israel have access to institutions and legal channels, contacts and work opportunities, and certain overall benefits such as social security, services and Israeli trade union membership not available to the population of the occupied territories. Palestinians' legal status in Israel and the policies pursued by the regime and Zionist institutions have produced a much greater degree of cooperation and identification of interests between certain sections of that community and the state than is the case in the occupied territories. This can result in very different conceptions of individual and community self-interest, desired paths of economic development and the political and legal prerequisites of social and economic change and prosperity.

On the other hand, the West Bank developed economic niches and institutions within the Jordanian and Arab environment between 1948 and 1967, some of which are still operative and relevant. Different historical determinants, resource endowments and regional and social links distinguish the various Palestinian experiences which, at the same time, are mutually relevant. Though study of the Arab experience in Israel demands its own outlook, approach and methods, its relation to the wider Palestinian context should always be borne in mind.

PALESTINIAN ARABS IN ISRAEL AND ISRAELIS

This sector of the Palestinian Arab people also has a significant position and role within Israeli society and its economy. The fact that a growing proportion of the Israeli population is Arab causes a growing demographic, political and economic dilemma for Israeli policy makers. By 1985, 15 percent of Israelis (excluding Jerusalem or 18 percent including Jerusalem) were Palestinian Arab - from Druze, Muslim, Christian, Circassian, Beduin and other ethnic or religious composition (Israel 1986: 26; 45). Certain productive sectors in the national economy, especially construction, but also some agricultural and industrial branches, utilise a relatively high proportion of Arab labour. While this was initially provided from within Israel, this labour now comes primarily from the occupied territories. As well as supplying a mobile labour force, the Arab areas also constitute an important market, consuming a significant portion of domestic output, most of which is produced outside the area. This implies a potential strategic role for this population and for a part of its labour force.

The Arab proportion of the Israeli population rose from 11 percent in 1951 to 15 percent in 1984 - excluding the Palestinian Arab population of annexed Jerusalem *(Ibid)*. This gradual but steady growth poses, in its own terms, serious ideological, political and security problems for the Jewish state. This is well attested to by the regular pronouncements of official or academic concern about the 'Jewishness' of the state, of labour, of land, or of the Galilee. State policy has oscillated over the years between the overriding prerequisites of maintaining the Jewishness of the state and the need to accommodate and integrate the Arab population and exploit its potential 'contribution' to Israeli economic growth.

Consequently, relations between the state and the 'Arab-Israeli' community have yet to stabilise into any defined, institutionalised and consistent pattern. Israeli policy makers are aware of the potential paths that Arab economic development in Israel could follow, especially those which contain any elements of autonomous, 'self-sustained' growth or bargaining power, and their implications. The state does all it can to maintain the initiative in this sphere so as to be best able to influence conditions, even if this means taking steps to bolster development only to forestall and preempt indigenous Arab initiatives.

PALESTINIAN ARABS IN ISRAEL AND DEVELOPMENT
The position of Arabs in Israel has also been examined in the context of its international developmental significance. Attempts have been made apply various methodologies derived from third world experience to this particular case: dualism and unbalanced development; internal colonialism; pluralist democratic models; control system theories; analyses of 'modernisation'. I do not aim to argue whether one or another theory best fits the specific context. Such an exercise in itself does not reveal any wider relevance, nor is it especially necessary in order to best describe the issues and conditions under consideration.

In fact, it might be more useful to first establish whether the position of Arabs in Israel rightly deserves consideration as an issue of 'third world development'. This is especially relevant since Israel cannot itself be considered to be part of the third world, either politically or economically. Specifically, it is of interest to examine if, and how, this particular case of 'development' differs from the norm. While it is not my concern to undertake the comparative study this would require, it is argued below that conventional developmental approaches applied so far have not successfully dealt with the issues. This is perhaps due to the fact that those used are either not strictly speaking methodologies of 'economic development', or that inappropriate economic analyses were adopted.

However, the disparities in development between Israeli Jewish and Arab society indicate the presence of phenomena of relevance and similarity to the wider third world experience, if only in the ways that they vary from each other. Issues of population congestion and urbanisation, artisanal and small-scale industries, traditional agricultural methods and stagnation and labour mobility/migration are all characteristic of the Arab situation in Israel and can be equally discerned elsewhere in the Middle East, as well as in much of Asia, Latin America and Africa. Perhaps where they differ most markedly is in the often close correspondence between specific socio-economic and political or national disparities witnessed in Israel.

In order to establish a wider international relevance of the

Arab situation in Israel, and to fully analyse its dynamics, it becomes necessary to embark on an effort different to those so far attempted. This effort is one that aims at analysing the particular situation being examined while bearing in mind its general developmental context. It is informed by a range of types and sources of information, analysis and polemic, and attempts to elaborate its own methodology on the basis of what has been already established. Indeed, an approach such as this might not have been feasible were it not for the attention paid to various aspects of this subject by diverse academic circles and political forces over the years.

To begin with, this calls for a review and critique of the ideological context in which those established data and analyses have been presented. This leads first and foremost to a 're-elaboration' of methodological and conceptual tools appropriate to our own treatment of the Arab economy. Subsequently, through a process which could be described as 'methodological illustration', it becomes possible to understand that economy as a dynamic and developing entity. It can be seen to be endowed with its own identity and sources of sustenance, yet also characterised by distinct linkages to, and interactions with, the national Israeli economy. This approach involves the adoption and application of tools and concepts of regional economic analysis, both for explanatory and critical purposes. It then becomes possible to perceive potential paths for the future development of an Arab, if not Palestinian Arab, economy in Israel.

NOTES

1. Throughout this book, use of the term 'Arabs in Israel' can be understood to be in reference to 'Palestinian Arabs' in Israel. Notwithstanding the growing 're-identification' of this part of the Palestinian Arab people with a Palestinian national identity and the fact that their 'Israeli national identity' is a contradictory, if not fallacious, concept, use of the term 'Arab' in the present context is stylistically more practical. This usage should not be considered to imply any opinion on the question of the extent of 'Palestinianisation' or 'de-Palestinianisation' of this people.

2. The Israel Central Bureau of Statistics publishes a comprehensive and generally reliable statistical series covering various aspects of the Arab population. For most aggregate data, this is the only statistical source available, but it includes in its figures for 'non-Jews' the Palestinian Arab population of East Jerusalem and the Golan Heights, occupied by Israel in 1967 and subsequently annexed. Legally, administratively and statistically these territories are treated in most respects as part of Israel. Official data used in this book covers East Jerusalem and its Palestinian population unless otherwise mentioned.

3. Extrapolated, at an assumed 3.2 percent annual growth, from figures for 1980 Palestinian population in (UNECWA 1983: 25).

One

PREVALENT ANALYSES OF THE ARAB ECONOMY IN ISRAEL.

There are two main shortcomings evident, either together or individually, in most examinations of the economic conditions of Arabs in Israel undertaken to date. On the one hand, many studies have been premised on, or overtly influenced by, a specific ideological viewpoint - primarily Zionist. As a result the descriptions of conditions (the what), analyses of the dynamics of economic activity (the how), and explanations of the causes of those conditions and dynamics (the why) have been prejudiced. Consequently they have been either partial or incorrect in their description of the issues of Arab economic development. On the other hand, a number of non-economic studies (e.g. political or sociological) have included references to economic issues usually as part of a study about a very different subject. The coverage of economic development in these studies has consequently been only cursory and secondary.[1] Political or ideological influences have also been discernible.

The pattern in both these types of study is to characterise the Arab economic system as part of, and in the same terms as, the political, social or geographic issues being investigated. There does not exist, among the wealth of data and analysis of the Palestinian Arabs in Israel any specific and clear explanation of the nature of their economy as a whole, nor of the dynamics of its relation to the Israeli economy and state. Attempts, sometimes only implicit, to perform this task using tools evolved for and relevant to non-economic issues have only served to further confuse the picture and disseminate or perpetuate misconceptions, distortions and in some cases, straightforward falsehoods.

The most obvious manifestation of this is the adoption, elaboration and misuse of terminology, most of which has little relevance in economic analysis and cannot help much in clarifying the specific economic issues and relations being discussed. It is furthermore often possible to identify and characterise these different approaches by the operative terms used to describe the Arab population, the political and economic system in which they live, and the nature of the development process they experience. I attempt to highlight this terminology in the course of the discussion as a way of distinguishing the different types of analysis.

A main contention, therefore, is that one predominant analytical typology has failed to correctly depict the Arab economic position in Israel primarily because of political/ideological commitments (mostly Zionist), but also due to its disciplinary confusion. The second typology has not succeeded primarily because inappropriate conceptual and disciplinary approaches have been used to try to explain the Arab economy, or aspects of it. These analyses have also been characterised by a high level of ideological preoccupations (largely non- or anti-Zionist). Subject to differing degrees of these two major weaknesses, both the typologies have simply failed to faithfully or coherently analyse and portray the Arab economic position in Israel. Consequently, it becomes necessary to examine these approaches' deficiencies before elaborating a more relevant analysis.

THE ZIONIST POLITICAL ECONOMY OF ARAB MODERNISATION

Early Approaches

The first typology mentioned above has emanated from a number of Israeli economists, sociologists and 'Arabists' active in official and other research institutions. Some of these studies have dealt with specific aspects of Arab economic activity and provide the most comprehensive data available on those subjects. Much of this research is based on field surveys and in-depth analysis of the voluminous official data. One of the earliest of these, and in many ways the most academically rigorous to date, was the pioneering work by Y. Ben Porath on the Arab labour force in Israel (1966). In his book, the author tries to trace the patterns and causes of the high physical mobility of Arab labour while examining in depth its various demographic, sectoral, and occupational characteristics. In the same period, S. Zarhi and A. Achziera produced the first comprehensive study examining, albeit briefly, the overall labour and living conditions, income position, sectoral product and state investment requirements of the Arab economy (1966).

Prevalent Analyses of the Arab Economy in Israel

These two works, which appeared before 1967, stand out among those produced by Israeli scholars in terms of their clarity and honesty. Unlike other Israeli studies, whose main aim appears to be to portray the position of Arabs and the state's role in the best possible light, these authors were as professional as possible (especially for that period). They had no hesitations in accurately portraying important aspects of the Arab economic position in Israel which other, more official, analyses avoided or tried to rationalise. Ben Porath discussed the negative effects on the Arab labour force of physical mobility, insecurity of tenure and the minimal opportunities for skill development. Zarhi and Achziera estimated the relatively low state investment required by the Arab economy to ensure its equal development, as compared to that afforded Jewish infrastructure, agriculture and industry.

However valuable an initial contribution their work might have been in terms of providing sound data and exposing the economic conditions of the Arab population to serious analysis, their work is flawed in two main areas. Firstly, they failed to consistently describe the nature of the relationship between the Arab population and the national political and economic system (the *how*). As with most later studies of this typology, the economic position of the Arab population is analysed as either a 'national minority', or the 'Arab sector'.

It is only in an insufficiently elaborated fashion that Zarhi and Achziera refer to the 'Arab economy'. It is also assumed by these analyses that relations between the minority-sector-economy and the Israeli state and national economy are conducted in an open, democratic and pluralist environment. At the time these authors were writing, during the period of military rule in Arab areas which lasted from 1949 to 1966, this was definitely not the case. Indeed, a wide section of the Arab population in Israel would until today vehemently contest such a characterisation.

These shortcomings arise partially from a failure to employ relevant methodology. Though this is not evident in the above-mentioned work, other Zionist political-economic studies have been undertaken by sociologists, geographers or U.S. trained political scientists. The weaknesses of this approach are equally due to the major fault in this typology's attitude, namely the political and ideological barriers to reaching the root causes of existing conditions and problems (the *why*). This lies in an unwillingness to examine how the prerequisites of development of the Jewish state can, and perhaps must, preclude equal development for the Arab population. Here, the disciplinary confusion takes the form of assumptions concerning the 'relevant and best' development process for the Arab population. Accordingly, this is one of 'modernisation' from socio-economic backwardness and underdevelopment, and 'integration' into national economic and political life.

'Rehovot Theses' of Modernisation and Integration.

It is unfortunate that subsequent studies not only develop these misconceptions, but add little to establishing more relevant and rigorous methodologies for the study of Arab economic conditions in Israel. 'Modernisation' is an emotive and attractive concept to those who consider themselves responsible for the development of the underdeveloped. However, it is not only laden with specific ideological, if not moralistic, overtones, but it is also a fairly useless tool for the analysis of the real pattern and content of economic development. Should modernisation be measured in terms of acquisition of consumer durables, average per capita income, attainment of social welfare benefits, change in technical or professional skill levels, a well organised market system, or the degree of capitalisation and technological application in production?

Whereas different researchers have adopted different parameters, the counterpoising of measurements of traditional and modern, backward and advanced, prosperous and stagnant, remain irrelevant to the real issues of Arab development. Moreover, discussions of such issues often neatly disregard the barriers to real economic growth inherent in the political system of the Jewish state and faced by the Arab economy. Researchers of this school focus upon static, absolute figures or time scale comparisons of such indicators as Arab agricultural output, labour force characteristics, state aid, number of industrial units, consumption of durables, or electrification of villages.

However, the real significance of such figures only comes to light when compared with the same figures nationally, something that most Israeli commentators fail to do. Ben Porath and Zarhi and Achziera did not actively engage in the sort of obfuscation of issues regularly undertaken by official government spokesmen. But a number of Israeli academics who subsequently studied the Arab economy share a heavy responsibility for popularising concepts of innate Arab backwardness, rapid Arab social and economic development in Israel and the benevolent, if not enlightened, role played by the state in that process.

The most sophisticated and best researched examples of this school of thought are the field studies of a number of Arab villages in Israel conducted in the early 1970s by a team of academics from the Rehovot Rural Settlement Centre. The work of this centre of Zionist political economy and some of its publications reveal their approach in their titles: *From Fellah to Farmer: A Study of Change in Arab Villages in Israel* (Arnon and Raviv 1980) and *The Modernisation of Traditional Agricultural Villages in Israel* (Yalan et al. 1972). The former is perhaps the most in-depth investigation that exists of the structure and performance of agriculture in five groups of broadly representative Arab villages in Israel. Despite some strengths, it suffers from the main weaknesses that run through most Israeli work on this subject, and as such deserves special attention.

Using 1971 census of agriculture data, supplemented by sample field surveying carried out in 1973, Y. Arnon and M. Raviv set out to investigate the causes of various significant changes in Arab agriculture. These include the transformation from subsistence to cash and export crop cultivation, the introduction of irrigation and mechanisation, the reduction in farm size and population, increased labour input requirements and changes in social attitudes. The copious presented data on these issues, is used mainly to substantiate the authors' main political argument. Arnon and Raviv hold that the modernisation of traditional ('age-old') Arab farming methods was the result of one essential factor: contact with and integration into the advanced Israeli economic system and enjoyment of the benefits that thus accrued, especially as offered through the state agricultural extension service. The study even postulates a dualistic national development model generated and organised by the modern (Jewish) sector and fuelled by the traditional (Arab) sector (Arnon and Raviv 1980: 208-17). For two other Israeli academics, investigating geographical changes in Arab localities (Bar Gal and Soffer 1981), modernisation is a process that one part of society can embark upon for the benefit of another. These authors describe an industrialised Jewish society which has initiated rapid changes in traditional Arab society, with a "material and cultural diffusion (occurring) from the Jewish to the Arab population" (*Ibid:* 84).

These claims cannot, however, be substantiated simply by reference to sample surveys of farmers' attitudes, even if it appears to them that contact with Israelis motivated their 'modernisation'. It is equally valid to argue that the basic need to subsist and compete in agriculture engendered by the pressure of this confrontation, was as much, if not more responsible than state policy for the adoption of new methods and the 'rationalising' of farm decisions. Though I do not reject the validity of a process of modernisation, by rendering it a major assumption, other phenomena of equal, or greater, impact on Arab society can be obscured or ignored.

Prevalent Analyses of the Arab Economy in Israel

Most of these authors would agree that 'traditional' agricultural methods and serious problems in performance still exist. This is explained away by reference to a vestigial 'peasant mentality', rather than being seen as inherent in the operation of state policy. Why should Israeli development policy be responsible for positive changes and yet not for the residual negative aspects of Arab agriculture? Why the absence of any examination of the relation between the state and the Arab population since 1948 in terms of how policy has failed or has disfavoured growth and development? Only by ignoring these fundamental issues does 'Zionist political economy' (as a quasi-discipline) remain valid. Once these problems are recognised, a less ideologically influenced or committed analysis becomes necessary. Their failure to clearly describe the *how* is compounded by their equally poor analysis of the *why* of Arab economic development (or underdevelopment) in Israel.

Arnon and Raviv correctly point out that the proportion of the Arab population dependent on agriculture fell after 1948 as a result of high rural population growth coupled with a fall in the area of cultivable land (1980: 168-75). However, there is no mention or analysis of the background to these developments, namely the widescale and significant expropriations of Arab cultivable land and the legal and institutional barriers faced by Arabs in pursuance of migration from Arab rural areas to settlement in Jewish urban localities (see, e.g. Jiryis, 1973).[2] The data presented on the introduction of mechanisation and technology in agriculture similarly ignores any comparison with Jewish agriculture (Arnon and Raviv 1980: 162-7). The evidence collected on Arab farmers' 'rationality' in responding to price incentives and cost/profit ratios and the abandonment of farm family self-sufficiency is presented as an achievement of state sponsored modernisation programmes (*Ibid:* 162; 166; 214-15; 222). The authors do not relate this behaviour to the stiff competition with Jewish agriculture and the forced reduction of Arab dependence on agriculture caused by the extensive land expropriations. 'Zionist political economy' assumes that Arab peasants do not enjoy the same 'rationality' as Israelis and other farmers and consequently cannot perceive the threats to their livelihood and means for confronting them.

'Arab-Jewish Sectoral Dualism': The Rise of Neo-Zionist Political Economy.

After any critical reading of this literature, we are left with a body of potentially usable data presented within a biased and essentially incorrect understanding of the relation between the so-called Arab sector and the national (Jewish) economy. The importance of distinguishing between these two aspects of much Israeli scholarship on the subject cannot be over-emphasised. Too many others, not necessarily sharing the same ideological commitments, have adopted the general and simplistic dichotomies associated with this typology (modernisation, traditionalism etc.) without starting to investigate their relevance or accuracy. Given the often sound data and research basis upon which these studies elaborate their particular ideological viewpoint, they maintain a prominent, and on the whole, unchallenged position in their claim to have correctly described the economic experience of Arabs in Israel.

A recent, and more sophisticated, research effort employing elements of this methodology is D. Czamanski and M. Meyer-Brodnitz's study of Arab industrialisation (1984). The authors attempt to guage the potential for industrialisation in Arab rural areas in Israel in light of evidence on the growth of 'Arab entrepreneurship'. They conclude, among other things, that the low incidence of entrepreneurship revealed by their data cannot be explained by a lack of production factors (land, labour, skills, capital) but primarily by weak institutional development *(Ibid:* 37-8). Like other Israeli researchers, they partly ascribe the origins of underdevelopment to the "traditions of Arab society"*(Ibid:* 37). Departing from the orthodoxy of most Zionist political economy, they do, however, take into account "externally imposed barriers" and the existance of a "dual society" *(Ibid)* which influence the prospects of Arab industrialisation.

Yet, though these factors are mentioned, further discussion of their origins and effect is avoided. The authors fail to follow up their observation by explaining the causes and mechanisms involved. They do not propose further study on the matter to supplement allegedly deficient data *(Ibid)*. Without wishing at this point to argue whether these 'external barriers' are major determinants of Arab economic activity, the relevance of the way in which Israeli authors avoid dealing with them cannot be missed. On the other hand, concepts of 'dual society', 'Arab and Jewish sectors' and an 'economy within an economy' are presented without looking at their implications and background. This is an example of the more honest, but ultimately ideologically distorted and methodologically inadequate, type of Zionist political economy. Similarly, claiming that not enough data exists to analyse the relationship between state policy and the 'Jewish sector' and the lack of Arab industrialisation allows these researchers to avoid taking a firm position on issues basic to their task.

If such researchers wish to be taken seriously, even in their own terms, they need to show a greater willingness to spell out the causes for, and implications of, phenonema inadequately described by terms such as 'Arab-Jewish sectoral dualism'. This school of thought has consistently failed to reach conclusions which might deny the legitimacy of the policies and processes they believe they can discern. The lack of disciplinary rigour in analysing the disparate, but large and sufficient, body of data serves to distort the often obvious implications of that data. Both the data and the resultant analysis are thus rendered insufficient and irrelevant to a faithful description of the economic position of Palestinian Arabs in Israel.

I have dwelt on the preceding methodology not in order to engage in a polemic against Zionist political economy. Indeed, I have tried to point out the general research contribution much of it has made over the years, especially in terms of collection and presentation of data. However, in understanding certain weaknesses and failures, it is possible to discern similar shortcomings in the non-Zionist body of research conducted on the same or similar subjects. This, in turn, can help in the elaboration of a different, more disciplined and accurate understanding of the process of Arab economic development in Israel.

Such an elaboration would benefit from the significant body of data available in preceding work, while avoiding the ideologically determined methodologies of much of that research. A basic observation underlying my analysis of the Arab economy is that its most enduring feature is its differential structure and level of development as compared to the rest of the Israeli economy. This is primarily a function of exogenous economic and non-economic forces. I do not give great weight to the play of internal non-economic factors; furthermore, it seems that only because of particular endogenous economic and other characteristics has its survival as a distinctly Arab economy been ensured.

An essential premise of my view of the dynamic of the state-sector (economic) relationship is that it is largely conditioned by effective (as opposed to declared) state policy (as revealed in official attitudes, plans and measures) and Arab perception of that policy. Any departure from the emergent pattern can then be understood as an exception to the rule. Such an approach helps to give greater meaning to some of the existing concepts used to describe the situation, integrate those observations which are relevant into our analysis, reveal others to be unnecessary and subsequently lead to more accurate methods of studying the Arab economy. Its main claim to accuracy would be that it is devoid of specific subjective motivations, ideological or other, and tries as much as anything else to analyse in relevant and flexible economic terms what is an economic issue. Before proceeding to that, it is important to introduce the other main typology of study of the Arab economy in Israel.

NON-ZIONIST POLITICAL ECONOMY: PROLETARIANISATION, INTERNAL COLONIALISM AND CONTROL SYSTEMS

There are four authors whose work on non-economic aspects of Palestinian Arabs in Israel best represents attempts from outside the discipline of economics to critically analyse the position of Arabs in Israel. These studies adopt terms and concepts relevant to their particular disciplines which do not always comfortably extend to the analysis of economic issues (minority, Arab sector, etc). Despite this, and unlike their Zionist political economist counterparts, their assumptions of the relevant development process affecting Arabs in Israel generally affirm that there is no significant development because of the unequal nature of the political and institutional system in Israel.

In their own terms, and given their own particular interests, each present strong and well substantiated arguments that seriously challenge the orthodoxy of Zionist political economy. While none of the studies directly attempt to criticise that doctrine in methodological or disciplinary terms, their own frameworks of analysis of the state-sector relationship implicitly reject modernisation theses. Broadly, these analyses can be identified by the three main arguments they present regarding the nature of the state-sector relation.

Rosenfeld and Makhoul: Social Structure and Proletarianisation

The earliest of these arguments was propounded by an Israeli anthropologist, H. Rosenfeld, in a series of articles about the transformation of traditional Palestinian Arab society (1962; 1964; 1976 and Carmi and Rosenfeld 1974). He focussed on the breakdown of family *(hamula)* ties and the role of Zionism (and the establishment of the state of Israel) in the proletarianisation of the Arab peasantry. His work, though from a liberal Zionist viewpoint, is not primarily determined by his adherence to that ideology and does not suffer the analytical shortcomings found in the previous typology. He departs from the view of the state as benevolent and modernising and defines the state-Arab sector relationship as essentially one of class/national oppression of the Arab minority by the state and its *Ashkenazi* (western) Jewish elite.

Prevalent Analyses of the Arab Economy in Israel

For Rosenfeld, a definite Arab class structure has evolved, dominated by what he terms a "deterritorialised proletariat". It arose through a number of historical processes. These included a Palestinian national movement restricted to the interests of a ruling class, the depressed state of peasants and workers during the mandate, the socialist perspective of the Jewish workers' movement in Palestine, the state-nation ideology and economy that prospered in Israel, the restrictions and confiscations imposed on Arabs on the one hand, and the changes for workers, self-employed and others in occupational status and economic conditions on the other hand. (Rosenfeld 1976: 399).

According to Rosenfeld, two interrelated factors helped to crystallize within this class a "comprehension of the limitations imposed upon their potentials" (*Ibid:* 403). These were an "accumulated growth, self-awareness and sense of security for Israeli Arabs that has come out of the work process" and the contradiction between this growth and the formal legal position of Israeli Arabs on the one hand and discriminatory and divisive state policy on the other (*Ibid:* 402).

His understanding and analysis of the significance of the effects of state policy towards Israeli Arabs and of migration and the "work process" breaks new ground. He makes a forceful argument against Zionist political economists' analysis of 'modernisation through integration' and describes what might be termed as a process of 'modernised underdevelopment through segregation and confrontation'. Moreover, his analysis postulates the existance of a definite Arab national class formation dominated by a dispossessed peasantry, proletariat and middle class. In his attempt to characterise the resultant structure of economic relations within Arab society and between it and the rest of Israel, Rosenfeld states that with the consolidation of the position of the Arab working class, there has emerged a 'village economy'. He cautions, however, that it is underdeveloped and "not a diversified economic unit of interdependent branches, groups or trades..." (*Ibid:* 399). Rosenfeld is ambiguous about the concept of 'village economy'. A few pages before introducing the concept, he affirms that "in fact, however, there is no village economy, since as mentioned, there are essentially villages of workers who live in one place and work in many others, who live among Arabs, work among Jews and who are employed almost entirely by Jews" (*Ibid:* 393).

Rosenfeld's departure from the tradition of Zionist political economy is characterised by his innovative analysis of the national status of Israeli Arabs, the system in which they function, and the mode of development open to them. Objectively, Rosenfeld holds, Israeli Arabs are not a minority but a 'class formation' and the

Prevalent Analyses of the Arab Economy in Israel

main aspect of the system within which this class exists and operates has been that of proletarianisation and national discrimination. The relevant developmental process for Rosenfeld, since economic advance has reached the limits possible through labour migration (*Ibid:* 399), is a struggle against discrimination, expressed in national terms, aimed at "closing the gaps in the social framework of the existing state" (*Ibid:* 404). This analysis contrasts sharply with Zionist political economy, which perceives a minority being developed and modernised towards a position of full equality and integration, within a free market system and through the benevolent intervention of the state.

More recently, a Palestinian scholar in Israel, N. Makhoul, based her stimulating analysis of the structural changes in Arab employment structure within a theoretical basis close to Rosenfeld's (1982). Makhoul highlighted the role of Jewish capital in the determination of the (class) position of Arabs in Israel. She argues that the simultaneous processes of "spatial mobility of Arab labour into Jewish-owned urban work-places, and the spatial mobility of Jewish-owned work places into the rural Arab residential places result in perpetuating a reality of proletarianisation without urbanisation" (*Ibid:* 83). Makhoul considers that the concentration of Arab labour in what she terms the "skilled manual/non-supervisory/productive" wage labour occupational categories confirms the predominance of a working class among the Arab population.

An interesting aspect of Makhoul's detailed statistical analysis of labour force data is the conclusion that the Israeli economy has "different labour markets: for Palestinian Arabs in predominantly proletarian categories of employment, for Jewish citizens in non-proletarian ones" (*Ibid:* 85). Implicit to Makhoul's analysis is a close alliance between Jewish capital and the state in the determination of the terms and scope for Arab development. It would follow from her approach that these are narrow, and the only path open to the Arab working class to development is that of struggle for equal rights within the Israeli system.

The preceding authors provide us with the first two examples of the second broad typology of research approaches to Arab economic conditions in Israel. This typology is characterised by a disciplinary approach that is associated with, but not rooted in, political economy, and which is influenced ideologically, though this has more a methodological than a political manifestation. Rosenfeld's and Makhoul's non/anti-Zionism is less prominent than is their Marxist outlook. They both emphasise the historical conflict between class/labour and capital in its particular Palestinian Arab versus Zionism format. The absence of implicit political or ideological motives in their work is welcome, though

Prevalent Analyses of the Arab Economy in Israel

this advantage is lost in their somewhat rigid definitions of a class determined analysis of the position of the Arab population and of its relation to the national economy. This relation is not adequately described by reference to the struggle of an Arab proletariat for equal rights.

While the Arab population might correctly be described in terms of their 'class formation', this only allows for a narrow and insufficient analysis of data related to economic activity. How can we even trace the industrial growth, agricultural performance, trade and marketing relations and savings and expenditure patterns of the Arab working class? To hold, as Rosenfeld and Makhoul do, that the main feature of the system of development relevant to Israeli Arabs is proletarianisation can only provide a partial explanation, since other processes have equal prominence in the experience of those parts of Arab society not 'deterritorialised' or 'proletarianised'.

Furthermore, Rosenfeld's prescribed path of 'working class struggle' for economic advancement has little relevance to a society still divided along regional, political, religious, ethnic and class lines. If there exists an element of solidarity and common interest in Arab society in Israel it is much more that of being Arab in the Jewish state than a feeling of class discrimination. I do not argue against the value of this sort of political economy and its important contribution to deepening understanding of the economic position of Arabs in Israel. But I do believe that it only partially contributes to the need for a broad economic analysis set out at the beginning of our discussion.

Zureik and Lustick: Control and Political Systems

The second prominent example of a theoretical treatment of Arab economic conditions in Israel not rooted in Zionist political economy is that by E. Zureik, a Palestinian sociologist. In his book, Zureik sets out to identify the most appropriate sociological model which can "delineate the institutional and ideological bases which govern the relationship between the subordinate Palestinian Arab minority and the dominant Zionist regime" (1979: 4). Zureik's analysis defines Israel as a colonial regime, and he considers that the model of internal colonialism best fits the situation of Palestinian Arabs in that state.

This model, in a version elaborated by Wolpe, provides for a social framework of class, ethnic, race, cultural and national relations, without articulating a link between class and non-class relations (*Ibid*: 17-18). An important feature of the model is the "imperialistic relation" between capitalist and non-capitalist

Prevalent Analyses of the Arab Economy in Israel

economies within one nation state, as manifested by the availability of "cheap labour power in the form of a non-capitalist commodity reproduced in (the dominated areas)" (*Ibid:* 18). Furthermore, political expression of this imperialistic relation takes a colonial form. And, trying to integrate certain of S. Lall's comments on development and dependency theory, Zureik holds that this is only the bottom link in a long hierarchy of dependent countries within a worldwide system of dependency (*Ibid:* 19-20).

Zureik proceeds to compare the salient features of Palestinian Arab society in Israel with those of internal colonies elsewhere (*Ibid:* 28-9). These are specified as structural transformation of the Arab society and economy both prior to and post 1948; the imposition of a capitalist economy on a traditional peasant order; geographic segregation of indigenous (Arab) and settler (Jewish) populations in the rural hinterland and urban metropoli respectively; and the creation of a justificatory ideology for the settler regime which dehumanises the culture and lifestyle of the indigenous population.

For Zureik, Palestinian Arabs in Israel are not a minority, a sector or a class, but the remnants of a colonised people (thus his emphasises on them being *Palestinians* in Israel); in fact they constitute an "internal colony" (*Ibid:* 140). The relevant system determining the status of this people is essentially one of colonial exploitation whereby, following Rosenfeld, the main developmental process has been one of proletarianisation. The peasantry has been transformed "into a lumpenproletariat with a 'declassed' status while at the same time diminishing the likely emergence of a viable bourgeoisie" (*Ibid:* 141). And the internal colonialism model allows for a clear path to effective development, namely a "structural transformation in the status of the colonised minority, such as proletarianisation" (*Ibid:* 198) which brings about a change in the level of consciousness. This leads to him to outline a number of modes of struggle (*Ibid:* 201): an intensified struggle for civil and political rights within the framework of the existing Israeli state; international pressure on Israel to change its policy; radicalisation of the Arab states in such a way as to resolve the Israeli-Arab conflict and the question of Palestine; and 'self-determination' for the Palestinians in Israel to decide upon regional autonomy or secession from Israel.

Despite his elaborate theoretical efforts, Zureik's model never seems to come to life in the substantive chapters of his book. While the fact that certain features of the state-Palestinian relationship might be similar to situations of internal colonialism (Zureik highlights South Africa), this in itself does not make it a valid concept for describing this particular situation. I would argue that while the three basic features Zureik proposes might be necessary conditions for the existence of internal colonialism, they are not generally sufficient, and in the case of Palestinians in Israel, they definitely are not. Just as Zureik fails to provide a working explanation of his model, he does not explain how it can be seen to work in Israel.

He does, however, review all the main data which describe the transformation of Palestinian economic structure in Israel, Palestinians' segregated status and other processes relevant to the internal colonialism model. But on what basis can it be affirmed that these add up to internal colonialism? The facts advanced could be (and often are) used in other methodological approaches attempting to prove different points. The main implication of the data presented by Zureik is that there are a range of socio-economic disparities and inequalities between Arabs and Jews in Israel, which are encouraged and manipulated by the state and the Jewish capitalist sector.

However, this is not in itself sufficient, if only in Zureik's own terms of trying to establish internal colonialism as a valid framework for explaining the status of Palestinians in Israel. Nor does it tell us whether there is an Arab economy *per se* in Israel, and if there is, what its features might be, how it works and where is it headed. Lustick has elaborated a valid critique of Zureik's approach:

> The problem with internal colonialism as an approach to the study of control in deeply divided societies is, then, not a lack of 'fit' between the phenomena under consideration and those that served as the empirical reference for classical theories of imperialism. Rather, the study of internal colonialism has been obstructed by a failure to elicit, from the rich diversity of European imperial expansion and from the full range of theories describing it, a set of defining characteristics. It soon becomes tedious rather than interesting to notice again and again that superordinate-subordinate relationships within societies have some features which resemble development patterns, social formations, psychological reactions or motivations characteristic of one or another example or theory of European overseas colonialism (1982: 74).

Unfortunately, Zureik's contribution does not provide the fresh analysis I believe to be necessary. Zureik's empirical assertions, especially regarding the specific class nature of Arab society and its political options, coupled with his fascination with the model undermine his ability to provide the approach he calls for in concluding:

> A research methodology has to be developed in line with the problem at hand. Artificial separation between the researcher and the phenomenon investigated is likely to lead to an imposed definition of and solution to sociological problems. The ultimate objective of such research must be to tap the authentic experience of the Palestinians... The purpose of the research must be neither to mystify nor to overwhelm the masses... (1979: 199-200).

An interesting contribution to a more relevant and dynamic analysis of the overall status of Palestinian Arabs in Israel is that provided by I. Lustick (1980). Though a study strictly within the discipline of political science, Lustick includes economic aspects in his description of the system of control of the Arab population. This both supports that analysis and promotes a better understanding of the dynamics of economic relations between the state and the Arab population.

Lustick notes that other writers, including some of those critics of Israel mentioned above, have stressed the repressive nature of state policy towards the Arab population. While he concurs that that a set of policies and practices exists which effectively control Israeli Arabs, he perceives a system of control which operates through different mechanisms and on several levels. In Lustick's view, it is the successful operation of this system which explains the phenonomon of 'quiescence' of Israeli Arabs despite their obvious dissatisfaction with the conditions in which they live. Also in contrast with other researchers, Lustick's central purpose is "not to assert that Arabs are controlled in Israel, but to analyse the system by which control has been achieved and maintained" (*Ibid:* 27).

Lustick describes three components of the system of control (*Ibid:* 77): segmentation, whereby Arab society is isolated and separated from Jewish society and fragmented internally as well; dependence, whereby Arabs are forced to rely on the Jewish majority for basic political, material and economic resources; and cooptation, whereby the state resorts to bribery, patronage and elite cultivation for surveillance of the Arab population and exploits its resources for certain (mainly electoral) purposes. These components exist and operate on three analytical levels: "the structural (basic historical, cultural, ecological and economic circumstances); the institutional (pertaining to the pattern of operation of Israel's major institutions); and the programmatic (concerning those specific policies designed and implemented by the regime for the purpose of controlling the Arab minority)"

(Ibid). While each of the components act separately on each of the three levels to enforce the system, they also operate interdependently ("synergestically"), reinforcing or replacing each other when one component cannot on its own achieve control.

The significance of Lustick's approach is not only in its success in flexibly explaining how this system works and how its different parts interrelate and operate. He has also taken earlier research further by incorporating into his system of control the various Israeli policies noted by other research, but whose function and interdependence had not been previously so dynamically analysed. Equally useful is that his application of the model of control is relatively free of any specific political, ideological or disciplinary motivations.[3] Since it is premised on the simple assumption that 'A controls B', it makes no value statement about that relation prior to setting out to show how, and with this approach why, control exists. Further, the author provides a wealth of well-documented, convincing and original data.

The fact that this is a model derived from and based within political science does not in itself detract from its potential contribution to a more strict economic analysis. In this particular case, the component of the system of control which most affects Arab economic conditions is that of dependence. On the structural level, Lustick notes historical gaps in development between Arab and Jewish communities in Palestine and the preservation of traditional social structure through economic insecurity caused by continuing dependence on employment sources outside the Arab areas. Institutionally, economic dependency has been maintained through prominent attention by the state to the rapid economic development in Jewish areas, the absence of cooperative efforts and organisations in Arab areas, and the consequent exclusion of Arabs from various benefits afforded Jewish productive and other enterprises.

On the programmatic level, dependency is reinforced through state policies of "economic discrimination, neglect, a studied attempt to prevent Arab owned centres of economic power from emerging, and a conscious effort to create and sustain ties of dependence... of Arabs on Jews and...of Arabs on Arabs serving the interests of Jews" *(Ibid:* 169). On this level, Lustick highlights land expropriation policies, the conscious decisions over the years not to promote industrialisation of Arab localities, development zoning and state aid policies, agriculture marketing controls and political blacklisting of individuals or entire villages. As a result of successful control through enforcement of dependency, Arab Israelis lack autonomous economic power bases, remain vulnerable to forms of state pressure, and have

Prevalent Analyses of the Arab Economy in Israel

become less likely to mount serious and effective campaigns for economic or political change.

The object of Lustick's analysis is therefore not a sector, class, internal colony or even primarily a minority. Rather, he understands Israeli Arabs as a population controlled through very specific mechanisms. The system in which they live as it has a bearing on them is one which aims to control them for its own purposes, and they have limited choices for their own future. This is not a system of democratic (or even as one Israeli sociologist would term it, "exclusionary")[4] pluralism, of class oppression or colonialism. It is simply one in which the Arab population's relation to the state and ruling elites is not determined by them but rather by their controllers' priorities and requirements. Therefore, barring the breakdown of the system (which Lustick discounts as a near or probable event), there is no real prospect of economic development which can respond to the controlled population's requirements. All that can occur are changes in local economic structure and activity concomitant with and relevant to those of the controlling regime.

ALTERNATIVE FRAMEWORKS

Economy or Class?

The preceding discussion has attempted to establish the relevance of various analytical typologies to the economy of Palestinian Arabs in Israel. Certain elements of the approaches reviewed have made important contributions to an understanding of the external and internal determinants of the Arab economy in Israel, as well as its central features. In the process, much valuable and interesting data has been amassed. The above review has revealed a certain amount of consensus, though within two quite opposed viewpoints. Nevertheless, much research ground has been covered and some basic economic features and processes understood.

It remains clear, however, that none of these approaches provide a working framework for economic analysis. There has been little, if any, study of the Arab economy itself - amidst a diversity of discussions of the issue under a variety of theoretical, ideological and disciplinary influences. All writers have noted the existence of an Arab 'entity' with specific economic characteristics and activities, differentiated from those of the national (or Jewish) economy. Yet, neither a minority, sector, class nor controlled population can, for analytical or practical purposes be considered an economic unit. Therefore, any attempt at analysis of the Arab economy in Israel without recourse to appropriate economic methodology remains inconclusive, and in my opinion, deficient.

A recent study by a Palestinian sociologist, A. Hayder, analyses the Arab economy in a new and radical way. He examined the emergence of an Arab industrial-commercial-landed bourgeoisie in Israel and the prominent features of that class (1986). In his unique field research, Hayder examined the influence of state policy and the major political and economic characteristics of Arab society. His approach is sociological and is confined to the rise of one particular section of society, but it is nevertheless of special importance.

Hayder's work represents an original and vital treatment of the Arab economy, and one which establishes new parameters for research on the subject.[5] Notwithstanding the deficiencies, for our research purposes, of analysis in terms of 'class', Hayder's work produced a wealth of field data and findings, and a rational analysis of them. Furthermore, it is a ground breaking contribution by a Palestinian Arab in Israel to analysis of a question that has for long been the domain of non-Palestinians. I examine his findings in greater detail in Chapter Five.

There are four important aspects of the economic status of the Arab population in Israel which are indicated in different terms by most of the preceding analyses, and which set the Arab community apart from the rest of Israel. Of perhaps the greatest significance in this context is a system or set of state policies and widespread attitudes specifically designed to deal with the Arab population and the resultant fact that, in most spheres, Palestinians are viewed and dealt with on a different basis from Israeli Jews. Also apparent are Arab geographic and physical settlement patterns with relative Arab concentration and separation from Jewish areas of habitation. Thirdly, despite the effects of 37 years of contact and a degree of assimilation into Israeli society, the Arab population still exhibits its own particular social structure and strongly entrenched traditions, culture and political institutions and attitudes. Finally, and of equal relevance to Arab-Jewish differentiation in Israel, is the range of differential features of economic activity, structure and power.

All of this implies that there is something particular, unique, and separate about the Arab population which merits analysing it as a distinct economic unit within the context of the Israeli economy. The most appropriate concept provided by economic theory stipulating a relation between a subnational and national unit and which accommodates at once spatial, physical, social and economic differentials between the two is that of an economic region. The appropriate disciplinary approach, capable of

Prevalent Analyses of the Arab Economy in Israel

integrating both economic and extra-economic analysis, is that of regional economic analysis.

A 'Regional' Treatment of the Arab Economy

While regions are generally thought of as geographic units, regional development theory has advanced a range of more detailed and flexible criteria, though retaining the geographic component. By extending and adapting these criteria to the case of Palestinian areas in Israel, it becomes possible, if not attractive, to employ such a concept and methodology here. It helps to facilitate analysis, clarify and highlight certain essential patterns and relationships relevant to Arab economy in Israel, and provide a notional basis for future treatment (academic or otherwise) of the issues involved. My introduction of the approach should therefore be understood within such a pragmatic and flexible, yet critical and innovative, context.

Traditionally, economists can be said to recognise three types of region: "the homogeneous region whose sub-areas have some characteristics, such as income level or cropping pattern in common; the polarised (or nodal or functional) region, whose sub-areas are interrelated by flows of some kind; and programming regions, whose sub-areas fall under the jurisdiction of a planning or administrative authority..." (Gore 1984: 10). As the above typologies indicate, a mixture of geographic and other considerations is essential to an application of regional criteria, and especially in a case such as that with which we are presently concerned.

In much of contemporary regional development theory, the process of any further definition of regions is avoided, since regions are usually well defined by administrative boundaries and data is not available for other spatial units. Often it is politically or economically convenient to delineate 'regional problems' according to conventional (geographic) borders. The geographic element of regions can become paramount in analysis, if not actually misconceived and misrepresented. This is even though other factors can be crucial to the operation of regional dynamics.[6] Instead of the region being "constituted as an effect of analysis... it serves as a methodological tool used in analysis, or a starting point in which the problem under study... is given definite boundaries" (*Ibid*: 11).

In fact, for our purposes, the uniqueness of the Arab situation in Israel allows and requires such an application of regional analysis.[7] This is useful not only in order to outline a regional profile of the Arab economy corresponding to broad typologies of economic regions. It further becomes necessary at a stage when economic analysis is used for prescriptive, planning purposes. Though this is not our concern here, as is discussed in Chapter Six, it is an option which could, and should, be examined by those concerned with the long-term welfare and development of the Arab community (and region) in Israel.

In its broadest definition, our conception of the Arab region in Israel can be understood as a synthesis of the three regional typologies mentioned above. It can be construed as a homogenous region in light of common features (economic, social and geographic); a functional region in terms of the importance of its relation to the national economy and polarised patterns of differentials in many regional-national characteristics; and a programming region in terms of the systemised context of Arab-state relations in Israel and the existance of specific state policies towards Arabs. Moreover, it is possible to specifically define the region since it is constituted both as an 'effect of analysis' (it is an entity whose existence emerges through a process of interrelated observations on the position of Arabs in Israel) and a methodological tool (as it provides for an analysis which integrates various observations of Arab separateness in Israel while also leading to new findings).

A working definition of a region provided by one regional economist that will suffice for our limited theoretical purposes is "a subnational area with at least one urban place and an associated hinterland, an area that is part of a larger system and in which economic relationships over its internal space are an economic development concern" (Bendavid Val 1983: 3). If looked at in terms of the argument for recognition of the 'Arab (economic) region in Israel', this could be a most satisfactory description. The Arab region is thus seen to be constituted by the areas of predominantly Arab settlement of the Galilee in the north, the Triangle in the centre and the Negev in the south (with their exclusively Arab localities), in addition to those distinct Arab quarters in the eight mixed population cities and towns.[8] As already indicated, it is defined by the exclusively Arab population of these area, their distinct social and economic features, national position and role, and the comprehensive and effective set of state policies towards Arabs in Israel (and thus towards the areas they inhabit).

In opposition to the above approach, it might be held that the geographic discontinuity of the Arab areas in Israel invalidates defining them together as a region. Furthermore, the absence of any state or administrative definition of an Arab region and the limited historic basis for such a classification (the concept has only been relevant for some thirty-five years) could be cited against

Prevalent Analyses of the Arab Economy in Israel

adopting the idea of an Arab region. However, we have already noticed an Arab separateness, a geographic proximity of Arab localities (though with a significant interspersal of Jewish localities) and a certain uniformity of treatment by the state and behaviour by the inhabitants, all of which cannot be disregarded by any economic analysis. The official non-recognition of regions has not in itself been able to prevent the emergence, and eventual recognition, of regions elsewhere over the years: the once underdeveloped U.S. southern states, the poorer south of Italy, the recently impoverished and drought stricken countries of the African continent, and even the so called 'development zones/towns' in Israel.

Consequently, the concept of an Arab economic region (with sub-areas north, central, south and in the mixed cities) is not only useful, but analytically necessary, especially in light of the limitations exhibited by earlier analyses. A pioneer of regional economics described three types of economic areas:

> ...simple market areas, nets of such areas, and systems of nets. Or, if we want to give popular names to each, we may speak of markets, belts and regions. In this sequence they become more complex, more self-sufficient, and unfortunately, less real... A clear economic region is a fortunate accident rather than a natural subdivision... A region is a system of various areas, an organism rather than just an organ (Losch 1964: 115).

The only attempt to date to propose this as the most suitable analytical approach to the question at hand was made in a short article by F. Gottheil (1973). For Gottheil, the Arab region in Israel witnessed a historical transition process which diverted it from the standard third world development course. From a subsistence agricultural economy with a nascent industrial and commercial structure, it became a consuming entity with its productive capacity resting primarily in the reproduction of exportable labour power. This process gave rise to various distortions which define the regional-national relationship. The region was integrated as an external factor into the national economic structure, much as a trading partner or source of foreign labour would be (*Ibid:* 239-40). Understanding the economic and other differentials between Arabs and Jews in Israel as 'Arab-Jewish dualism' (*Ibid:* 240), Gottheil applies the hypothesis popularised by G. Myrdal which argues against necessary spread effects of regional development, an assumption which underlies Israeli regional development policy (in Jewish areas).[9]

Gottheil's proposition that Arab economic development in Israel be considered an issue of regional development introduced a unique and new element into the discussion. It is unfortunate that he did not go further into the subject and attempt to specify just what sort of region it was and what the nature of its relation is to the national economy. Though he argues for an official 'Arab regional development policy approach', Gottheil does not sufficiently consider the obstacles inherent to state policy. Namely that there is little evidence of a state desire to develop the region. However, the absence of an official (Arab) regional policy does not negate the existence of a region; on the contrary, it has been an important factor behind the emergence of a distinct Arab region in Israel.

***

The four defining factors of the Arab region, state policy, geo-physical features, social and political characteristics, and economic differentials contain elements which are at the same time barriers and/or incentives to the region's development. The discussion which follows in Chapter Two analyses the region in terms of the first three of these determining factors and their operation. These can be considered as exogenous to the dynamic of Arab economic development insofar as they do not substantially alter as a result of changes in economic activity. They influence economic development without being influenced by it in turn (at least in the short and medium term). Within the broad heading of economic determinants, there are two types. The first is discussed in Chapter Two within the context of state/national economic policy towards the region and includes those (exogenous) national economic parameters whose dynamic is determined outside the region (and with little, if any, reference to the Arab region).

The operation of 'endogenous' economic factors is then discussed in detail, both in terms of their 'determining' and 'determined' nature. The main features of the regional economy are examined in Chapters Three, Four, and Five. It thus becomes possible, on another level, to examine the regional-national link with reference to some basic tools of regional economic analysis. This will highlight features that have already been noticed by others, though in terms relevant to their regional developmental significance, and not simply as static indicators of inequality or vague concepts of 'Arab underdevelopment'. The growth prospects of the Arab region are then evaluated in Chapter Six in light of the preceding diagnosis and with reference to regional growth patterns.

Prevalent Analyses of the Arab Economy in Israel

NOTES

1. See (Nakhleh 1977) and (Scholch 1983) for concise and valuable critical reviews of social and political studies of the Arabs in Israel.

2. The issue of Arabs being prevented from living in the exclusively Jewish town of Carmiel and attempts at preventing them from moving into the Jewish town of Upper Nazareth are only two examples of effective segregation; these and other issues are widely reported in the Israel press. For regular English language translations from the Hebrew language Israeli press, see (*Israeli Mirror*, 1980, *passim*).

3. It should be noted that Lustick states in his preface that all his life he "has been involved, as a participant, leader and resource person, in Jewish and Zionist organisations" (1980: *xi*). This makes his critical approach towards Israel all the more serious and considered.

4. In his book (1978), a reputed Israeli expert on Arab society, S. Smooha, attempts to reconcile Israel's democratic political system with its character as a Jewish state and understand the place of Palestinian Arabs within that contradiction.

5. The first available published account of Hayder's research (Hayder, 1986), indicates that his Ph.D thesis presented in 1986 at the Hebrew University in Jerusalem was entitled "Economic Initiative in Selected Galilee Villages". It is interesting to note that Professor H. Rosenfeld was one of the supervisors of this research.

6. One regional economist has strongly criticised regional theory for what he terms its "spatial separatism - that is, the structuring of the theory in a way which separates space from social processes" (Gore 1983: 263). Some of the issues raised by Gore are returned to briefly below in Chapter Six.

7. It should be stressed here that regional development theory is undergoing something of a crisis of identity and credibility as a discipline in its own right. I have attempted to refer to its more practically oriented aspects and avoid the somewhat debilitating effects of entering the theoretical debate. However, in (Gore 1983), all this ground is comprehensively covered in a stimulating critique of much conventional theory.

8. These localities are Acre, Ramleh, Lydda, Jaffa, Haifa, Upper Nazareth, Maalot/Tarshiha and Jerusalem. See Chapter Two for further details.

9. Myrdal holds that unbalanced development produces nationwide imbalances; spread effects are secondary to backwash effects of the development process, ultimately resulting in a reinforced regional economic divergence (Gottheil 1973: 240). Israeli regional development policy is discussed in Chapter Two.

Two

HISTORY, POLICY, PEOPLE AND SOCIETY - THE DETERMINANTS OF THE ARAB REGION

Israel's official policy towards its Arab citizens rests on a series of laws and regulations which explicitly or implicitly constrain the scope of Arab development in Israel and effectively nullify the legal principle of equal rights.[1] These are applied in the spheres of land ownership and use, agricultural and industrial growth, occupational advancement, and allocation of natural, state and public resources and utilities. They are systematically enforced so as to maintain the 'Jewishness' of the state and the supremacy of its interests at all levels of political and economic power. State policy towards Arabs in Israel has been an important influence in the emergence of a national identity and role to the Arab region.

This system originates in the basic Zionist premise upon which Israel was founded, namely that of safeguarding Jewish interests and exclusivity. While laws and regulations might not aim at depriving Arabs for the sake of depriving Arabs, many ultimately do so in order to avoid losing the rationale of their existence. The interdependence of these restrictions is not coincidental: where laws do not exclude Arabs or deny them the enjoyment of rights or benefits intended for Jewish citizens, the state has usually been able to resort to some quasi-legal arrangement or 'unwritten law' to ensure that 'national' interests prevail. This system and its historical antecedents has been well and extensively documented elsewhere and is not in itself the main object of our examination (see, e.g. Weimer 1983; Lustick 1980; Rosenfeld 1978; Jiryis 1976; 1973).

What is of concern here is to understand in a broad sense the role of 'structural' determinants in blocking and/or promoting the growth of an Arab region in the Israeli economy. In this chapter we shall begin by examining the 'development gap' between the

Arab and Jewish economies in Mandatory Palestine. This will provide an introduction to a discussion of the evolution from 1948 and into the 1980s of the policies of Zionist institutions and the state towards the Arab population of Israel and their effect upon economic activity and development. This review of history and policy is followed by a discussion of the demographic, geographic and social factors which at once help to determine and characterise the region.

THE DUAL ECONOMY OF MANDATORY PALESTINE[2]

The underdevelopment of the Arab economy in Israel today has its roots in the situation which prevailed prior to the establishment of Israel in 1948. It is necessary to affirm this partially because of a tendency of some critics of contemporary state policy towards the Arab population to suffer from a certain historical myopia. Accordingly, present problems of the Arab economy are often ascribed to the machinations of the Jewish state and it is forgotten that Palestine experienced some of the same problems of other developing economies. An understanding of pre-1948 Palestinian economic conditions highlights the extent to which Palestinian Arabs were already handicapped in relation to the Jewish economy, even before the advent of the state of Israel.

Further, it becomes possible to see how, because of others' (i.e., Israelis') prerequisites, Palestinian Arab economic development in Israel was diverted from the course it might have otherwise followed in different political circumstances. This is important when considering the claims of Zionist political economy to have developed and modernised the traditional Arab economy - to what extent was that process relevant to the dominant (Jewish) economy and detrimental to the subordinated (Arab) economy?

By 1948, after over 50 years of immigration and colonisation, a strong, viable and autonomous Jewish economy had been built in Palestine. The development of this infrastructure, alongside a correspondingly secure political and social structure, was a prerequisite for the establishment of the Jewish state. It had in fact been the primary objective of the Zionist movement throughout the period (see, e.g. Lustick 1980: 218-40; Weimer 1983; Rosenfeld 1978: 381-6). To ensure success and to minimise competition or the effects of boycott by the Arab population, it was necessary that this economy be substantially Jewish, sustained by Jewish labour and capital, and benefiting the Jewish population.

This Jewish infrastructure, however, was neither isolated from, nor balanced in its relation with, the existing Arab economy of Palestine. While the Jewish economy did not, as a matter of principle, employ Arab labour, it definitely benefited from the Arab consumer market. Jewish economic growth was greatly enhanced by the ability of Jewish industry to penetrate Arab markets, both in Palestine and in neighbouring countries. A Jewish writer of the period observed:

> Jewish industries are built in part at the expense of Arab consumers, but they do not return to them any benefits in terms of absorbing Arab workers, and the establishment of free markets to (absorb) the produce of the peasants. In both instances we face the problem known by the name of 'conquest of labour'...which lies at the heart of the relationship between Zionism and the Arabs. (Kolton 1932: 76, in Zureik 1979: 55-6)

Through selective and measured interaction, the Jewish economy influenced Arab economic development without being significantly affected itself. This can also be seen in the gradual acquisition by the Zionist movement of a relatively small proportion of arable land in Palestine and the successful establishment of a thriving and advanced agricultural sector. In 1945, Jews owned almost 13 percent of the arable land in Palestine (Hadawi 1970: 19), but in 1944 Jewish agriculture contributed 30 percent of national income generated in that sector (Zureik 1979: 59). Depending on the producing unit involved, Jewish agriculture in the mid-1940s marketed between 60 percent to 90 percent of output (Lustick 1980: 154).

The growth of Jewish agriculture not only contributed to the creation of a sizeable Arab rural based, urban employed labour force, but also to the transformation of the structure of the Arab agricultural sector. There were important changes in modes of Arab cultivation, with a shift away from cereals and subsistence agriculture into cash crops - vegetables, tobacco and fruits (especially citrus) - involving an overall increased marketing of output and commoditisation of the agrarian economy (see, Carmi and Rosenfeld 1974 and Nathan *et al.* 1946).

Arab industry remained concentrated in the more traditional branches of soap and olive oil processing, manufacture of certain textiles, leather, and building materials, in addition to the smaller workshop based economy of wood-working and carpentry. Jewish industry exhibited greater diversification and regularly sought new areas for expansion (see Nathan *et al.* 1946). By 1944, Arab manufacturing produced only 12 percent of the industrial national income, having contributed over 33 percent of industrial income in 1936 (Zureik 1979: 58). Jewish industry, sustained by substantial capital investment (see, Picadou 1982: 357), grew rapidly throughout the Mandate period. During World War II, for instance, output doubled and there was a constant expansion in the export of Jewish manufactures, particularly polished diamonds (National Institute 1948: 98-9).

Overall, there were few positive developmental results from the coexistence of the Jewish and Arab economies in Palestine in this period; the Jewish economy was fully occupied with its prerequisites and the Arab community was still emerging from the legacy of the Ottoman period. Only in citriculture were there appreciable joint efforts and interaction (see, e.g. Zureik 1979: 57; Himadeh 1938; INSEE 1948). A British government statistician confirmed the clear division between the two economies which existed in mandatory Palestine:

> It is of fundamental importance, that for all important economic purposes, Palestine contains two distinct economies... Branches of economic activities called by the same name have yet such profound differences as between the two communities that it is necessary to carry into the economic field the distinction between the two races which, in the past, has been avoided as an apparent denial of the common citizenship of Jew and Arab (Loftus 1944: 24).

As noted by Zureik, the apparent 'separate development under similar circumstances' of the two economies has been used to advance arguments about the 'non exploitative character of Zionist colonisation'; the stagnation of the Arab economy is considered to arise from its 'internal structure' (1979: 54-9). One writer, however, observed that this "closure between the Arab and Jewish sectors disguised a deeper down complex articulation", between an advanced capitalist mode of production and a pre-capitalist one, mediated by Mandate government policies (Picadou 1982: 363-4). Indirectly (and in some cases, directly) Jewish economic growth in Palestine created the conditions for changes in Arab social and economic structure that were predominantly reactive, rather than determinative.

At the start of the British Mandate, in 1919, the 67,000 Palestinian Jews constituted some 10 percent of a total population of 673,000 (Carmi and Rosenfeld 1974: 470); through large scale immigration this number had risen by 1946 to 583,000, or some 31 percent of the total (Lustick 1980: 36).[3] In the Mandate period, the Arab population maintained its basically rural, agrarian character though its national position and relations began to alter fundamentally. Partly, though not primarily (see Carmi and Rosenfeld 1974), as a result of land loss, and partly due to the inability of Arab agriculture to competitively employ the growing Arab rural labour force, this significant sector of the Palestinian Arab population commenced a long process of proletarianisation.

Carmi and Rosenfeld have shown that this process was "...one defined by employment opportunities that stemmed from outside the village, and the condition and quality of those opportunities - that is, and mainly, the interchangeable status of the peasant-wage worker in the labour market..." (1974: 479). A process of rural-urban migration continued through the Mandate period especially in response to expanded employment in the public (British) sector.[4] But "the Arab town-city social economy was a weak factor for creating proletarianisation and urbanisation..."*(Ibid)*. Potential developmental benefits of Arab proletarianisation were lost to the imperatives of the Jewish and public sector growth; the former through creating national economic conditions which led to Arab labour migration and the latter through offering alternative employment opportunities. By the time the British left Palestine in May 1948, this situation, and the devastating changes wrought in Palestinian Arab society by the 1948 war were to have a profound influence on the future course of Arab development in Israel:

> Given the well-known tendency of capital investments to flow to those areas in a developing country in which electrical transmission lines, roads, railroads, telephone lines, skilled manpower, piped water, and an industrial base already exist, and given the near total absence of such facilities and resources in Arab areas in 1948-1949, there were strong structural constraints against the industrialisation or rapid economic development of the Arab sector in Israel (Lustick 1980: 155).

THE EVOLUTION OF POLICY SINCE 1948

Bitter Realities for Arabs in the New Jewish State

The hostilities that accompanied the establishment on 15 May 1948 of the State of Israel ended in early 1949. Dramatic transformations had taken place in Palestine. A totally new state had come into being in a substantial part of Mandatory Palestine, a very different Jewish state, both in size and composition, than that envisaged by the 1947 UN Palestine partition resolution. It presented a new reality which the Palestinian Arab people and their Arab neighbours had never expected.

The scale of the human tragedy was devastating:[5] of the approximately 1.3 million Palestinian Arabs in 1948, some 750,000 were expelled or fled from Israeli controlled territory (58 percent of the total and over 80 percent of those previously resident in the territory of the new state). One million people were living in the areas now known as the West Bank and the Gaza Strip. The 150,000 who remained within the borders of Israel and separated from their compatriots, became what Lustick termed 'an instant minority' (1980: 47). The 15,000 Arab inhabitants of the cities of Tiberias and Safad were all made refugees, while the urban centres which contained the core of Palestine's Arab economic, social and political leadership and elites were emptied of 94 percent of their Arab inhabitants. The Arab population of West Jerusalem, Jaffa, Haifa, Lydda, Ramleh, and Acre fell from 266,000 to some 15,000 (Lustick 1980: 49). During and immediately following the war, a total of 386 Arab villages within the borders of Israel were abandoned or forcibly emptied, and destroyed (Abdulfattah 1983: 109).

The period immediately following the war was tragic for most Palestinian Arabs. Families were divided; land, homes and property lost. Those remaining in Israel were unemployed and many lived in open fields and suffered food shortages while the refugees crowded into hastily assembled camps. The social and economic structure of Arab Palestine had suffered a blow (*al-nakba*, the catastrophe) from which it continues to suffer today; the state of Israel had meanwhile 'inherited' a wealth of real estate and buildings, farming land, economic installations, and household and personal property.[6] The magnitude of the physical and other losses of Palestinian Arabs in 1948 has been valued at up to 1 billion Palestine pounds - equivalent to some $127 billion in 1984 prices.[7]

Though the Zionist movement had discussed the eventual attitude of a Jewish state to its Arab population prior to 1948, the only relevant consensus that existed was that first and foremost the rights and interests of the Jewish inhabitants of a Jewish state were to be advanced. Views ranged from those advocates of mass expulsion to the vision of a socialist bi-national society (see, Lustick 1980: 28-40; Weimer 1983: 26-34; Rosenfeld 1978: 381-9). However, from the earliest days of Israeli rule, the social perspective for Arabs was that at best "their legal rights as citizens of Israel would be protected" (Rosenfeld 1978: 389). There was no immediate rationalisation of an economic policy towards the Arab population, but policies relevant to the building of the Jewish state took their toll on Arab economic structure and the scope for its development from the very start. Over subsequent decades, this was to prove to be the essential dynamic determining policy towards the Arab region in Israel.[8]

It is clear that there has been an evolution of official policy towards the Arab population since 1948, changing under the influence of the imperatives of Zionist interests and those of national economic growth. Contrary to more simplistic characterisations of Zionist attitudes to Palestinian Arabs in Israel, there has not been one all-embracing (or all-exclusive) policy towards Arab economic development in Israel.[9] This has been well documented by Weimer who points out that:

> to characterise the 'Arab problem' as an 'unseen question', as 'colonialism' or as 'modernisation *versus* traditionalism' neglects the fact that Zionism itself is neither static nor does it end in 1948, but continues to be one of the ideological pillars of the State of Israel, subjected to the socio-economic realities of the state (1983: 58).

This evolution of policy can be broadly divided into three main periods, each with its own salient features. As indicated by Weimer's analysis, these stages were determined largely by developments in the requirements of the building of the Jewish state on the one hand and national economic growth on the other. An important additional factor was the extent to which policies of the preceding period had achieved their aims and could be abandoned. It should be reaffirmed that on the whole, there has been no conscious and systematic policy towards Arab economic development as such, in the same sense as national or conventional regional development policy. Rather, the intentions, provisions, measures and attitudes towards the Arab population can be understood within the present analysis as 'policy towards the Arab region'. Before detailing the main elements of policy, I shall review the stages in the development of the system in which they operated.

Military Rule Over Arabs to Help Build the Jewish State

The first policy period ran from 1948 until the early 1960s. This stage was crucial to the new state, and was characterised by high Jewish immigration, massive investment, the consolidation of a balanced and integrated economy and a vigorous Jewish settlement drive throughout the country. Though there were still some advocates of the expulsion of the remaining non-Jewish population, these were in a minority (Weimer 1983: 36). The main explicit policies towards the Arab minority were political and security based.

Though Arab society was in disarray and weak, it was imperative that it be well isolated from any possible contact with the rest of the Palestinian and Arab peoples over the borders. Further, any Arab opposition to the state and its policies could not be tolerated, especially at this early stage. Finally, if the Arab population's remaining resources, primarily human, could be harnessed in the interest of national economic priorities, that was of course desirable.

The most effective way to ensure these aims towards the minority was found in the establishment of military government in Arab areas. Though officially established in 1950, military rule in Galilee, the Triangle and Negev areas of Arab habitation had been in effect since 1948. The military governor was entrusted with wide judicial and executive powers. Any areas could be declared 'closed', movement was controlled through strict permits, Arabs were kept from migrating to Jewish or mixed cities, and Arab citizens could be arbitrarily arrested, banished from certain areas or put under town or house detention (see, Jiryis 1976 and Lustick 1980: 123-9). In short, the military government interfered in and effectively controlled all aspects of Arab life.

Military rule, assisted in the process of expropriation by the state of vast areas of Arab owned land which was the most significant policy enacted with bearing upon Arab development in this stage (see below). It also regulated the supply of Arab labour nationally, through the pass system and segregated labour exchanges (Ben Porath 1966: 51-2; Weimer 1983: 37-8). The only explicit policy guideline of the military towards Arab economic development was that it should be "carried out in such a way as not to create a self-contained Arab economy, for this would encourage hostile activity" (quoted in Lustick 1980: 184). The military government provided a convenient way for the Israeli political leadership to isolate and neglect Arab affairs in general, leaving policy in the hands of the military (see, Weimer 1983: 34-41; Lustick 1980: 52). As an Israeli journalist of the period observed,

> ...the authorities did not even try to think, after the establishment of the State, about the possibility of 'Israelising' the Arab minority. Instead they preferred to go the way that seemed, on the face of it, to be easier and more convenient, and that was the segregation of the minority and its limitation... (in Lustick 1980: 146).

Liberalisation to Allow Jewish Economic Expansion

The final abolition of the military government in 1966 was preceded by a gradual lifting of restrictions. This was the result of several factors, including growing Arab protest supported by certain members of the liberal Zionist establishment (see, Jiryis 1976: 36-9). However, as has been argued by Weimer and others, the growing labour requirements of the national economy at the bottom of the occupational scale (created by Jewish immigration patterns) was important in effecting the policy shift:

> Strict segregation, which had been the condition *sine qua non* for the economic integration of the new immigrants had become obsolete with the increasing... consolidation of the Israeli economy and had to give way to economic pressures which the *laissez-faire* attitude of the Israeli government could not ignore (1983: 44).

By the mid-1960s, therefore, there had taken place a significant shift in policy: a certain liberalisation of attitudes to Arabs and the beginning of active efforts towards some sort of integration. The motivations for this change, as mentioned, were initially economic as well the need to provide some response to criticism. But an equally important influence was the realisation that the minority was not only growing in size, but also in overall significance and some way must be found to ensure that its subordinate position, albeit as citizens, be maintained. Israeli policy makers had:

> accepted the fact that the Arabs were there to stay and the premise upon which this policy was based was that - so long as the correct measures were applied - the aim of reconciling the Arabs with the existence of and their position within the Jewish state could be achieved (*Ibid:* 46).

In this second period, concerted attempts were made by the central authorities to effect some degree of Arab development. In 1959, the *Histadrut*, the national trade union federation, decided to accept Arabs as full members, though their affairs were to be dealt with by a special Arab department. Two 'Five Year Plans' were formulated in the 1960s to develop the Arab economy (see below). Zionist parties intervened more actively in local Arab social and political activities, as the 'cooptation' of elites and clans became an important aspect of electioneering (Lustick 1980:

Chapter Eight). The first successful applications of technology to Arab agriculture also came in this period.

Policy in the 1960s was characterised by less aggressive and provocative measures than during the period of military rule. But this is not especially surprising since by that time, the harsh policies of the 1950s had largely achieved their aims. The consolidation of the Jewish state and its majority population had been successful; the Arab minority had been effectively isolated from the volatile political currents then sweeping the region; the state had taken the maximum amount of land and Arab resources that could be successfully and usefully absorbed. Overall, the growth of the Israeli economy from the 1960s allowed, and even necessitated, a removal of the barriers in the way of full utilisation of the human resources in the country. While this second period was more liberal than the era of military rule, there was no active promotion of Arab industrialisation or development approaching the scale existing in the Jewish economy.

Stemming 'Palestinianisation' and Arab Development

The second period of evolution of official policy continued into the mid-1970s. This liberalism was threatened, however, by a combination of demographic and political consequences of the occupation of the West Bank and Gaza Strip in 1967, the increasing 'Palestinianisation' of the Arab population in Israel, and growing economic difficulties. The state economy was overburdened by the large military budget and politically stimulated investment in Jewish settlements. It was already clear from the 1960s and early 1970s that state investment in electricity, roads, and other infrastructural projects and local authority aid in the Arab region would be minimal. Arab development was, and still is, considered primarily a political issue: "The decision of the government not to push hard for the economic development of the Arab sector was largely based on a desire to prevent the emergence of Arab owned centres of economic power" (Lustick 1980: 184).

The considerations governing policy in the 1970s and into the 1980s were similar to those of the 1950s. Now, however, the state had become less capable of overtly offensive measures against the Arab region. The Arab population was more effectively and radically organised politically, as evidenced by the 30 March 'Day of the Land' demonstrations against land expropriations in 1976. It had also made significant educational, material and occupational advances. Zionist ideals were also seriously threatened by the demographic implications of falling

Jewish immigration and a large Arab population under Israeli rule, both in Israel and the occupied territories. While the overall system of minority control was still operational, it had become less efficient and under greater challenges than ever before.

The policy measures which characterised the latest and present stage combine reformulated elements of the previous two periods. On the one hand, the economic problems faced by Israel have put growing pressure on its limited natural and material resources; as might be expected, this has meant correspondingly decreased resources available for the Arab sector. This has led to a new form of official and public neglect and isolation of the Arab region, more or less leaving it to its own devices, so to speak. Secondly, rather than attempting any effective integration by bringing Arabs into the national (Jewish) political, economic and social structure, an effort has been made to penetrate the region and extract resources from it, primarily in the industrial sector (see Chapter Five).

The past decade has seen increased debate and concern within Israel about the 'demographic danger' of Arab population growth. In some ways, this debate is reminiscent of that which took place during the period of intensive settlement and expropriation in the 1950s. The response to this perceived problem has included the the so-called 'Judaisation of the Galilee', as discussed further below. Countering such aggressive trends, efforts have again been mounted in recent years by state and Zionist circles to 'coopt' Arab social and economic elites, resembling those of the early 1960s. However, despite recent reorientations, policy towards Arab development remains basically determined by the same considerations that have always guided it, namely the pre-eminence of Jewish development in Israel.

Nevertheless, the key concept still propounded by government officials in this sphere is that of 'integration'. The most recent version of this policy was instituted by the Cabinet Minister with special responsibility for Arab affairs, Ezer Weizmann and his advisor, a renown Arabist, Professor Yosef Ginat. Their period in office witnessed a number of measures aimed at redressing certain Arab and Druze grievances, and won noticeable support among a relatively wide sector of the Arab population. These included returning certain Arab agricultural land which had been requisitioned for military use, some re-zoning and planning of Beduin communities in the Negev and Galilee, attempts to increase government aid to Arab local authority budgets, raising funds overseas for the establishment of Arab community and educational projects and proposing new formulas for a solution to the burgeoning Arab housing problems (see, *Jerusalem Post,* 14 October 1986).

The replacement of Weizmann after the 'National Unity' government's 'rotation' in 1986 by Moshe Arens appeared to signal yet another retreat by liberal policy in favour of a more rigid and selective application of the concept of integration. This approach firstly focussed on greater benefits and privileges to the Druze population of Israel, whose dissatisfaction with state treatment grew noticeably in the mid-1980s. This was accompanied by renewed calls by government spokesmen for integration of the Arab population in Israel, but this time coupled with demands for Arab fulfillment of 'obligations', such as so-called 'civilian service' (instead of military service), in return for granting of 'rights'.

As viewed by Arens, integration required that Arabs in Israel fully embrace the state's Jewishness, and particularly the significance of the Holocaust in the Jewish experience: "In the state of Israel, there is something uniquely Jewish. Will Arab Israelis be able to identify with this unique quality, which is a Jewish quality?" (*Jerusalem Post,* 10 February 1987). It is not altogether surprising that the heads of Arab local councils to whom Arens addressed himself, received his appeal with scepticism and hostility. As the moderate head of Baqa al Gharbiya local council replied: "Everyone wants integration and coexistence. But it should not be that of a horse and his rider. The question is whether we can be partners in our fate" *(Ibid).*

THE RANGE OF POLICIES, PAST AND PRESENT
The laws and policies which have most debilitated the Arab economy in Israel are those affecting ownership and control of land. Some 34 different laws have legitimised the expropriation of private Arab lands in Israel, belonging both to residents and refugees, with the process continuing until today (see, Oded 1964; Jiryis 1973; Kislev 1976; Lustick 1980: 170-82). These confiscations have alienated an estimated 75 percent of the holdings of Palestinian Arabs prior to 1948 (Abu Kishk 1979: 128).[10] All confiscated land has been redistributed to Jewish farms and localities. Only one of the confiscation laws provides for compensation. Under this law some 700,000 dunums was expropriated. Only 25 percent of the confiscated land was financially compensated for, at rates which bore little relation to actual market values (Lustick 1980: 179-82). The continuing expansion of Jewish settlement, especially in the Galilee, has led to violent clashes in Arab villages where land was targeted for confiscation.

The legal stipulation that confiscated land is 'the inalienable property of the Jewish people' and regulations that only 'Jewish labour' be employed on 'Jewish land' ensures limited Arab leasing of 'Jewish land' or employment in Jewish agriculture. The leasing of 'national land' to Arab farmers is vigorously opposed in many Zionist circles; leases rarely run for more than one agricultural year. Farmers cannot therefore, invest in improvements or capital stock (*Haaretz*, 29 March 1985). The effect of confiscations has been devastating, severely restricting Arabs ownership of, or access to, their main productive base, while also constricting the area available for the expansion of towns and villages.

Problems associated with the shortage of land for housing are further complicated by the limitations placed by the state on building land in Arab villages and the long delays in authorising town zoning plans without which legal construction cannot commence. Many Arab localities have not yet obtained authorised plans and the housing problem is continuously growing (see, Lustick 1980: 196-7; Abu Kishk 1976, 1981; Bayadsi 1975). This has led to nationwide debates and threats to implement the pending court orders for the demolition of many of the thousands of 'illegal' Arab dwellings. The housing crisis is especially severe in the Arab quarters of the mixed cities, especially Haifa, Jaffa and Acre (*Jerusalem Post*, 20 December 1985; see also, Tessler 1980: 7; and *Haaretz*, 30 December 1984).

Over the years, the state has gradually abandoned some of the more flagrantly discriminatory laws and regulations affecting Jewish-Arab differentials in wages and social security benefits, and Arab access to national resources and institutions (Lustick 1980: 184-5). However, there remain important exceptions, in both the official and private domains. The explicit exclusion of 'non-Jews' from employment in military related industries, the larger public enterprises and the higher echelons of the state and civil service is maintained until today (see, Makhoul 1982; Waschitz 1975: 45-9; Farjoun 1980: 120-2). Similarly, political constraints and discrimination restrict Arab residence in Jewish population centres.[11] This has the dual effect of limiting employment and advancement opportunities, while perpetuating the dependency of the lower-skilled commuting Arab worker on Jewish employers. The fact that the bulk of the Arab population does not serve in the Israel military means they are excluded from a range of economic and social welfare benefits available to veterans.

State resource distribution policy, while not always codified in specific laws, also affects the scope for industrial and agricultural growth. These institutionalised arrangements include:
* the selective expropriation of the better, more irrigable Arab lands (see Abu Kishk 1976);
* the discretionary powers of the water authority in allocation of water supply quotas;[12]
* the exclusion of Arab farmers from the important cooperative systems which manage a significant part of the agricultural production and marketing processes;[13]
* the slow provision of electricity, water, sewage and roads;
* no state investment in Arab industry or designation of Arab areas as industrial zones (most recently confirmed by the Israeli Prime Minister in *Jerusalem Post International Edition*, 11 January 1986);
* the relatively small per capita allocation of state aid to Arab local authorities (see, Lustick 1980: 188-9);
* almost no Jewish or public investment in housing in Arab localities (*Ibid:* 185; Abu Kishk 1976);
* the decision not to bestow on any Arab locality the beneficial status of 'development town', as afforded to numerous Jewish localities in the Galilee (see below).

All of these are examples of ways in which regulations and institutional arrangements mitigate directly or indirectly against Arab development. While recognising the arguments advanced by Zionist political economy about the factors that supposedly necessitate such measures (i.e., the primacy of *Jewish* development in the *Jewish* state), any effective and honest analysis must give prominent consideration to the operation of such barriers and restrictions.

REGIONAL DEVELOPMENT POLICY IN ISRAEL[14]
The impressive range of activities carried out by various Israeli development encouragement agencies and government departments is in principle meant to cover the whole country and equally benefit all citizens. There are two ways in which the Arab region is effectively ignored. On the one hand, it is not recognised administratively or for regional development programme purposes as a region. The nearest Israeli governments have gone to devising or implementing specific development plans for the region is the occasional reference to the need for development of the 'Arab sector' or the 'minority villages'. These were the target of two Five Year Plans from 1962-72 which were comprehensively criticised at the time (see, e.g. Flapan 1962) for being too vague and inadequate in

specifying aggregate goals. In the event, they were only ever partially fulfilled and concentrated on infrastructure provision (see, Flapan 1963 and 1963a; Abu Kishk, n.d.; Arnon and Raviv 1980: 216; Lustick 1980: 190-2). Most ministries and quasi-state institutions (e.g. the Histadrut), including the Prime Minister's office have 'Arab' or 'minority' departments which are meant to integrate the specific needs of the region into the respective agencies' activities, though there is no inter-ministerial mechanism for planning or supervising this.[15]

On the other hand, the Arab region is effectively excluded from those development programmes promoted in areas where Arabs form the majority of the population. The Jewish Agency (which does not have an Arab department) has, since the early 1970s, been working on a plan for the 'accelerated development' of the Galilee to 'reach the highest possible rate of Jewish population growth'. This aim specifically excludes the majority Arab population from enjoyment of the plan's considerable benefits (Jewish Agency 1974: 3; see, also Katz and Menuhin 1978 and Katz 1982). A group of Israeli researchers investigating the regional development status of the Galilee wrote:

> ...there is little evidence of factually based planning for the 'minority sector' related to overall regional development. The official Government policy on minorities, as we understand it, is to close the gaps in levels of living between Jewish and minorities population. However, we have seen little field analysis of the problems and possibilities. Furthermore, we are not aware of any coherent plans and programs for their development, based on the dynamics of their 'sector' and consistent with overall development plans for the Northern District. They cannot be ignored (Katz and Menuhin 1978: 6).

> Yet, ignored they are, and effectively. It would appear in the Northern District, the very issue of Arab economic development is considered by policy makers and planners as prejudicial to national interests.

> This is consistent with the nurturing of a national dividing line that runs through the economy and society and premised on the view that 'development is equated with national character, as is backwardness... expressing a view of superior and inferior national groups with qualitatively different cultures' (Rosenfeld 1976: 391-2).

Though this national division is regularly crossed through the cooptation or 'integration' of Arab elements, it remains a stronger tendency in state policy than occasional liberal initiatives.

National goals ignore the specific interests of the Arab population by focussing on maintaining the Jewishness of the state and the nature of its economic development and by not allowing the expression of any specific Arab regional goals. Both public and private economic sectors maintain the stagnation of the Arab economy by ensuring an allocation of its resources which is most beneficial to the national economy. Through this double edged strategy of passive neglect and aggressive containment, the Arab region has been by-passed in the four decades of impressive economic growth and institution building in Israel. Though state policy does not recognise the 'Arab region' as such, a certain dynamic has prevailed whereby an Arab region emerged, both actually and conceptually. Accordingly, Arab 'regional' economic behaviour has arisen from, *inter alia,* the effects of a range of national policies which set Arabs apart in most spheres of national life. To this extent, therefore, systematic state policy towards the Arab region is a reality and discernable.

Whether there exists a conscious collusion between the state and the Jewish business sectors towards the Arab region is immaterial. The effective coincidence of interests by these two has ensured a successful implementation of strategy towards Arabs. The private and public sectors' main interest and involvement in the Arab region is characterised by maximum export of value added to outside the region. This is coupled with the allocation of the region's most abundant resource, cheap and relatively unskilled labour, to Jewish sectors most in need of it.

This view of national policy towards the Arab region conflicts sharply with that advanced by official spokesmen who hold that the state is the primary sponsor of any development so far realised. The official version, also promoted by some academics, is advanced not only for public image considerations. More importantly it perpetuates the dual strategy of neglect and appropriation of resources - on the basis that the state knows best and has the Arab population's best interests at heart. Thus, a government spokesman in the mid 1970s can portray the decline of Arab agriculture as a modernisation process which 'allowed' people to move out of agriculture. The Government is credited with having successfully implemented two Five Year Plans, while ministries established industrial areas in the Galilee and Triangle, granted 'Approved Industry' status to new enterprises and made easy credit available for the electrification of Arab villages (see, Shemesh 1975). And,

> despite the impressive achievements of the state of Israel in the advancement of the Arab community in various fields...there are still several targets which have not been fully reached... It is the policy of the government to give Israeli Arabs a feeling of belonging and identification with the country by means of a process of integration and partnership, in planning, decision making and implementation... (*Ibid:* 30).

REGIONAL EFFECTS OF NATIONAL ECONOMIC ACTIVITY

The structure of the Arab regional economy is largely determined by the national economy. Consequently, the strengths and weaknesses of the Arab region's economy follow lines established by the national economy's overall development and the specific dynamic of the national-regional relation. Here it only will be possible to briefly outline those aspects of the national economy that have direct bearing upon the Arab region.[16] The past period of Israeli economic growth has revealed clear structural trends in each of the main economic sectors. They can be construed as barriers to Arab development insofar as they are linked to national economic goals which predicate the close involvement of state and Jewish institutions as the prime guarantors for their achievement.

Industrial development has been guided by a strategy with four important elements, which will continue to condition investment:

* integration: backward and forward linkages such that agricultural production can support processing or textile industries, and heavy and medium metal industries can provide raw materials for the production of a range of capital goods;
* import substitution: Israel can now produce most consumer goods and durables; in the current economic climate, this strategy is being re-emphasised;
* a high degree of export orientation in military as well as plastic, textile, electronic and food products;
* advanced and well-financed research and development facilities provide vital support to local production. Israel now exports the products of its science based industries and its research and development capacities.

Agricultural structure, though increasingly less centralised and regulated, is still characterised by rigidities with regard to farm structure, production controls, purchasing and input provision arrangements, pricing and marketing (see, e.g. Hunt 1974; Ministry of Agriculture *passim;* Doherty 1980). A central element in Israel's agricultural development has been a high level of technological innovation and application. State policy aims at food self-sufficiency, necessitating a number of steps over the years. These include the promotion of agricultural exports; import replacement (especially animal feed, wheat and cereals); the settlement of marginal land through application of soil, water and fertiliser enhancing technologies more efficient utilisation of scarce water resources; the harnessing of new forms of energy and encouragement of small farm units (family or cooperative).

Some other sectors are less regulated and more open to new ventures of any kind; a relatively high level of small Arab commercial activity and personal services testifies to this. Tourism, an important Israeli industry both in terms of its foreign exchange earning power and its contribution to Gross National Product (GNP), is largely controlled by the Jewish sector even though sites in Arab areas are a major attraction. The Jewish control of this sector has been maintained by an active policy of collusion between the state and the private Jewish sector though there are no serious structural barriers to Arab entry. The financial sector is monopolised by state and Zionist concerns and there is very little room for independent Arab initiative, a factor which has encouraged illicit usury among and between Arabs.

In addition to the above factors, there are four aspects of Israeli economic policy and conditions in the 1980s which have a direct effect upon the Arab sector. The first of these is related to attempts to cut back state expenditure which in most cases hit the Arab region hardest, both in terms of social services and state aid to local authorities and infrastructural investment. Though already relatively low, any further decrease in the relative level of state aid will mean fewer approvals of towns plans and industrial zones, stricter allocation of development zone funds and tighter credit facilities.[17] The economic crisis of the mid-1980s has lead to greater overall unemployment and consequently more unemployment of Arabs as they are the more expendable part of the workforce.[18] In addition to increasing economic hardship, this might encourage greater labour mobility (both geographic and occupational/sectoral), maintaining relatively low skill development. The high rate of inflation and government austerity measures also hits the Arab population hardest, because they have lower incomes and relatively fewer assets and savings to fall back on. Finally, as a result of the general crisis, growth in the Jewish sector has fallen, causing a shift in the prevailing industrial mix and a consequent withdrawal or redistribution of private investment (sub-contracting and subsidiaries) in the Arab region. This was most recently manifested by the collapse of the large Israeli textile and clothing manufacturer *Ata* and the closure of its factories in the Arab region.

As has already been shown, there is little evidence of centrally planned efforts at integrating Arab regional economic structure into the broad strategic path of the national economy. Most of the linkages that exist are determined by national prerequisites. Little attention is paid to the needs of the region or the contributions it could make nationally which would also have local benefits. The main national-regional flow has been one of movement of cheap Arab labour inputs and specific agricultural production lines to national economic sectors and the movement of goods and services from the national economy to regional consumption centres. The region has been largely a passive reactor to national economic development.

The Myrdal spread/backwash relation appears here to be valid since the region has had to respond and adapt itself to national trends without enjoying most of those developments within its borders, as shall be shown below. Arabs have a distorted share of the benefits of national economic development while bearing equally (and often unequally) its costs. This is yet another piece in the emerging picture of national-regional inequality and helps to define the particular path of Arab economic development in Israel. As shall become clearer in Chapters Three, Four and Five, the resultant patterns of the Arab region's economic activity reflect both the obstacles which perpetuate its underdevelopment and the potentials which act as incentives to its growth.

The Arab experience in Israel has shown that there are limits to the ability of the state to arbitrarily deprive, coerce and subjugate the Arab population. This can be seen in various ways:
* the strong Arab commitment to the remaining land and to maximising its productive potential;
* the desire for educational advancement and acquisition of much demanded skills, however relatively inferior to those of the Jewish work-force;
* the stubborn insistence on obtaining the 'modern conveniences' of electricity and piped water, usually at localities own expense and effort;
* the examples of those individuals who found a way around restrictions to establish businesses or small industries.

Overall, the Arab population has learned through bitter experience to resist further encroachments on rights and property. At the same time, this has entailed a learning process of how to utilise the Israeli legal system to their best possible advantage, and to at least minimise its use against their interests. As a natural communal response to state neglect and discrimination, this constitutes an incentive to the region's growth. This dynamic, of state policies being met and tempered by popular reaction, has had an important role in defining and shaping a distinct Arab regional economy in Israel.

THE GEO-DEMOGRAPHIC FRAMEWORK OF THE ARAB REGION[19]

Arab Geographic and Residential Concentration

Arabs in Israel live in 157 exclusively Arab localities, plus eight mixed towns; this total includes East Jerusalem, five villages surrounding it annexed in 1967, 28 recognised or spontaneous Beduin localities in the Galilee and central districts, and 31 Beduin settlements in the Negev (Israel 1983a: 286-96). Excluding the Negev, of the total 126 Arab localities, only three have municipal status,[20] 51 are local councils and the remaining 72 are grouped in regional councils with Jewish localities or have no local authority status at all. There are also 31 localities in the Negev inhabited either by settled or semi-settled Beduin tribes.[21]

The distribution of Arab population is diffused from around the largest Arab population centre, the town of Nazareth. Some 25 percent of the Arab population in 1983 (excluding the inhabitants of Jerusalem) resided in the sub-districts of Yizre'el, Kinneret and Safad, which comprise central, lower and upper Galilee (see Table 2.1). Another 39 percent are found in this area's northern and western periphery, the Acre and Haifa sub-districts, which together comprise the rest of Galilee. Thus, almost 65 percent of the Arab population live in the Galilee region. Extending south from the Galilee to the once large Arab cities of Jaffa and Ramleh, the Hadera and other central sub-districts, known as the Little Triangle, hold 27 percent of the regional population. The rest of the Arab population of Israel is found in the Negev (8 percent).

In the Northern District alone (which excludes Haifa), Arabs form just over 50 percent of the total population. In the Northern and Haifa Districts (including the now mainly Jewish city of Haifa) together, they make up almost 47 percent of the total population. In the two sub-districts of Yizre'el and Acre, they were 50.5 percent and 64 percent respectively of the total population. In the central Hadera sub-district, Arabs formed 44 percent of the population. On another level of differentiation, 74 percent of the Arab population in 1983 (excluding Jerusalem) lives in localities with less than 15,000 inhabitants, while 17 percent live in the four larger Arab towns (see Table 2.2).

History, Policy, People and Society

Table 2.1: Population in Israel, by District, Sub-District and Population Group, Selected Years
(Thousands)

DISTRICT AND SUB DISTRICT	8 XI 1948	22 V 1961	YEAR 20 V 1972	4 VI 1983	31 VII 1985
TOTAL POPULATION	872.7	2,179.5	3,147.7	4,037.6	4,266.2
Jerusalem District	*87.1*	*191.9*	*347.4*	*4722.9*	*506.2*
Northern District	*144.0*	*337.1*	*473.9*	*656.0*	*706.7*
Zefat Sub-District	10.8	45.6	56.7	64.8	68.5
Kinneret Sub-District	19.5	43.3	49.6	62.6	67.4
Yizre'el Sub-District	59.0	120.1	173.7	232.5	249.7
Akko Sub-District	54.7	128.1	193.4	276.3	298.6
Golan Sub-District[a]	-	-	0.6	19.7	22.4
Haifa District	*175.1*	*370.3*	*483.8*	*575.3*	*592.7*
Haifa Sub-District	125.5	276.2	356.7	409.6	416.0
Hadera Sub-District	49.6	94.1	127.1	165.7	176.7
Central District	*122.3*	*407.0*	*579.7*	*830.7*	*889.1*
Sharon Sub-District	36.9	102.5	143.5	190.4	203.7
Petah Tiqwa Sub-District	48.9	136.5	202.8	297.5	320.6
Ramla Sub-District	4.4	68.3	89.2	109.7	112.9
Rehovot Sub-District	32.1	99.7	144.2	233.1	251.8
Tel Aviv District	*305.7*	*699.3*	*90.2*	*1,000.2*	*1,015.3*
Southern District	*21.4*	*173.9*	*354.2*	*478.8*	*510.1*
Ashqelon Sub-District	7.2	76.7	53.0	203.7	213.9
Be'er Sheva Sub-District	14.2	97.2	201.2	275.0	296.2
ARAB POPULATION	156.0	247.2	461.0	687.6	749.0
Jerusalem District	*2.9*	*4.2*	*86.3*	*126.1*	*34.2*
Northern District	*90.6*	*142.8*	*217.6*	*329.0*	*355.2*
Zefat Sub-District	1.9	3.0	4.1	5.3	5.8
Kinneret Sub-District	5.1	7.9	11.2	15.7	17.1
Yizre'el Sub-District	34.9	53.5	81.4	11.4	126.5
Akko Sub-District	48.7	78.4	120.8	177.6	92.0
Golan Sub-District	-	-	-	12.9	13.7
Haifa District	*27.4*	*48.0*	*75.0*	*110.2*	*119.3*
Haifa Sub-District	9.1	18.6	25.9	36.5	39.2
Hadera Sub-District	18.3	29.4	49.0	73.6	80.1
Central District	*16.1*	*26.9*	*44.4*	*65.9*	*72.0*
Sharon Sub-District	10.4	17.4	27.5	39.1	42.5
Petah Tiqwa Sub-District	3.0	4.7	8.2	12.5	13.8
Ramla Sub-District	2.6	4.4	7.8	13.3	14.7
Rehovot Sub-District	0.1	0.4	0.8	0.9	1.0
Tel Aviv District	*3.6*	*6.7*	*7.3*	*11.3*	*12.3*
Southern District	*15.4*	*18.6*	*30.4*	*45.0*	*56.0*
Ashqelon Sub-District	2.4	0.3	0.6	1.3	1.4
Be'er Sheva Sub-District	13.0	18.3	29.8	43.7	4.5

NOTE: a. In 1972 includes only Jewish localities; in 1983 includes whole population.
SOURCE: From (Israel, 1986: 30-33).

History, Policy, People and Society

Table 2.2: Population in Israel, by Type of Locality and Population Group, Selected Years (Thousands)

Type of Locality and Population Group	22 V 1961	20 V 1972	4 VI 1983	31 XII 1985	No. of Locs. on 31 XII 1985
TOTAL POPULATION	2,179.5	3,147.7	4,037.6	4,266.2	1,137
Urban localities	1,837.6	2,789.1	3,616.0	3,815.2	156
200,000 +	736.61	897.2	981.7	1,005.1	3
Jerusalem	167.4	313.9	428.7	457.7	1
Tel Aviv-Jaffa	386.1	363.8	327.1	322.8	1
Haifa	183.0	219.6	225.8	224.6	1
100,000-199,999	a	218.1	818.4	954.7	8
50,000-99,999	144.8	476.8	345.9	262.1	4
20,000-49,999	471.0	501.3	699.5	758.2	23
10,000-19,999	175.3	350.6	350.9	391.5	27
2,000-9,999	309.8	345.1	419.7	443.8	91
Rural localities	341.9	358.5	421.6	451.0	981
Moshavim	120.6	125.1	140.8	146.4	411
Collective Moshavim	4.0	5.5	9.1	10.6	47
Kibbuzim	77.1	89.7	115.5	125.2	268
Institutional localities	6.0	9.4	13.3	13.5	33
Other rural localities	101.0	81.7	102.7	112.5	222
Outside localities[b]	33.2	47.2	40.2	42.8	-
ARAB POPULATION	247.1	461.0	687.6	749.0	131
Urban localities	157.0	366.2	595.1	654.2	72
200,000 +	17.7	102.3	149.2	159.0	3
Jerusalem	2.4	83.5	122.4	130.0	1
Tel Aviv-Jaffa	5.8	6.4	9.5	10.2	1
Haifa	9.5	12.4	17.4	18.8	1
100,000-199,999	-1	0.2	3.2	3.7	-
50,000-99,999	0.3	0.9	1.5	1.5	-
20,000-49,999	35.3	49.5	90.7	98.2	6
10,000-19,999	2.3	38.3	95.7	128.1	9
2,000-9,999	101.5	175.1	254.8	263.8	54
Rural localities	90.2	94.7	92.5	94.8	59
Moshavim, Kibbuzim, Institutional localities	0.8	0.5	1.4	1.9	1
Other rural localities	60.4	48.4	56.8	55.9	58
Outside localities[b]	28.9	45.8	34.4	37.0	-

NOTES: a. For comparison, Jerusalem and Haifa are included in the group 200,000+ in 1961, although their population had not reached that size then; b. Including 36 Beduin tribes (Negev and Galilee).
SOURCE: From (Israel, 1986: 44-45).

Of the Arab population including Jerusalem, some 25 percent live in the eight mixed cities and localities (Jerusalem, Haifa, Jaffa, Acre, Lydda, Ramleh, Maalot-Tarshiha, Upper Nazareth). If Jerusalem is excluded from the calculation, the mixed localities' Arab population constitutes only 9 percent of the total Arab regional population. This means that a total of 547,000 Arabs live in exclusively Arab localities (in 1983), while 55,000 live in almost exclusively Arab quarters in predominantly Jewish cities. Despite the existence of Jewish quarters, towns or settlements next to or interspersing these Arab areas, this high degree of residential segregation is significant and constitutes an essential element in creating a uniquely (Palestinian) Arab lifestyle and living conditions in Israel.

Only in the more extreme circumstances (e.g. due to high population congestion in Nazareth or the old Arab quarter of Acre) has there been any arbitrary movement of Arab households into Jewish areas. Otherwise, residential migration has been rare. Figures available for the first time, (in Israel 1985: 56-7) indicate that only 4 percent of the Arab population in 1983 had lived in another locality in 1978, compared to a corresponding figure of 13 percent for the Israeli Jewish population. There has been a relatively small degree of Arab inter-district migration; the Northern District (especially the Nazareth area) was the main source of migration, while the Haifa, Hadera, and Beersheba sub-districts absorbed most of the Arab migration flow between 1978 and 1983. As regards the types of localities affected by the Arab population movements, there was a negative migration balance in rural localities (under 2000 inhabitants) and in Arab urban localities (Nazareth and Umm al-Fahm) and the mixed cities. The small 'urban' Arab localities (2000-9999 inhabitants) and Haifa and Tel Aviv/Jaffa were at the receiving end of the Arab migration flows, and exhibited positive migration balances.

It took over a generation for most Arab localities to be connected to the national electricity grid, and a number remain without electricity, piped water, paved roads or main arterial roads leading to regional centres (see, e.g. Lustick 1980: 191). Only one Arab town, Shefa'amr, possesses a complete sewage treatment and disposal system (*Haaretz:*, 14 October 1984). In the rest, cess-pits and unsanitary open canal systems are widespread. Recently, locally inspired and funded efforts have been mounted to attempt to fill the vacuum created by official neglect of such basic services. As only three localities have municipal status, most Arab towns and villages benefit minimally from the state and local authority utilities, services and infrastructure so vital to economic development. While the issues of provision of this infrastructure are very much tied to the problems of approval of zoning plans for Arab localities, this is itself another aspect of official policy disfavourable to the Arab region.

The Arab 'Demographic Threat'

In official statistical series, 66 Arab localities are described as 'urban'. This is, however, extremely misleading in almost all cases, especially when comparison is made to even the smallest Jewish locality or settlement anywhere in the country. In Israel, a locality with over 2,000 inhabitants is officially defined as urban, but even the larger Arab towns (those with over 14,000 inhabitants - Nazareth, Umm al-Fahm, Taibeh, Shefa'amr, Tamra) have maintained their rural, even village character.[22] The average Arab household numbered 6.14 persons in 1983, compared to the Jewish level of 3.34 persons. Housing density is greater among Arabs than Jews: an average density of 2.2 persons per room compared to 1.1. While some 29 percent of Arab households live three or more persons to a room, only 1 percent of Jewish households live in the same conditions. This can be seen in Table 2.3.

Table 2.3: Households in Israel, by Size of Household, and Head of Household's Population Group, 1985

Pop. Group	Households (thous.)[a]	Total	Persons in Household (percentages)							Average persons per household[b]
			1	2	3	4	5	6	7+	
TOTAL POP.	1,151.5	100.0	15.4	22.1	13.9	18.9	15.0	6.9	7.8	3.5
JEWS	1,036.7	100.0	16.5	23.6	14.3	19.7	15.2	6.2	4.5	3.35
ARABS	114.9	100.0	5.9	8.6	10.3	11.3	13.5	13.2	37.1	5.71
Muslims	79.3	100.0	5.6	7.4	10.2	11.0	11.3	12.2	42.4	5.98
Christians	24.0	100.0	7.6	14.0	8.4	11.6	20.1	18.2	20.1	4.80
Others	11.6	100.0	(4.9)	(5.6)	15.3	13.2	14.3	(10.1)	36.5	5.76

NOTES: a. Excludes institutions and Bedouins in the south; b. Includes single households.
SOURCE: From (Israel, 1986: 71).

In the 1972-82 period, Arab population growth averaged 3.7 percent per annum compared to the Jewish rate of 2.1 percent (in Israel 1986: 27). It is this relatively high rate of population growth, though decreasing (annual growth had fallen to 3.1 percent between 1983/5, compared to a Jewish rate of 1.6 percent), which has led to Arabs becoming an increasingly large minority (see Table 2.4). In 1983, 45 percent of the Arab population (excluding Jerusalem) was aged between 0 and 14, 43 percent between the ages of 15 and 44, 9 percent between 45 and 64, with 3 percent 65 years or over. These proportions differ sharply from Jewish levels which exhibit a much 'older' age structure (30 percent, 43 percent, 17 percent, and 10 percent for the same age brackets respectively).

Table 2.4: Sources of Population Increase in Israel, Selected Years
(Thousands, unless otherwise stated)

Period	Pop. at beginning of Period	Natural Increase	Migration Balance	Total Increase	Pop. at end of Period	Annual Percent. Increase
	1	2	3	4=2+3	5=1+4	6=4:1
Total Population						
1948-1985[a,b]	805.6	2,002.7	1,412.2	3,414.9	4,266.2[c]	4.5
1948-1960	805.6	475.4	869.4	1,344.8	2,150.4	7.6
1961-1971	2,150.4	562.0	339.8	901.8	3,120.7	3.4
1972-1982[d]	3,115.6	752.7	183.3	936.0	4,036.6[c]	2.4
1983-1985[d]	4,033.7	212.4	20.1	232.5	4,266.2[c]	1.9
Jews						
1948-1985[a]	649.6	1,487.0	1,403.8	2,890.8	3,517.2[c]	4.6
1948-1960	649.6	392.3	869.3	1,261.6	1,911.2	8.3
1961-1971	1,911.2	412.9	337.9	750.8	2,662.0	2.8
1972-1982	2,662.0	532.3	178.5	710.8	3,373.2	2.1
1983-1985[d]	3,349.6	149.5	18.1	167.6	3,517.2	1.6
Arabs						
1948-1985[b]	156.0	515.5	8.7	524.2	749.0[c]	4.0
1948-1960	156.0	83.1	0.1	83.2	239.2	3.3
1961-1971	239.2	149.1	1.9	151.0	458.7[c]	4.1
1972-1982	453.8	220.3	4.8	225.1	690.4	3.7
1983-1985[d]	684.1	63.0	1.9	64.9	749.0	3.1

NOTES: a. As from 15 V 1948; b. Population for 1948 was estimated according to data for later periods; c. Includes census adjustments and addition of Arab population of East Jerusalem as of 1967 and Golan Heights as of 1982; d. Discontinuity due to census results.
SOURCE: From (Israel, 1986: 27).

The consistent growth of the Arab population has been the source of increased fears among Israeli policy makers about the

History, Policy, People and Society

'demographic threat' and was the basic departure point of plans to 'Judaise' the Galilee and areas of Arab concentration. The lines of differentiation within Arab society with regard to religious customs and affiliation are fairly clear. Of the total Arab population, including Jerusalem, 77 percent are Muslim, over 13 percent are Christian and under 10 percent are Druze or of other sects (see Table 2.5). Though there are a number of towns and villages with a mixed religious composition, the different groups tend to live separately even in these (e.g. Nazareth and especially Shefa'amr). This accentuates and further delineates the regional disparities of some social, demographic and economic characteristics.

Table 2.5: Population in Israel, by Religion, Selected Years
(end of year population, thousands)

YEAR	JEWS	MUSLIMS	CHRISTIANS	DRUZE	TOTAL ARAB	GRAND TOTAL	ARAB %
1949	1,013.9	111.5	34.0	14.5	160.0	1,173.9	13.6
1954	1,526.0	131.8	42.0	18.0	191.8	1,717.8	11.2
1959	1,858.8	159.2	48.3	22.3	229.8	2,088.7	11.0
1964	2,239.2	202.3	55.5	28.6	286.4	2,525.6	11.3
1969[a]	2,506.8	314.5	73.5	34.6	422.6	2,929.5	14.4
1974	2,906.9	395.2	78.7	40.8	514.7	3,421.6	15.0
1979	3,218.4	481.2	87.6	49.0	617.8	3,836.2	16.1
1980	3,282.7	498.3	89.9	50.7	636.9	3,921.7	16.2
1981	3,320.3	513.7	91.5	52.3	657.5	3,977.9	16.5
1982[b]	3,373.2	530.8	94.0	65.6	690.4	4,063.6	17.1
1983	3,412.5	542.2	95.9	68.0	706.1	4,118.6	17.1
1984	3,471.7	559.7	98.2	70.0	727.9	4,199.7	17.3
1985	3,517.2	577.6	99.4	72.0	749.0	4,266.2	17.6

NOTES: a. Figures from 1969 onwards include annexed East Jerusalem; b. Figures from 1982 onwards include annexed Golan Heights.
SOURCE: From (Israel, 1986: 26).

Arab society has undergone an educational experience very different from that of Israel's Jewish population.[23] Both in terms of access to facilities and educational advancement and quality and conditions of education, the Arab population in Israel has been especially disadvantaged. Most simply, this can be seen in the fact that of the Arab population aged 14 years and over in 1985 (including Jerusalem), 13.6 percent have never been to school, 35.5 percent only reached primary school, 12.4 percent left school at intermediate levels, 2.4 percent studied at vocational secondary schools, 28.3 percent attended general secondary schools, and 7.8 percent went to university or other post secondary institutions (Israel 1986: 568). This compares with Jewish levels of university and post secondary education (22.2 percent), secondary (24.6 percent) and vocational (24.8 percent) and a smaller proportion who only attained primary level (20 percent) or who never attended school (5 percent).

These various distinct demographic and physical formations and patterns of the Arab region are among the strongest factors determining its existence and growth. More than three decades of residential segregation, differentials in local and physical planning and allocation of resources, and the consolidation of a particularly Arab demographic structure (which has more in common with that of the West Bank than of the interspersing Jewish settlements of the Galilee) have created facts which cannot be ignored. In themselves, and despite the effects of contact with different ('modern') demographic attitudes and the geographic discontinuity of the Arab areas, these factors have enough weight to substantiate the argument for the recognition of an Arab region in Israel. However, there are other important features of the context and content of Arab economic activity which substantially strengthen the case. These include some of the salient features of Arab society.

SOCIAL STRUCTURE IN THE ARAB REGION

The broad subject of Arab social structure in Israel is not one that can be competently dealt with here, nor does it directly affect our central interests. However, the dynamics of change in Arab society have important implications for the continuing process of defining the region's relation to the national economy. It would be too ambitious a task to attempt to advance a comprehensive view of the many social barriers which contribute to the shaping of a distinct Arab region in Israel. The various strands of social conflict (generational, geographic, religious, familial, tribal, ideological, etc.) active in Arab society all can, and do, play a role at different stages in accelerating or blocking change. In addition, many of the prevalent distortions of social structure created and perpetuated by the legal/political barriers discussed above are important to the overall system of control. It is possible to perceive four main axes along which Arab social change operates with a bearing on the process of economic development. These are briefly identified below.

History, Policy, People and Society

'Regionalism' in the Region

Arab society is differentiated geographically on several levels: between villages and large towns such as Nazareth or Umm al-Fahm; between the three main components of the region, Galilee, the Triangle and the Negev; between the predominantly rural Arab Galilee and Triangle and the urban Arab population of the mixed cities. On another level, the population is split between those living in the mixed cities and the vast majority in villages and the larger semi-urban localities. This segmentation can have various negative effects.

The separation of Arab population centres is in itself a barrier to balanced and comprehensive economic development of the Arab 'region' because it partially determines the economic differentials within the region as a whole. However, the minimal intra-regional market and labour linkages, and the more recent phenomenon of intra-regional rural-urban migration attest to a more complex internal structure than might otherwise appear to be the case. The non-recognition of an Arab region has been especially important to those Israeli policy makers and academics, who are keen to demonstrate the success of a (non-existent) policy of integration and equality between Jewish and Arab citizens.

Religious and Ethnic Differences

The religious and ethnic composition of Arab society is another potential hindrance to development. By emphasising the religious and family/tribal composition of Arab society in Israel, state policy attempts to deny legitimacy to alternative Arab communal identities, be it regional, national, class or other (see, Lustick 1982: Chapter Four). The fact that certain religious or ethnic groups (e.g. Druze, Beduin or Circassians) receive preferential treatment from the state (due to their military service) can detract from their ability or willingness to identify with other, more deprived sections of the Arab community in Israel. For example, in 1985/6, when Arab and Druze local authorities were confronting the government over aid and subsidies, the Druze local authority federation refused to participate in joint negotiations and action with its Arab counterpart. Furthermore, religious and ethnic differences have traditionally facilitated state efforts to control the population, by favouring certain groups, such as the Druze, Beduin and Circassians, in return for explicit allegiance, in the form of military service or electoral support (Lustick 1980: Chapter Six).

History, Policy, People and Society

On another level, the strength of sectarian feeling between some villages can fortify regional differences. An important historical effect evident in the religious composition of Arab society is that to an extent, educational, income and occupational differentiations follow religious lines. Therefore certain areas of predominantly Muslim composition, for example, have lower standards of education, living and skills than others. Similarly, the predominantly Christian and Druze villages of central and upper Galilee exhibit more indicators of prosperity and more advanced local services and infrastructure. The occasional communal conflict that erupts between families or villages (e.g. in Kfar Manda in 1984 and the violent clashes prior to that in Kfar Yasif) can also run along the lines of religious or ethnic differentiations - though the motives and causes are rarely, if ever, sectarian as such.

'Modernisation' and Contact with Israeli Society

Though not a clearly delineated division, the experience of 'modernisation' and the development away from traditional values, methods and structures is a significant phenomenon within Arab society.[24] While this partially follows natural generational differences, it is also a result of the direct contact and experience of an oppressed, less developed society with a westernised and 'modern' regime. A distorted and uneven local adoption of external values and methods can be a natural result of the forced or unequal exposure of less developed societies to 'advanced' industrialised societies in general and of Palestinian society to western Zionism in particular.

Yet, the particular mixture of the traditional and the modern that has resulted in Arab society cannot readily be identified elsewhere in Israeli society, including among Jewish immigrants from Arab countries. This is a situation which arises out of the clash between the need to 'keep up' and the material limitations of Arab economic potential. By virtue of the fact of the continued existence and apparent viability of this Arab 'mode' of life, it is the level of development most appropriate to the region. As such, it constitutes another element of the parameters which define that economy.

Cooptation to Zionist Interests

A final issue of relevance is the extent to which state policies of control, cooptation and integration of local elites and traditional

leaders has succeeded in fragmenting Arab society along ideological and political lines (see, Lustick 1980: Chapter Six). This is significant to our present analysis because of the importance of the process of 'selective integration' to the continued subjugation of regional to national interests. Almost four decades of Zionist rule can be seen to have split Arab society into a number of typologies:
* those groups coopted into state or Zionist political interests and who actively collaborate in return for favours;
* many who have been unconsciously coopted but are indifferent, having abandoned any specifically Arab identity or commitment;
* activists (organised or individual) who are excluded and isolated from benefits and position for expressly political reasons;
* the vast majority who are effectively spectators to political and development processes, primarily concerned with the immediate problems of ensuring basic welfare and security needs.

While these differentiations can be perceived and defined from the outside, their influence is not always actually felt or relevant, especially in light of the function of other deeper (religious, family, regional) divisions. As with other obstacles to cohesive regional development, reactions to this type of social differentiation can also have an unexpected unifying effect. This becomes all the more true as the crude machinations of cooptation prove to be increasingly obsolete and ineffective in the face of broader levels of social and political consciousness. Such breakdowns in the system of control are especially noticed in issues related to the Palestinian identity of the Arab population as a whole. Yet, with further disintegration of the traditional Arab family, other avenues for 'consciousness raising' also appear.

Social Divisions: Obstacles or Incentives to Development?

The origins of most of these barriers lie in the historical development of Arab society in Israel. They do not exist in order to further the aims of any specific power, though they are regularly manipulated and aggravated by the state in the interests of its policies towards the Arab region. Though the regime is in a good position to deepen and increase various social divisions to thwart possible development efforts, there are clear limits to this capacity. This is defined in part by the process of Arab social and economic development itself.

The increase in communication and links between the components of the Arab region decreases the possibilities of external manipulation and intervention. At the same time, the different sectors of the Arab population are able to perceive themselves not as isolated local minority groups, but as part of a significant national minority, with the potential confidence and strength to play a serious role in determining its own affairs. Traditionalism and religious solidarity have proved their staying power, often to the ire of the state or Zionist interests; this in itself has helped to solidify a distinct Arab social structure with needs and aspirations of its own.

However, the gradual 'modernisation' of society has succeeded in producing institutions and methods which in themselves are not harmful to local needs, but which have until now been controlled by state or affiliated interests. This balance of power could change as new social elements, not sharing the interests of those in control and favoured by them, gradually and naturally move into the 'modern sector'. Finally, the growing political awareness and organisation of the Arab population and its identification with Palestinian aims and aspirations has shown itself to be the greatest threat posed so far by this minority to the system by which it is ruled. In the sphere of social structure, therefore, the barriers to development carry within them the seeds of development. Needless to say, the transformation of barriers into incentives is a process with its own momentum and subject only to the influence of the main actors: the state and the concerned population.

NOTES

1. This principle of equal rights for all Israeli citizens, including Palestinian Arabs, was first enshrined, and clearly stipulated, in the Israeli Declaration of Independence of 1948. Israeli laws are founded on a variety of covenants, articles and legal statutes borrowed from legal systems previously operative in Palestine, including Ottoman and British regulations; there is no Israeli constitution *per se*.

2. There is a vast body of literature on this subject, and the following discussion draws on a few of these sources: (Nathan *et. al*. 1946); (Granott 1952); (Hobman, ed. 1946); (Himadeh 1938); (INSEE 1948); (Abu Lughod, ed. 1971); (Carmi and Rosenfeld 1974); (Rosenfeld 1976); (Zureik 1979); (Lustick 1980); (Weimer 1983).

3. There are a number of different estimates of population distribution by this date as the last comprehensive census had been carried out in 1931. Another source quotes a smaller total population of 590,000 in 1919 of which Jews constituted 9.7%, rising to a total of 1,835,559 in 1946, of which Jews constituted 35% (Zureik 1979: 47). In any case, the Jewish population had become a sizeable minority on the eve of Israeli independence.

History, Policy, People and Society

4. Though, as shown by Carmi and Rosenfeld's evidence of similar urban and rural wage rates, this was by no means of the type, or for the motivations, usually experienced in developing countries where the 'expected rural-urban income differential' is considered to be the determining factor in the process (see, e.g. Todaro 1969).

5. The total population figure was arrived at by extrapolating from the 1946 population in (Zureik 1979: 47) at 4% population growth per annum. While there are different estimates for the number of refugees, the 750,000 out of a total Arab population of 900,000 in the area that came to be controlled by Israel quoted in (Lustick 1980: 28) is modest. Israeli statistics indicate 160,000 Arab inhabitants in 1949 (Israel 1983b). There were continual population movements in the immediate post war period, with a certain return flow of population, clandestine or permitted, in addition to an increase of some 30,000 Palestinians in the Little Triangle region ceded to Israel as part of the 1949 Armistice agreement with Jordan (Lustick 1980: 49).

6. A new and illuminating account of the conditions and policies faced by the remaining Palestinians in the new Israeli state can be found in T. Segev's history of the first year of the Jewish state (1986). R. Sayigh provides a masterful and incisive record of the transformations in Palestinian social structure as lived by refugees in Lebanon (1979).

7. Several estimates, including that made by the UN Palestine Conciliation Commission, made in the years succeeding 1948 produced lower figures than those arrived at by two Palestinian experts, one of whom participated in the original UN effort - (see, Hadawi and Kubursi, forthcoming) and (UN Conciliation Commission on Palestine 1950, and successive years).

8. Policy is here understood to encompass legal provisions and official government policies and measures, in addition to those of the large Histadrut and public sector (including Zionist institutions such as the Jewish Agency). Another element that should be included because of its great influence and effect upon Arab conditions is that of Jewish public opinion and attitudes to Arabs.

9. Israeli policy towards the economy of the occupied West Bank and Gaza Strip is, for example, depicted by some of its critics as 'aiming to destroy the economy', as 'discriminatory', 'racist' etc. All of these characterisations may or may not be true. They are, however, inadequate for any serious analysis of how and why Israel controls, exploits and consequently dominates the occupied territories. This (non-) methodology can also be found in some critiques of Israeli policy towards Palestinian Arabs in Israel. It should be noted that the shortcomings of this approach are less problematic than those arguments which defend or attempt to rationalise Israeli policy.

10. Abu Kishk elsewhere cites a figure of 2.2 million dunums of land expropriated from Arabs in Israel until 1960 alone (1981: 125). Kislev mentions up to 2.5 million dunums expropriated until the mid-1970s (1976: 28).

11. The problems encountered by Arabs trying to take up residence in exclusively Jewish quarters or localities were most pointedly exhibited (and widely reported in the Israeli press) in the opposition put up by Jewish

residents to Arabs renting flats in the late 1970s in Carmiel and more recently in Upper Nazareth.

12. This was highlighted in the results of a sample survey of two Arab farming localities, Jatt in the Triangle and Shefa'amr in the Galilee (Khalidi and Sabbagh 1985a), in which a high proportion of farmers complained about the restriction of irrigation water quotas of 500 cubic metres per dunum as opposed to the higher quotas alloted to Jewish settlements - see Chapter Three.

13. A decision to admit Arabs to the Histadrut sponsored national Farmers Union was only taken at the Histadrut Convention of 1985; it will be four years before the decision takes effect.

14. More specific facets of current state policy affecting Arab industrial and agricultural development will be discussed in the following chapters when examining problems in those fields.

15. In the 1984 Israeli 'National Unity' government, the Minister without Portfolio, Ezer Weizmann, was accorded special responsibility for Arab Affairs. He was succeeded in 1986 by the former Defence Minister, Moshe Arens. The post carries no executive powers. This was the first time that Arab affairs had been given direct ministerial supervision. Previously it had been the domain of a department in the Prime Minister's office.

16. A source of regular, authoritative and up-to-date information on Israeli economic and technological developments and events can be found in the monthly *Israel Economist*. Numerous more comprehensive or specialist historical and contemporary accounts are also available.

17. The Union of Arab Local Authorities, which represents all Arab municipalities and local councils, called several successful strikes in 1985 to protest the failure of the government to disburse the $6 million due them as state grants (see, *Jerusalem Post,* November and December 1985). Their protests were called off only when the Prime Minister intervened and guaranteed payment of part of the sum due (*Jerusalem Post International Edition,* 11 January 1986). However, the failure of the government to release all promised funds led to a resumption of protest activity by Arab local councils late in 1986.

18. There were regular references in the Israeli press as of late 1985 that in the ongoing economic crisis, Arabs would be the first to be laid off - first from the occupied territories and then from the Arab region in Israel.

19. Unless otherwise indicated, all the figures in this section on demographic and geographic indicators are 1983 figures, derived from the results of the 1983 Census of Population and Housing, which can be found in (Israel 1985: 32-79).

20. The second largest Arab locality, Umm al-Fahm, only received municipality status in 1985, and is the first Arab municipality to come into existence since Israel was established in 1948. The other two, Nazareth and Shefa'amr, have been municipalities from the era of the Ottoman Empire

21. Strictly speaking, these are not localities, but rather geographic and administrative reference points designated by the state for eventual settlement of the Negev Beduin. This is a process which successive governments have tried to encourage since the 1950s, in continuing efforts to displace the Negev Beduin from their traditional areas of settlement into these new 'localities'. However, these efforts have not met with great success, since the

History, Policy, People and Society

Beduin have continued to manifest a strong attachment to their historic farming and grazing rights in the areas of the Negev expropriated during the early day of the state. Meanwhile, state incentives (schools, clinics, employment opportunities) were not strong, or indeed credible, enough to effect this 're-sedenterisation' (state managed or spontaneous). The particular conditions and history of the Beduin in Israel is not dealt with here and can be consulted in a number of comprehensive accounts (Davis and Richardson 1985); (Falah 1985); (Goering 1979) and (Amiran *et al.* 1976). Spontaneous settlement has been noticeable among the Beduin of the north, as depicted in an interesting account by a Galilee Beduin (Falah 1983).

22. One Israeli geographer (Meyer Brodnitz 1971) has used the term '*in-situ* urbanisation' to describe the process particular to Arab localities of population growth and 'de-agriculturisation' without a concomitant development of infrastructure, services and urban economy. Though not coined in reference to Arab localities, the term 'rurban village' is appropriate here.

23. For authoritative accounts of Arab education in Israel, see (Nakhleh 1979) and (Mari 1978).

24. To be understood as the adoption of new values and the abandonment of certain traditions; this is a process which most societies pass through and I would differentiate it from the sort of 'modernisation' which Zionist political economy alleges is the main feature of Arab economic development. I do not believe that 'modernisation' is a phenomenon with much relevance to economic growth/development/change, though it can be seen to have greater meaning in a broad social sense.

Three

AGRICULTURE:
A RESERVE FOR REGIONAL GROWTH

The factors discussed in Chapter Two which define and shape the Arab region have operated mainly as barriers to development. Historic legacies, state policy, and the prevailing geographic and social structure have on the whole helped to inhibit Arab economic advancement in Israel. Yet, paradoxically perhaps, they have been important influences in the emergence of a distinctly Arab political, social and geographic unit which has provided the context for the development of patterns of distinctly Arab economic activity. The economic structure of the Arab region, is therefore, conditioned by these non-economic factors, but equally by the forces and effects of its own development. The operation of the former as barriers to growth can conflict with the interests of the region's growth as fuelled by Arab economic resources and aspirations. But the two sets of factors, the economic and non-economic, are not necessarily opposed and can coincide.[1]

This dynamic is of interest not only because it has allowed Arab agricultural activity to continue to provide the livelihood of a large Arab farm population. Equally, it has accentuated some of the unique characteristics of Arab agriculture, thus awarding it an important position in a distinctly Arab 'region'. The consolidation of *Arab* economic processes in Israel can have wide ranging implications both for the developmental prospects of the Arab region and for future state policy towards an increasingly sizeable and vocal sector of the population. Though this trend can be reversed, through repressive or conciliatory policy measures, or through an eventual dissipation of Arab cultural political or economic identity in Israel, there is no indication of this occurring. Indeed, continued operation of this regional constraint/determinant dynamic further strengthens an awareness of shared Arab economic interests within the national economy.

Agriculture: A Reserve for Regional Growth

My analysis of the regional economy examines it through reference to three issues of greatest concern. This chapter begins by looking at the position of the agricultural base, caught between the process of continued decline and that of self generated growth. The subsequent chapters discuss the main forms of regional industrial and commercial activity and the role of Arab labour in the national economy. I shall attempt to elaborate a profile of the region that will demonstrate its specificity, while the nature of the regional-national relation is also highlighted, aided by recourse to some basic tools of regional economic analysis. Thus, the validity of a regional rationale to Arab economic behaviour in Israel, rooted in the dynamics of its own economic processes, becomes all the more difficult to refute.

ARAB AGRICULTURE IN ISRAEL: THE HISTORICAL LEGACY

More than any other issue of Arab development in Israel, that of agriculture has been the focal point for conflict and controversy, even from before 1948. The crucial issues of ownership and access to land and water have placed the 'agrarian question' at the forefront of the concerns of generations of Zionist and Palestinian policy makers, activists and farmers.[2] For the Zionist movement and Israel, the acquisition and exploitation of the land was a major element in the successful establishment of the state, and agriculture represented a significant growth centre in the economy for many years. For the predominantly peasant Palestinian Arab population, agriculture was historically their main pillar of subsistence. The land has since become the basis for maintaining an existence in their country as well as a highly emotive symbol of national identity. A look at the experience of Arab agriculture in the initial period of Israeli rule helps to better explain its present position.

The development of a self sufficient, increasingly capitalised and export oriented agricultural base has been a national priority since the foundation of the state. It is an example of one of the more successful Israeli economic experiences.[3] Growth has been possible largely through massive public investment, the establishment of a variety of highly efficient forms of agricultural organisation (the *kibbutzim* and *moshavim* in particular), and the development of an elaborate, well coordinated and comprehensive distribution, marketing and export support system. However, the most crucial ingredient in the successful engineering of this programme was neither ingenuity nor capital. The appropriation of land previously owned by Palestinian Arab peasants, either refugees or new Israeli citizens, provided Jewish

The Land Issue in Israel

On the eve of the hostilities that erupted in the wake of the 1947 UN resolution calling for partition of Palestine, Jewish owned land totalled some 1.6 million dunums (Zureik 1979: 47), of which some 1.2 million was cultivated (Hadawi 1970: 19). When the war ended in 1949, Jews were already cultivating 1.3 million dunums; with the consolidation of conquered or expropriated land in the early 1950s, the Jewish cultivated area had by 1959/60 reached 3.3 million dunums, an increase of 175 percent on pre-1948 levels (Israel 1966). Jewish cultivated area continued to grow during the period of military rule in the region through expropriations, but also through reclamation and the bringing of marginal land into cultivation.[5]

Much of the land lost by Arabs in the 1948-52 period (when most confiscation laws were implemented) was either owned by refugees (exiled or those still present within Israel) or was public (state) land which had been traditionally cultivated by local villages. However, there were also significant expropriations in the Triangle in the mid-1950s, while later in the decade, Arab land was confiscated in the Galilee to build Jewish 'development' towns such as Upper Nazareth and Carmiel.[6]

The land issue has had the most profound effect on Arab agriculture's subsequent development.[7] More than the loss of the political, commercial and financial leadership, more than the disruption and displacement that occurred in family and social relations, more than the cultural and psychological ramifications of suddenly being subjected to the rule of a foreign, and effectively hostile power, the loss of land threatened the very basis of continued Arab existence in Israel. Needless to say, it was an all pervasive determinant of the scope for development of Arab agriculture. The situation was further complicated by the fact that Jewish agriculture added in one decade some 2.1 million dunums of Arab land to its cultivated area, a considerable bonus, indeed, to any agricultural development effort.

The 'Vicious Circle' View of Arab Agriculture

Other problems also handicapped Arab agriculture in this period. Fragmentation was a paramount obstacle to any efforts at introduction of irrigation, large scale mechanisation or cropping patterns that required larger areas. Over and above this, Arab farmers did not have the financial means to institute such improvements, and the state did not make any investments in this sector.[8] Even had investment been available, Arab agriculture was still geared to traditional methods of extensive cultivation of subsistence crops. Considerable effort and transformations would have been required to ensure effective and optimal allocation of aid. Commoditisation had not penetrated throughout the sector even before 1948 when citriculture increased.

In the wake of the 1948 war, the Arab citrus branch on the coastal plain had been destroyed, the land expropriated, and its skills and labour force mainly transplanted to Palestinian refugee camps in Lebanon.[9] Furthermore, the important class of Palestinian merchants and land owning financiers capable of helping to sustain Arab agriculture had lost all and/or fled. An important additional barrier to development of Arab agriculture was the exclusion of Arabs from the important cooperative marketing and export infrastructure to which Jewish farming units were linked. This increased the isolation of the region in what two Israeli academics have termed its "vicious circle perpetuating the low productivity of subsistence agriculture" (Arnon and Raviv 1980: 209).

This widely held view is the starting point for those who credit the Jewish economy with eventually modernising Arab agriculture. In their view, the low productivity of traditional agriculture is due to two major mutually reinforcing factors: low labour and land productivity. This in turn leads to low farm income and consequently low savings and reinvestment. So, unable to produce better and higher yields, the established pattern cannot be broken "by the sole efforts of the traditional farmer. This situation explains the third characteristic of traditional agriculture...namely, its unchanging character, or rather the state of stagnation from which it cannot free itself by its own efforts" (*Ibid:* 208).

As correctly held by this same analysis, the eventual elimination of rural underemployment through absorbtion of surplus labour in the Jewish urban economy did not, as in similar situations, lead to the abandonment of agriculture in favour of urban, non-agricultural occupations.[10] Thus, modernisation is seen to have been made possible by the migration process; continued migrant ties to the village allowed for the creation of investment capital. Subsequent central authority guidance through extension services helped Arab farmers follow a correct and appropriate introduction of agricultural technology.

There are a number of problems with this account which merit clarification that we better understand the numerous factors which 'modernised' Arab agriculture. Well prior to the establishment of Israel, traditional Arab agriculture had already entered the process of commoditisation (citrus, cash crop vegetables, the shift away from cereals, etc). This was part of the overall development process in the first part of the century and the 'state of stagnation' was gradually becoming less prevalent. Indeed, there is no reason to believe that the breaking of the 'vicious circle' had not begun to take place before 1948, and that the path to modernisation (savings, investment, technological application) would not have occurred anyhow.

In fact, perhaps the major factor in Arab agriculture's reentry into the 'vicious circle' after 1948 was the loss of the bulk of the agricultural land base and in many cases, the better quality land. This was aggravated throughout the 1950s by being barred from any chance of realising productivity and income gains through effective exclusion from the market. The surplus labour that had previously been free to obtain employment throughout the national economy was for the best part of a decade unable to enter the narrow, Jewish dominated labour market that existed. Once these restrictions had either been lifted, or adapted to, agriculture was able to reestablish itself along a more 'normal' development path.[11]

The divergences between Jewish and Arab agricultural performance in this period are clear.[12] Arab agriculture cultivated 28 percent of arable land in 1949/50, while only producing 9 percent of the total national value of output. With the consolidation of confiscated land under Jewish cultivation, by 1954/55, the Arab share of cultivated area had fallen to 17 percent and its share of value of output was now 6 percent. By 1965/6, reclamation and settlement of some outstanding claims on land had increased the total Arab cultivated area to 860,000 dunums, while the Arab share of value of output was 7 percent. In the period, the ratio of Arab to Jewish land productivity (value of output per cultivated dunum) remained constant at 33 percent from 1949/50 to 1954/5. It fell to 24 percent in 1964/5 and has dropped to under 20 percent since. Figures for labour productivity indicate a similar divergence (Zarhi and Achziera 1966: 21). Over the years, these significant differentials have since changed little, except for some further deterioration.

The underlying causes are not difficult to ascertain. Fragmentation, accentuated by often indiscriminate expropriation of parcels of land, the low level of Arab capital investment in biological, chemical and mechanical inputs, minimal irrigation of Arab land, and the loss in value added because of exclusion from distribution and export networks were all factors. However, the reasons that this situation prevailed (and have yet to alter

Agriculture: A Reserve for Regional Growth

significantly) are not, as many researchers have held, to be found in the Arab farming unit itself. Jewish agriculture has always been highly capitalised and well-subsidised sector, integrated with the rest of the economy. The same cannot be said for Arab agriculture, except that it was always at an earlier stage of development.

It thus can be said to have exhibited more of the features of 'underdevelopment' - subsistence oriented production, inefficient resource allocation, low savings and investment levels, slow penetration of education and technological advances etc. Nevertheless, it cannot be argued that 'traditional society and attitudes' are the main reason for the perpetuation of this state.[13] The essential ingredient absent from the mix of production factors was state support and central guidance. These were, and remain, centrally important to the success of Jewish farming.

State Planning and Aid for the Arab Rural Sector

Lack of state investment in the Arab region contributed in great measure to the slow advance of agriculture, as well as to the broader economic and social problems of the region. In the final years of military government in the Arab region, two investment plans were announced. This was mainly in answer of growing criticism, but it also represented an attempt, however misguided, to elaborate a coherent state policy towards the region. The first, was termed the 'Five Year Plan (1962-7) for the Development of Arab and Druze Villages' but was criticised at the time for being too general, without clear targets and generally insufficient (see, Flapan 1962; Lustick 1980: 190-1). It proposed investment of some $18 million in infrastructural, housing and economic development, $3.3 million of this in agriculture.[14]

In agriculture, the planned investment was low, both relative to the level of investment in Jewish agriculture and in terms of the level of Arab agriculture itself: in 1962, the value of Arab farming output was some $17 million. Additionally, the state intended to provide only 45 percent of the Plan's total investment, with banks providing loans for some 20 percent and the Arab private sector investing the balance of 35 percent. Such expectations of possible levels of Arab savings and investment were highly optimistic, to say the least. In agriculture, it was envisaged that the state would provide credits of 25 percent of the sum, with the Arab private sector providing most of the rest.

The subsequent plan, meant to supplement but not replace the earlier plan, was announced in 1963 by Minister of Agriculture, Moshe Dayan, based on a detailed census survey of

Agriculture: A Reserve for Regional Growth

Arab agriculture (Flapan 1963; 1963a). Its recommendations focussed on the 28 percent of villagers with farms above the allegedly viable size of 31 dunums. It contained various specific measures and targets, avoiding some of the problems raised in the 1962-7 Plan. These included reclamation, additional water allocations to make possible more irrigation, expansion of plantations, industrial crop and irrigated field crop area, at a total investment of $15 million, 45 percent of which was to be provided by government grants and the remainder through commercial loans.

While this plan attempted to overcome the shortcomings of its predecessor by establishing clear targets on the basis of detailed surveying, it too fell far short of being capable of structurally improving Arab agriculture. A prominent Israeli critic of state policy in that period detailed the plan's inadequacies, including its failure to effectively deal with problems of fragmentation, discriminatory price levels, marketing, credit, tax assessment, technical instruction, and overall lack of attention to village social development:

> If we examine the extent to which the Dayan Plan contributes to reducing the gap between Arab and Jewish farming, we find it so obviously inadequate that it does not deserve the name of a development program; in fact it is a conservation plan... In short, the gap in technical level, incomes and other respects will remain the same, if it does not grow worse (Flapan 1963a: 5).

The efforts of the early 1960s were followed by a second 'Five Year Plan (1967-72)', with a forecast investment of some $32 million, 34 percent to be provided by government grants, 51 percent in government loans and the rest from Arab investors (Lustick 1980: 191). Government officials defend their record by stressing that no such special expenditures exist for other other sections of Israeli society. However, it remains the case that state development aid disfavours the Arab region. Expenditure in the Arab sector as a proportion of total state development budget expenditure rose from 0.2 percent to between 1.3 percent and 1.5 percent from 1957/8 to 1971/2 (*Ibid:* 192). Without being able to undertake here an evaluation of the extent to which the plans achieved their targets, it is clear that they did not approach the level of involvement and aid required for any serious change. "The basic reason for the failure of the development plans to have more than a marginal impact on the economic development of the Arab sector was the lack of government funding" (*Ibid:* 191).

Agriculture: A Reserve for Regional Growth

Despite these initial outlays,[15] the lack of and need for effective state investment in the Arab economy remained a cause of concern for some Israelis. In 1966, Zarhi and Achziera estimated that a net investment of some $430 million ($630 million gross) over 10 years was required to reduce the Arab Jewish development gap (1966: 23-4). They noted that,

> ...although such an investment is considerable, in comparison with capital investment in the Israeli economy as a whole it is not particularly high... That is to say that investment needed for the development of the Arab settlements will be less than 5 percent of total investments (Ibid).

Several years later, in the early 1970s, another economist predicted that development of the region would require an investment over 10 years of some $29 million annually, equal to about 1 percent per annum of Israel's 1969 GNP (Gottheil 1973: 246). However, further government engineered development plans never materialised.

Arab agriculture and the rural areas, the supposed main beneficiary of state inspired development efforts, have lagged far behind their Jewish counterparts. The following sections will analyse in detail the different aspects of this situation, though a comparative analysis only serves to highlight the problems. It is important to stress that despite the constraints on Arab agriculture, and the losses it has suffered in the past 40 years, it has maintained a significant place in the regional economy. This is partly due to its national role, but also to the base it provides for other regional economic activities, especially in the provision of a certain subsistence reserve in many localities.

The maintenance of a distinct Arab agricultural sector, with its own mode of production and relations to the national economy also acts to consolidate a physical framework and environment for other complementary or alternative economic activities of the Arab population. Thus have the factors which have acted as obstacles to agricultural growth (state policy, geographic and social constraints) come together to help form a sector of a regional economy. Paradoxically, this economy's developmental dynamic is defined and strengthened by some of those very factors which mitigate against it.

Agriculture: A Reserve for Regional Growth

FACTORS AND ORGANISATION OF PRODUCTION: LAND, THE REGION'S INHERITANCE[16]

Area, Quality and Distribution of Arab Land

The total Arab cultivable area in 1981 was 756,700 dunums, of which almost 50 percent was in the Negev. The region's arable area constitutes a small proportion of national arable land (over 18 percent of the total cultivated area of 4.1 million dunums). This figure includes the Negev desert where Beduin cultivated 375,000 dunums in 1981, most of which is used for irregular and non-intensive rainfed cultivation of field crops - only 0.1 percent of land in the Negev is irrigated. Jewish agriculture in the Negev cultivates a total of 1.26 million dunums, of which some 47 percent is equipped for irrigation. Therefore, excluding the Negev,[17] the northern and central areas of the Arab region constituted some 10 percent of total arable area in Israel in 1981. Arabs cultivate the available land somewhat more intensively than the national average: the Arab cropped area is 96 percent of arable land compared to a national level of 92 percent.

The only available data on the geographic distribution of Arab land are from the Agricultural Census of 1972, since which date there has been little change (in Abu Kishk 1984: 166-9). The central areas are composed of the three remaining Arab villages in the Jerusalem district and the fertile land of the Triangle, in the Hadera subdistrict. Together, these areas cultivated 12 percent of the Arab region's land in 1972 (23 percent excluding the Negev). The northern area of the region is composed of the Arab parts of the subdistricts of Acre, Yizre'el (Nazareth and its surroundings) and Haifa.[18] Together, these cultivate 39 percent of the region's land (77 percent excluding the Negev). The bulk of the land in the north is located in the central Nazareth area and just inland from the Acre coastal plain (some 80 percent) with the rest extending into Upper Galilee.

There are discrepancies in the quality of the available arable Arab land between the two main areas of cultivation, the Triangle and the Galilee (Arnon and Raviv 1980: 14-15; 26). In the former, mild climates, plentiful underground water and relatively high rainfall assist in raising the productivity of the diverse and fertile soil types allowing for the specialisation of this area in mainly vegetable and fruit cash-crops. In the mainly hilly Galilee, diverse ecological conditions between the hills and the valleys, and primarily rainfed cultivation, has led to specialisation by the hill villages in olives, tobacco and field crops, while valley villages concentrate on rainfed or irrigated cereals, industrial

Agriculture: A Reserve for Regional Growth

crops, olives and vegetables. In the Negev, conditions are most favourable for rainfed crops, especially wheat and barley, though olives and certain fruit trees are also cultivable. The almost complete absence of irrigation fairly definitely excludes any alternatives.

Land can be classified according to eight types, four of which are cultivable, though requiring a variety of soil erosion measures: waterways, contouring, or terracing (Abu Kishk 1985). Improvement is either very costly or requires a level of cooperation not easily achieved on the other four types of land (marshy, hilly, pasture and wild). For example, the Battuf valley in central Galilee is covered by water throughout the winter with no drainage outlets. Some 20,000 dunums are closed off by surrounding hills and farmers have to wait until the water dries off the surface before they can work the soil.

As mentioned above, Arab cropped area is a relatively higher proportion of arable land than is the case nationally. However, there are indications that problems in differential land quality still prevent full utilisation of available resources. For example, in two Arab villages in the Galilee and the Triangle surveyed in 1985, almost half of a representative sample of farms reported some degree of arable land left uncultivated due to its salinity or hilly and rocky nature (Khalidi and Sabbagh 1985a).[19] Of these, half were unable to cultivate over 50 percent of their arable land. It is not altogether surprising that some 20 percent reported that the same parcel of land was cropped more than once a year, for a summer and a winter crop, and sometimes for a third.

Ownership of Arab land is almost totally private, unlike Jewish settled land which is mainly quasi-public, held by bodies such as the Jewish Agency, and thus 'the inalienable property of the Jewish people'. Only 1 percent of Arab farm area in 1981 was on 'national land' compared to 81 percent nationally. Since 1948, very little land has been sold out of the Arab sector, while some exchanges or sales take place involving family members or neighbouring farmers and a degree of consolidation has been achieved. Arab farming is organised around family units with widespread leasing practises, on annual or sometimes longer terms from non-cultivator Arab owners (a contractual arrangement known as *daman)*, and to (less so) from Jewish owners.[20] Though convenient for both parties, this practice, as with most sharecropping or leasing arrangements between cultivators and non-cultivator landlords, can discourage substantial investment in land improvement.

Agriculture: A Reserve for Regional Growth

Constricted Land Resources Aggravate Fragmentation

The quality and distribution of land, the main agricultural production factor, is an essential determinant of the sector's performance. The strongest factor determining the quality of land left to the region is of course the effect of the widescale expropriations by the state since 1948, which have often been targeted at the best land, leaving farms divided into disparate plots. The prevailing social structure encourages small family farming, leading to fragmentation and making cooperation difficult, in turn lessening the chances for a strengthening of viable parts of the sector. Arab inheritance practices, whereby a deceased father's land is divided equally among his remaining sons, have also affected the distribution of land, lowering the relative size of Arab farms.[21] In the two Galilee and Triangle villages surveyed, 75 percent of the sampled farms cultivated a number of fragmented plots (Khalidi and Sabbagh 1985a). While most parcels were under five dunums, this reflects the generally small farm size as well as that of the plots. However, whereas the average size of the sampled farms was 37.5 dunums, the average parcel size was 6.3 dunums.

This fragmentation reduces the potential for economic farming and breaks up the better quality land. The 'hand and foot' inheritance division system splits plots between the better and poorer quality land or the land is in long, narrow strips. The irrigation of a 1000x10 meter strip requires pipes of such length as to make it uneconomic. Where communal *mushaa'* land is still cultivated, each farmer has a right in each village plot, thus further complicating the production process.

There are a total of 13,695 Arab farms (11,468 excluding the Negev), constituting 34 percent of the national total. As indicated, plots are mostly small and fragmented, often to the point of making cultivation uneconomic. This is illustrated by the fact that whereas 61 percent of the cultivated national area is found in farms of 500 dunums or more, only 14 percent of the cultivated Arab area is in farms of that scale (figures here including the relatively larger Negev Beduin farms). And in that same category of farms over 500 dunums, the national average farm size is 3265 dunums while the average Arab farm is 866 dunums. Overall, the average size of Arab farms is 55 (arable) dunums while the national average farm size is 100 dunums. If Beduin farms in the Negev are excluded, average Arab farm size is 33 dunums, slightly more than the average of 31.5 dunums for the central and northern areas (Abu Kishk 1984: 166-9).

If the level of 30 dunums is accepted as the minimum 'viable' farm size,[22] 14 percent of the Arab cultivated area can be said to be in 'unviable' farms, compared to 8 percent nationally. However some 62 percent of all Arab farms are under 30 dunums; this is a proportion which has been declining since 1962 when it stood at 71 percent *(Ibid)*. In those twenty years, the number of farms has not decreased, indicating an extraordinary rigidity in farm structure and the degree to which the Arab agricultural base is tenaciously maintained. In the central Hadera area, there are proportionately more Arab farms under 30 dunums (80 percent of the total) than in the north (59 percent).[23]

This factor appears to primarily reflect the differential quality of land, since the central area is all plain land, amenable to smaller-scale, cash-crop farming and smaller farms can be profitable. The Galilee area is mostly hilly and more suited to olive, tobacco and field crop cultivation, which is less lucrative on a smaller scale. This fact, taken with the minimal increase in the average farm size, might indicate that the problem of fragmentation has been stemmed. On the one hand, a certain degree of consolidation has taken place in the past decade; on the other, when smaller sized plots are profitable, further subdivision is tolerated.[24]

The state has not played an active role in trying to improve this situation, nor can it be expected to, given our analysis of its policies. Basically, its overall interests do not include the emergence of a strong Arab agricultural sector. Officials defend the state's record on the issue of fragmentation by highlighting those few efforts that have been made, primarily in the mid-1960s. They assert that cooperatisation, a prerequisite for consolidation, is not something to be enforced, but must come from within Arab society. Notwithstanding the validity of such an attitude, this is undermined by the overtly preferential aid and treatment accorded Israeli Jewish cooperative institutions.

Nevertheless, neglect of Arab agriculture is indicative not so much of deliberate policy as of the exclusionary environment *despite which* Arab farmers have maintained a strong involvement with their land. Where consolidation has been possible, major problems remain in exploiting this through capital and technological intensification. The cost of land improvement and reclamation is usually too great for an individual or group of farmers to bear alone. So, some centralised guidance and aid to any cooperative efforts, Arab or otherwise, remains a necessary (and in this case, absent) element of any improvement of the physical organisation of Arab farming in Israel.

FACTORS AND ORGANISATION OF PRODUCTION: WATER AND IRRIGATION, THE REGION'S HANDICAP

Access to national water resources is restricted by the policies of the state water authority (see, e.g. Davis 1983). The Israel Water Commission, *Mekorot*, provides only 59 percent of all domestic, industrial and agriculture water in Israel (Israel 1985: 452). However, it is responsible for allocating water quotas from wells, even the private artesian wells which are prevalent in the Triangle (Abu Kishk 1985).[25] That area has always been more advanced agriculturally and farmers there obtained permits to dig wells in the 1950s before the authorities began to implement more stringent plans for water distribution and storage. Once the well is dug, the Commission determines how much water can be pumped and for what period, sometimes specifying the crops on which it can be applied. There are no other significant water sources except for the few springs which do not provide large quantities of water. Reservoirs have not been a viable alternative because of the absence of land for dams and the cost of compensating owners.

Water is a scarce resource in Israel, and Arab agriculture is allocated less than its proportional share. Arab irrigated land constitutes 2.6 percent of the national irrigated land area (Israel 1983a), much less than its proportion of cultivated area. Excluding the Negev, only 16 percent of Arab cultivated land is irrigated, compared to a national proportion of 56 percent *(Ibid)*. Consequently, it is not surprising that Arab agriculture consumes only 2.2 percent of all water used by agriculture (Israel 1985: 452).

The Triangle is the major area for Arab irrigation. According to Jewish Agency figures for 1978, in the Hadera subdistrict, some 41 percent of the cultivated area was irrigated, constituting over 70 percent of the total Arab irrigated area of 55,000 dunums (in Abu Kishk 1984: 163). In the Nazareth and Central Galilee area the proportion of irrigated to cultivated Arab area was 3.3 percent. In the Western and Upper Galilee the proportion was 2.8 percent.[26] Yet even in the Triangle, 89 percent of Jewish land is irrigated. These comparative proportions have improved only slightly in the past 20 years.

Irrigation methods are generally less sophisticated and widespread than those used in Jewish agriculture. In general, when feasible, irrigation is used for crops with a high export value. The earliest irrigation system used in Arab villages is furrow irrigation; another method is through cisterns which distribute the water to individual fruit trees and is also used for some vegetables. Sprinklers have been introduced and must be used according to the strength of water pump motor and factors

Agriculture: A Reserve for Regional Growth

such as soil type and wind. The most recent irrigation method is drip irrigation which involves a network of plastic hoses with distribution holes, requiring strict attention to pumping hours and evaporation. It was found that in the two surveyed Galilee and Triangle villages, 90 percent of sampled farms used both sprinkler and drip irrigation systems, to the almost complete exclusion of other (Khalidi and Sabbagh 1985a). Further, irrigation appears to have been introduced gradually, with only 13 percent having installed irrigation before 1965, some 20 percent between 1965 and 1974, and 33 percent since 1975.[27]

Mekorot allowed Arab farms 500 cubic metres (cu.m.) of water per cultivated dunum in the 1985 agricultural year, less than the quota allocated most Jewish farms *(Ibid)*. An example of the problems faced by Arab farmers in water provision is found in the experience of the village of Jatt in the Triangle. Farmers discovered in the 1960s that the only way to get permits to irrigate their rainfed land would be through formation of cooperative societies. It was only after several years of negotiations with *Mekorot* and nearby Jewish settlements, and through substantial investments by the farmers themselves, that an irrigation system finally became operative.

Now, the 500 cu.m. quota applies to all members of the cooperatives, though they have been awaiting for three years *Mekorot* approval of their application for an increase in the quota to 700 cu.m. Neighbouring Jewish settlements and villages have quotas of between 800 and 1200 cu.m. The quota system is further regulated by price. The farmers of Jatt were paying $0.04 per cu.m. of water in early 1985. However, for all water consumed above the 500 cu.m. level, the price quadruples. Farmers cannot afford to consume much above the 500 cu.m. allotment.

Additionally, there are continuous disputes between the farmers and *Mekorot* about actual and recorded consumption levels. A Jatt cooperative was able to prove in court that *Mekorot* water metres on irrigation pipes were faulty, and that cooperative members for consumption of 48,000 cu.m. which had not been consumed. The cooperative eventually succeeded in obtaining compensation. Jatt farmers also suffer from a high salinity level in much of their land and the pressing need for drainage of other areas. While nearby Jewish settlements have the means to undertake this costly operation, few Arab dunums have been so improved. Thus, significant quantities of potentially useable rainwater are wasted while good land is left unexploited.

Another example of the problems affecting usufruct of Arab land can be seen in the (mainly) melon growing Battuf valley (Abu Kishk 1985). After the winter rains, the land dries out gradually, strip by strip and as soon as the soil is dry enough for ploughing, melons are planted. They are therefore harvested at different stages, producing several crops in one season. The cost of draining the Battuf is prohibitive without the same combination of capital, supervision and cooperation mentioned above. The water cannot be pumped out because there is nowhere to dispose of it or build a reservoir. To make a drainage waterway, it must be planned so that there is no erosion.

The Battuf is itself a low lying plateau and a reservoir cannot be made on the surrounding hilltops. The water could be collected in an underground reservoir which covers less area, but this too is costly. The establishment of a drainage district would require an authority to appropriate areas in the lowest part of the valley to collect pumped out water, undertake levelling, and build an underground drainage and filtering system. In the end, with the soil enriching water pumped out, the valley would thus be turned into the usual rainfed land which is much less fertile than the existing use of the area.

Despite these constraints, the value productivity of a unit of Arab water for agriculture (value of agricultural output per unit of water) was almost double that of the Jewish sector in 1981/2 (calculated from Israel 1983b: 414-17; 419). This is despite the fact that Arabs possess under 3 percent of the national irrigation capital stock (Israel 1984: 422), cultivate less than this percentage of total irrigated area and receive a similarly disproportionate share of water for agriculture. This exhibits an efficiency that goes well beyond anything created by the Israeli sponsored 'modernisation' process.

While there is nothing surprising about state water resource distribution policy, Arab expertise in utilisation of a scarce resource reflects a unique tenacity and ability. It has been explained how the system of water resource allocation leaves very few practical options for ameliorating the position of Arab access to water. Furthermore, were it legally or politically possible, any effort to improve Arab water sources and utilisation would involve large capital outlays, farmers capable and willing to cooperate and close technical supervision. Excepting perhaps the second, none of these factors are at hand today.

Agriculture: A Reserve for Regional Growth

FACTORS OF PRODUCTION: CAPITAL, TECHNOLOGY AND REGIONAL ISOLATION

Factors and Patterns in Adoption of Technology

Most available indicators confirm the existence of a major regional-national divergence in technological application in agriculture. It has already been noted that Arab agriculture's resource base is constrained by both the past and continuing influence of state policy, and social and geographic determinants. Yet, as has also been argued, this has encouraged specific responses: ways have been found to adapt, improvise and avoid the effects of the more detrimental constraints. Evidence noted above of more intensive Arab cropping patterns, the maintenence of a defined Arab cultivated area and relatively higher productivity in water application all support this contention. The following section shows how Arab agricultural labour processes have further helped to accomodate the sector to the pressures it faces. Yet in the sphere of input provision, there are few alternatives to the basic requirements of the seeds, fertilisers, pesticides, machinery and ancillary equipment which are central to improvements in production.

Undoubtedly, some of the problems faced by Arab agriculture in utilising its resource base (land and water) are compounded by the relatively small application of complementary inputs. This is mainly due to the lack of funds for investment, as discussed below. Other factors inhibit advance in this important area, prominent among which is the durability of established methods and farming attitudes. While farmers in the Triangle, for example, have shown themselves willing and capable of innovating in the production process, this has not always or everywhere been the case. It takes more than lectures by extension service agents or the demonstration effect of application of inputs by other farmers to change well-tried methods.

The problem here is not simply the failure to introduce fertilisers and pesticides, new seed varieties or crops. The process of modernisation, in its technical sense, involves a package of measures and incentives. Reorganisation of local agrarian relations, strict climactic and soil conditions, experimentation and repeated efforts, encouragement and guidance, availablity of mechanical and other inputs (greenhouses, plastic covers, appropriate irrigation systems), are all necessary elements in the successful introduction of improved chemical and biological inputs. Such a package is not available to Arab cultivators, mainly because it is usually the state or other public agencies which provide or subsidise these.

There are considerable differences in findings on the extent of, and factors behind, adoption of agricultural technology. Most Israeli academic research contends that Arab agriculture has witnessed significant progress, and that this was possible due to the establishment of the state of Israel. The major source of field survey data on the subject is provided by Arnon and Raviv (1980). Their results point to a number of innovations, varying in intensity between hill villages in the north and plains villages in the Triangle, and mostly from before 1967. They note increased use of plastic cover for out of season crops, almost total abandonment of draught-drawn animals in favour of tractors, high application of fertilisers and pesticides, especially in irrigated plains, the adoption of more sophisticated irrigation equipment, and a smaller degree of weed control and use of livestock equipment (*Ibid:* 164-6).

A more recent and less comprehensive survey produced some similar findings: extension service and the media were the most often utilised sources of new farming information (65 percent of reported sources), with other farmers also playing a role (30 percent); a range of fertilisers and pesticides were used in almost all farms surveyed in both the hill and plains villages, though more so in the latter which also irrigates more widely; generally, introduction of fertilisers preceded that of pesticides, though in most cases both took place from 1966 onwards (Khalidi and Sabbagh 1985a). In one significant difference between the surveys, the latter indicated a large proportion of farms using no machinery (25 percent), with most machinery being introduced since 1969 (over 50 percent since 1970).

Certainly, as has been argued by some Israeli scholars (e.g. Weigart 1977), the problems in technological advance are aggravated by the lack of cooperative organisation among Arab farmers. This is attributable in part to prevailing social relations. However, Arnon and Raviv observed in their field survey of several Arab villages in Israel, that "...while socio-cultural factors may have strengthened the economic forces impeding progress, as soon as favourable conditions occurred for the modernisation of Arab villages in Israel,... the process was not hampered by religious or social traditions" (1980: 153). They continue by asserting that their results indicate that where irrigation was introduced, "a 'package' of factors, including the efforts of the extension service, were responsible for the changes that had taken place in Arab farming", while "economic factors, such as the availability of capital and marketing facilities as well as professional know-how, were hardly ever perceived by the villagers to be important factors for change" (*Ibid:* 166).

Agriculture: A Reserve for Regional Growth

The problems that pervade much of such research have already been discussed. In this instance there is a clear problem with the interpretration of such field surveys. For example, the Arnon and Raviv research indicated a relatively high proportion of farms which had not introduced any new practices or inputs into the production process (*Ibid:* 162). However, another sample survey of one large, relatively advanced hill locality revealed that all farmers used pesticides and fertilisers while a proportion did not use machinery (Khalidi and Sabbagh 1985a).

Discrepancies of this sort need not in themselves shed doubt on research results, since survey methods and samples, the date of research and other factors can cause contradictory results. What is problematic, however, is that micro-level data are used to justify broad generalisations which substantiate ideological, methodological or political concerns. After reviewing the significant changes in agricultural technology that occurred in the surveyed villages, it is concluded that as a result of various state initiated efforts:

> ...progress in the Arab agricultural sector, following the first 5-year Development Plan (1962-1967) and in the course of the Second Plan (1967-1972), has been rapid and spectacular...Within a remarkably short time a level of sophistication and productivity was achieved by the Arab farmers which is now the equal of that of the Jewish agricultural sector (Arnon and Raviv 1980: 216).

Access to Capital and Opportunities for Investment

In fact, that data which allows for broad comparisons between technological application in Arab and Jewish agriculture point to wide gaps and serious underdevelopment of the Arab sector. To begin with, Arabs use of agricultural machinery is proportionately less than the Arab share of cultivated land: Arabs possess only 8 percent of all self-propelled agricultural machines, of which 92 percent are wheel tractors used mostly to operate manual implements (Israel 1983a: 274-5). Just under two thousand Arab farm owners possessed some type of propelled machines. These machine-owners constituted 12 percent of both Arab owners and of total owners, while 38 percent of Jewish farmers possessed similar machines.

While this reflects in part the different types of land available to the two sectors and differences in farm organisation, the low level of mechanisation is also due to the overall shortage of capital in Arab agriculture. This factor cannot but limit the ability of Arab farmers to adopt new inputs, mechanical or other. The fact that some Arab farmers have reached levels equivalent to those of Jewish agriculture is secondary. The previously examined performance of state policy and plans in the region, as well as the aggregate data presented further below on capital formation in agriculture belie the picture drawn by many Israeli researchers.

Some of the reasons behind the low level of capitalisation have already become evident: if it cannot be effectively applied, there is little point in accumulating capital stock. However, the Arab sector is largely bypassed by the development funding that exists for agriculture, because of their exclusion from the benefits available to Jewish cooperative systems. There are three types of state investment in agriculture (Szeskin 1979). Commercial infrastructure (including irrigation schemes, roads, crop grading, packing and marketing facilities) is supported, though none of these facilities exist in the Arab region. The state also helps in the building of production units on individual holdings, something in which *moshavim* and *kibbutzim* are naturally favoured. Finally, the state can provide farmers with working capital.

Agricultural credit can be obtained in the form of seasonal loans from funds made available by the Ministry of Agriculture for the purpose (Abu Kishk 1985). The size and terms of the loan depends on what and how much is grown by the applicant. The interest rates on these loans are usually low. Additionally, development loans are given by the Israel Bank of Agriculture for improvement of irrigation facilities, construction of greenhouses, further development of avocado and grapefruit plantations, livestock breeding, and for packing and trans-shipment facilties for export crops. These are obtained from banks upon Ministry of Agriculture approval, which is of course crucial.

For instance, no Arab farmers have obtained licenses for poultry breeding or citrus cultivation, or modern dairy farming. Licenses for these branches makes farmers eligible for loans, which in turn involve complicated application procedures. These branches have thus remained almost exclusively the domain of *kibbutzim* and *moshavim*. There are also loans available for drainage of water from land with a natural outlet but in need of improvements such as levelling. The fragmented and family based organisation of Arab farms discourages eligibility.

The production of intensive crops for export is highly capitalised. Through the 'Supervised Credit Scheme' (initiated by the Bank of Agriculture), the central authority exercises a virtually controlling influence over this type of development. Grants and loans on highly favourable terms are only available for approved projects. Participating settlements are required to submit detailed financial statements summarising past activities and budgets and accounts reflecting future plans. The Bank and then the Ministry check these before the approved plans are passed to production or marketing boards for implementation. The need for cooperative or communal organisation is also apparent here, and thus Arab farms are generally excluded from the benefits of this scheme.

Therefore, given the existing limited Arab capital accumulation in agriculture and the difficulty of obtaining state support, the Arab farmer has little recourse to increased capitalisation via the state. In the field survey of two villages in Galilee and the Triangle (Khalidi and Sabbagh 1985a), 70 percent of sampled farmers reported never having received any form of credit; 10 percent had benefited from some form of state or cooperative credit and 7 percent from bank credit; 13 percent reported having received family or private loans. Some 22 percent of farmers sampled considered lack of finance to be among the major problems they face.

Aggregate figures for capital accumulation in agriculture confirm that Arab agriculture has been largely bypassed by the impressive developments in technological innovation in Israeli agriculture. In 1981, the Arab region contributed under 6 percent of national capital input to agricultural production (Israel 1985: 414) and possessed 6 percent of the national capital stock in agriculture, equivalent to approximately $190 million (Israel 1984: 422; 251; also see Table 3.1 below). The Arab share by type of capital stock was mostly in fruit plantations (15 percent of total in that branch), livestock (12 percent) and agricultural equipment and machinery (8 percent).

Together, these three types of asset accounted for 88 percent of all Arab capital stock (with 53 percent in plantations alone). Irrigation systems and green houses constituted most of the rest. However, the Arab share of these types of asset was nationally insignificant (just over 2 percent). The distribution of capital stock nationally indicates a much greater diversification of investment: fruit plantations, livestock and agricultural machinery accounted for 44 percent of capital stock, structures (grading, storage, packing etc.) for 31 percent, irrigation systems for 20 percent and greenhouses for 5 percent.

The clearest indication of the extent of the regional-national differential in capitalisation can be seen in comparative crude capital-output ratios. Calculated (from Israel 1985: 414) in terms of capital to value of production, it is found that the regional ratio (of units of capital per units of value of production) in 1981 was 1.00 while that of Jewish agriculture 1.45 (a regional-national ratio of 0.69). In small Arab villages, the ratio approaches the national level, at 1.17, while among the Negev Beduin, it was especially low, at 0.77. Only in *kibbutz* agriculture, which is relatively small scale and places greater stress on application of labour, was the ratio slightly below the Arab level. In light of this data there are few conclusions to be drawn except those which point to the overall isolation of Arab agriculture from the process of capitalisation of Israeli farming as a whole and the shortage of the necessary reserve for effective growth and agricultural development.

Table 3.1: Input and Output in Agriculture - Selected Data, 1981

Type of Locality	Input				Gross Value Added					
	Growers	Labour	Water	Capital	Production	Total	Plantations	Field Crops	Vegetables	Livestock[a]
	No.	Man-Yrs	Mill M^3		IS Mill.					
TOTAL	43,008	78,737	1,315	34,394	24,372	12,553	3,745	4,076	1,486	1,634
ARAB	14,166	8,526	35	2,013	2,004	792	201	117	231	237
Small Village	3,074	1,419	4,630	315	269	115	30	11	32	32
Large Villages	8,994	5,724	30,334	1,495	1,472	540	166	63	198	107
Bedouin in Negev	2,098	1,383	913	203	263	137	4	43	-	89
Arabs % of Total	32.9	10.8	2.7	5.8	8.2	6.3	5.4	2.9	15.5	14.5

NOTES: a. Livestock excludes poultry.
SOURCE: From (Israel 1985: 414-5).

FACTORS OF PRODUCTION:
LABOUR, THE REGION'S COMPARATIVE ADVANTAGE

Within the national economy labour is a scarce and relatively expensive resource. Crops that have expanded most recently are those amenable to mechanisation. Intensive crops demand close observation and timely attention to detail. This is generally not compatible with mechanisation. One observer has noticed that:

> ...family labour on a smallholding is a low cost and flexible commodity since it is rarely counted or costed very carefully, is available for long periods each day in peak seasons and 'rests' at low cost at other times. Furthermore, it tends to

Agriculture: A Reserve for Regional Growth

become intimately involved in making a success of a particular crop since the family's standard of living depends directly on it (Hunt 1974: 17).

This labour mode has been, and continues to be, the predominant one in Arab agriculture, and has helped guarantee the Arab agriculture sector a small, but solid, position in the national economy. Its maintenance has not been without its price, both in terms of agriculture's inability to provide a livelihood for communities historically dependent on it, and in light of the difficulties in competing with Jewish agriculture.

The Contraction in Arab Agricultural Employment

The view of Arab agricultural development in Israel that influences Israeli research of the type epitomised by Arnon and Raviv is dominated by the view that the modernisation process involved the freeing of surplus rural labour. It is assumed that this labour was in a state of underemployment, if not disguised unemployment, and that this, coupled with consistent production methods and low levels of output, characterised traditional subsistence agriculture (Arnon and Raviv 1980: 150-7). Yet, these analyses provide little firm evidence corresponding to the various theories regarding agricultural underemployment (*Ibid:* 22-5). The reasons given for underemployment of the Arab rural labour force after 1948 are limited to those of population pressure and the limited land resources available.[28] However, as has already been explained, the problem facing the region is not simply that of the quantity of land available. Just as crucial is the quality of land and access to capital and other requirements for making the best use of it.

According to this analysis, "the most revolutionary change in the life of the Arab village is that in employment opportunities for members of both farming and non-farming families" (*Ibid:* 168). While certain factors, such as reductions in the cultivation of field crops, have resulted in smaller labour requirements, the introduction of labour intensive crops have had the opposite effect. The net effect has been, according to Arnon and Raviv's survey results, a reduction in agricultural labour requirements. Thus, the establishment of a modern and growing Israeli Jewish economy provided a sort of escape valve for the underemployed rural Arab population, raising agricultural labour efficiency and allocating rural labour elsewhere in the economy. "All redundant family labour can find employment off the farms, as was not the case in the past" (*Ibid:* 173).[29]

Agriculture: A Reserve for Regional Growth

Countering this approach is one which emphasises the effect of land loss on the possibilities for agricultural subsistence (see, e.g. Zureik 1979: Chapter Five). 'Proletarianisation' is considered central to an understanding of the transformation of agriculture, with land confiscations being a prime determinant of the process. While there is a strong argument that proletarianisation began prior to 1948 and was not solely linked to land loss (Rosenfeld 1978), it is by no means clear that unproductive Arab agriculture was liberated of the burden of unemployed labour by the simple process of exposure to Israeli created work opportunities. In fact, it was after the first decade of the existence of the state, once military rule began to ease in the early 1960s, that Arab labour began to find employment outside the villages.

It is not surprising therefore that after a number of years of isolation in the Arab region with insufficient land and no external investment or support, a development process could resume once certain barriers were lifted. To argue otherwise only perpetuates the incorrect view that there was no 'development' in the pre-1948 Palestinian Arab economy, and that the only true development process is that engineered and sponsored by a 'modern', capitalised and westernised society. An examination of the data will help to clarify the experience of Arab agricultural labour in Israel.

There has, of course, been a substantial move of Arab labour out of agriculture since 1948, continuing a process that had begun during the Mandate. Both in absolute numbers and proportionately, the agricultural labour force has contracted dramatically in the past three decades. In 1955, by which time the bulk of expropriations had been effected, 49 percent of the Arab labour force was still employed in agriculture, (Zarhi and Achziera 1966: 6). By 1959, the proportion had fallen to 45 percent, while the total number was constant around 21,000.[30] In the early 1960s, there was a growth in agricultural employment, reaching 25,600 by 1968, equivalent to 31 percent of the employed Arab labour force. This was due both to the increased physical mobility of Arab labour permitted with the easing of military rule, as well as the fact that Arab agriculture had begun to reestablish itself in its new environment.

It was only in 1969 that agricultural employment began to fall again, reaching 15,000 by 1974 (14 percent of the Arab labour force), but fluctuating between that level and 19,000 (16 percent of the labour force) through the decade. Since 1981 there has been a sharp fall in the total number of Arabs employed in agriculture, reaching its lowest level ever, just over 13,000, in 1984, (9 percent of the employed Arab labour force). However,

Agriculture: A Reserve for Regional Growth

the Arab agricultural labour force had, by 1985 regained a larger share of the total Arab labour force (10.5 percent), with employment in the sector rising to over 16,000. It is possible that this increase reflects the sector's ability to absorb labour in periods of recession in other sectors, an important indication of its role in regional subsistance, if not development.

The Myth of Underemployment in Arab Agriculture

Notwithstanding the most recent rise, the data appears to confirm the basic theory that over this period, surplus underemployed labour in Arab agriculture was eliminated. However, there are strong indications that the decrease in the total amount of labour employed in regional agriculture has not been to a level that would point to any serious degree of underemployment. By examining two sets of figures, for employed or employing others on farms, and for employees in agriculture, this contention becomes clearer. There are no consistent figures on labour in Arab agriculture *per se*, though events after 1967 provide some indication.

In 1966, some 12,000 employees worked in both Arab and Jewish agriculture. By 1969/70, the number of Arab employees from Israel working in agriculture had fallen to 8,300. Since 1979/80 the figure has fluctuated between 6,000 and 4,500. It can be safely assumed that less than half these were employed in Arab agriculture. This assumption is based on the observation that Arab agriculture is neither organised nor capitalised to the extent that wage labour is a major option.[31] This contention holds up in light of the following calculations.

The growing number of agricultural labourers from the occupied West Bank and Gaza Strip in Israel all work in the Jewish sector. Once it became possible to employ the more flexible and less costly labour force from the occupied territories, the numbers and proportion of Arab waged farm labourers from within Israel began to fall. While there were 12,000 Arab employees in agriculture in 1966, the number had risen to 13,000 by 1969/70; but of these, 8,000 were from the occupied territories. Since these had all displaced Arab labour from Israel, the balance of Arab labour supply in 1969 of 5,000 was provided by the Arab region and was distributed, as before 1967, between Israeli and Arab agriculture. On the basis of the above assumption, the distribution between the two sectors would have been around 2,000 and 3,000 Arab employees in the Arab and Jewish agricultural sectors respectively.

Agriculture: A Reserve for Regional Growth

In 1966 the 12,000 Arab employees can be assumed to have been distributed similarly, except with approximately 2,000 in Arab agriculture and 10,000 in Jewish agriculture. This figure tallies with the post-1967 distribution whereby, in the immediate post-war boom, demand for Arab labour in Jewish agriculture grew from the 1966 figure of 10,000 to some 11,000, supplied by 8,000 labourers from the occupied territories and 3,000 from the Arab region. The capital intensity of Jewish agriculture and restrictions on employment of non-Jewish labour on Jewish land make it seem unlikely that subsequent demand for Arab wage labour exceeded by very much the number of Palestinians employed from the occupied territories plus those from Israel.

Until the end of the 1970s, the number of Arab self employed and employers was fairly constant at between 12,000 and 13,000. Since 1981/2, the number has fallen, though it was just under 9,000 by 1984/5. In light of the above calculations, it is likely that in 1959/60, of the 10,000 Arab employees in agriculture, between 7,000 and 8,000 worked on Jewish farms, eventually to be displaced by Palestinians from the occupied territories. When the remaining 2,000 to 3,000 employees working in the region are added to the 13,000 self employed, employers and family labour in Arab agriculture, this totals some 15,000 to 16,000 Arabs working in Arab agriculture in 1959/60.

It can be safely assumed, therefore, that of the 6,400 employees in agriculture from the region in 1984/5, between 2,000 and 3,000 were still able to find employment in Arab agriculture, while there were just under 9,000 self employed in the sector. This means that a total of between 11,000 and 12,000 were employed in regional agriculture in 1984/5. Therefore, the decrease in the region's agricultural labour force has been between 4,000 and 5,000 in twenty-five years, a fall of between 25 and 30 percent, rather than the much larger percentage implied by the total figure of Arabs (self employed and employees) employed in (Jewish and Arab) agriculture.[32]

Though large, this would not appear to be a significant enough amount to warrant any firm conclusions regarding the extent of underemployed labour in Arab agriculture, except that which is naturally and gradually displaced through any process of mechanisation, consolidation, and non-cultivation of marginal land. I do not wish to argue that modernisation has not occurred in Arab agricultural methods and production modes. Nor do I ignore the significant results of those micro-level surveys which confirm the existence of an unexploited labour force in rural areas out of season. Indeed, given the constrained resource base available, and the context of development, Arab agriculture has proven to be increasingly productive and modern, though not for

Agriculture: A Reserve for Regional Growth

the reasons, nor in the manner, claimed by Zionist political economy.

It is unfortunate that a complete theory of transformation of Arab agriculture from a traditional, subsistence mode to a modern, capitalist one has been built on a dubious and effectively prejudiced, set of observations. Calculating the reduction in labour in Jewish agriculture for the same period shows that, including Arab wage labour, employment in Jewish agriculture was at 106,000 in 1959/60 and 75,000 by 1984/5. The percentage decrease in labour requirements of this sector was therefore some 29 percent, almost the same as that calculated for regional agriculture. Yet no theories exist to explain this contraction in Jewish agricultural labour in terms of 'modernisation' or ending the 'vicious circle' of traditional subsistence farming and underemployment.

Labour Input in Arab Agriculture

The above calculations regarding Arab labour working on Jewish farms are supported by labour input figures for the Arab rural population. According to official criteria, rural Arab localities are those with a population of less than 2,000. Such localities contained only 16 percent of the Arab region's population in the census year of 1983, excluding East Jerusalem (Israel 1985: 44-5). While this delimitation between 'rural' and 'urban' is arbitrary and unrepresentative of actual rural-urban divides in Arab society, it remains a statistical constant that must be accepted. As detailed figures have recently become available for this section of the Arab population, it is instructive to examine them closely, in order to shed further light upon patterns of agricultural labour allocation.

There are, of course, a number of differences between this part of the population and the remainder, though it is doubtful that these are especially significant. For example, this part of the Arab region is generally less integrated and more isolated physically and economically than the 'urban' localities where the bulk of the population is found (i.e. larger towns, whose population is still significantly involved in agriculture). Generally, it is also likely that the rural Arab population will be more dependent on and involved in agriculture. Further, it can be expected that in small villages, there will be a greater reliance on family, as opposed to wage, labour than elsewhere in the region and that most of the wage labour utilised is hired locally, from within the rural sector.

Agriculture: A Reserve for Regional Growth

In 1981, of the total labour input of the Arab rural population (calculated in units of 'work years'), 24 percent was employed in agriculture.[33] The degree of on-farm employment was greater in the rural areas of the Triangle than in those of the Galilee, indicating the greater viability (and ability to support the local population) of the Triangle farming sector. The highest rate of on-farm employment of labour was in those localities with between 76-99 family farming units per locality. A correlation between a high rate of on-farm employment and a high rate of employment on families' own farms was also found, confirming the relation between good farming possibilities in an area and successful family farming. The overall rate of agricultural labour input by the rural labour force into other farms (either Jewish or Arab) is low, at only 10 percent of the total (see Table 3.1 above). The rate of wage labour is highest in the Galilee, at 12 percent of agricultural labour input, compared with 7 percent in the Triangle. Given the relatively low level of Jewish agricultural activity in the Galilee and the fact that Arab wage labour probably does not travel far for employment, it is likely that the large proportion of this waged labour force is employed in Arab agriculture.[34]

Arab agriculture is totally dependent on a regional labour supply. This is a specific dependence upon self-employment and unpaid family labour. According to the above calculations of the proportion of wage labour in Arab and Jewish agriculture, there is a lower level of family, or self employed, labour in Jewish than in Arab regional agriculture. Of the 75,000 people working in Jewish agriculture in 1984/5 (including those Palestinians from the occupied territories from Israel), only 60 percent were non-waged (Israel 1985: 398). In the Arab region, this proportion was between 70 and 80 percent for the same period (assuming 2,000 to 3,000 wage labourers in regional agriculture).

There is general agreement that Arab agriculture is notable for its relatively high degree of intensive labour. This observation is supported by data on overall regional labour input in agriculture. In 1981, the region's labour input in agriculture (in man-years) was 11 percent of the national total, most of it supplied in the larger 'urban' localities (Israel 1985: 414). Measurements of application of labour can be made through calculating ratios of labour to output, capital or area cultivated. Because of the marginal or poor quality of a significant proportion of Arab land (especially the vast areas of the Negev), it would not be expected that overall Arab labour input be higher than labour input in Jewish agriculture.

Indeed, the Arab figure for the ratio of labour:area (in man-years per thousand cultivated dunums) is about half of the Jewish

Agriculture: A Reserve for Regional Growth

figure - 11:1 compared to 20:1 (calculated from *Ibid* and figures quoted earlier in the chapter). When the Negev Beduin are excluded from the calculation, the Arab figure rises to 17:1. However, both of the alternate ratios (labour to capital or output) show greater Arab application of labour than in Jewish agriculture. The labour:capital ratio is 4.2:1 in Arab agriculture and 2.2:1 in Jewish agriculture; the labour:output (value) ratio is 4.3:1 in the region and 3.2:1 in Jewish farming.

Another angle from which to view relative labour application is through constructing an index of different inputs per unit of Arab and Jewish labour as shown in Table 3.2 :

Table 3.2 : Comparative Ratios of Labour Input in Arab and Jewish Agriculture, 1981

	Per Unit of		
	Land	Capital	Value of Output
1 Unit of Arab Labour	0.09	0.24	0.23
1 Unit of Jewish Labour	0.05	0.45	0.31

SOURCE: Calculated from (Israel 1985: 414).

This labour mode is obviously the safest and most cost-efficient for Arab farmers given the particular constraints within which they operate. It permits concentration on the labour intensive crops that Arabs have increasingly tended to produce in past years. It reflects an Arab preparedness to perform the tedious and menial tasks these crops require, a result of the national-regional division of agricultural labour. It also minimises the relative losses incurred from non-mechanisation and the limited availability of water and complementary inputs compared with Jewish agriculture. Thus the pursuance, albeit unplanned and in response to external constraints, of the 'comparative advantage' of labour intensification has allowed Arab agriculture to survive and thrive, relative to the extent of subsidisation afforded the Jewish sector. It is shown below how this has manifested itself in the region's production.

SHIFTS IN PRODUCTION PATTERNS: THE REGION SURVIVING

The nature of the production process in Arab agriculture has undergone substantial transformation since 1948. This was not a process which commenced with the establishment of Israel; rather it was one which resumed several years after the ramifications of 1948 were realised. Crop diversification and comparative specialisation, the move away from subsistence cereal crops into cultivation of more intensive vegetables and fruits, and the introduction of new technologies and methods had all begun during the British Mandate.

Though interrupted in the aftermath of the establishment of the new state, these developments were subsequently renewed with increased vigour and under a totally new set of conditions and influences in the late 1950s. Since then, Arab agricultural production has developed within the context of new and specific determinants. These have operated with differing degrees of intensity, modified over the past 30 years. Yet their collective influence has established the boundaries of most developments in Arab agricultural production.

The legacy of traditional farming continues to influence Arab production. In terms of both methods and composition of output, certain production patterns, such as the cultivation of olives and most field crops, are a direct continuation of proven farming traditions. Though mainly integrated into the national economy, Arab agricultural production still plays a certain subsistence role. That part of the population directly dependent on the family farm continue to produce some of their basic food needs. As such, family farms' output, and a part of their productive land, will continue to reflect subsistence requirements. However, other factors now play the major role in determining what is produced and how.

Foremost among these is the quality and topography of Arab land, which places clear limits on the types of crops that can be grown. Factors of farm size (scale economies) and soil quality influence the extent to which certain crops, requiring specific inputs, can be grown in any area. Closely related to this is the particular mix of production factors available to Arab farming: the weakness of capital and technological inputs as compared to the region's relative strength in labour supply. It has been argued by Israeli observers that an abundant Arab labour supply has led to the increased cultivation of more 'appropriate' crops:

> The basic difference between Jewish and Arab farming in Israel is no longer in the respective level of technology but in the consideration of labour requirements as the main criterion in the choice of crops. In Jewish agriculture, the dominant factor is the need to reduce labour input; Arab farming gives marked preference to labour intensive crops... (Arnon and Raviv 1980: 160).

Agriculture: A Reserve for Regional Growth

Factors Influencing Choice of Crops

It has been shown in the previous section that in fact the capital and technological differentials between Jewish and Arab farming are far greater than these authors would accept. Arab agriculture has been effectively maneouvered into a position where labour intensive cultivation has become the only feasible basis upon which to continue operating. It is not simply a matter of free choice or conventional farm economics. Prominent among the factors encouraging this 'preference' are the structural constraints inherent in central policies of pricing, production quotas, licensing and marketing.

Israeli agriculture is characterised by a complex system of price controls, subsidies, production licenses and quotas, all geared to a sophisticated marketing and export network. This system is in principle applicable to all producers, and Arabs are not singled for special treatment. These regulatory arrangements, however, have been devised to service the collective and cooperative productive sector which is totally Jewish and accounts for the bulk of Jewish farming (in terms of number of owners, farms, capital, labour and value of production). Subsidies usually apply only to cooperative institutions and their collective bargaining power ensures that they are allocated the licenses and favourable quotas for the more profitable and secure crops. Due to the specific organisation and low level of capitalisation of Arab farming, it does not qualify for many of the incentives offered Israeli farmers. These are discussed in greater detail in the following section, but the significance of their role in determining the composition of Arab crops cannot be overemphasised.

Another element that guides Arab farmers in their choice of crops is, as with most economic decision-making processes, the market. Though mediated by the national regulatory and marketing bodies, market indications provide the Arab farmer with the profit/loss parameters within which production decisions are made. However, because of the institutionalised intermediation between producer and market, these signals mostly reach the Arab region in the form of quotas, licenses and contracts, rather than as incentives to produce whatever is most attractive, feasible and renumerative. In effect, therefore, the crop production decisions of the Arab farmer in Israel, to a greater extent than his Jewish counterpart, are made well before the farmer himself has the chance to express his 'preference'.

Agriculture: A Reserve for Regional Growth

Cereals and Field Crops

The most significant change assumed, by Israeli researchers, to have occurred in Arab agriculture in the past decades "is that wheat is no longer the dominant crop and subsistence crops have, to a large extent, been replaced by commercial crops" (*Ibid:* 158). This claim, based on field survey results from the northern and central areas, does not hold true for Arab agriculture as a whole. As Beduin farming became increasingly tied to rainfed field crops in less fertile areas of the Negev, the total area of Arab field crops, wheat included, has increased markedly since the 1950s. In 1959/60, the region cultivated 550,000 dunums with field crops, (constituting 76 percent of the total Arab cultivated area).[35] This area rose to 638,000 dunums in 1969/70 (75 percent of the Arab cultivated area) and began falling soon thereafter, reaching 533,000 dunums in 1980/1 (73 percent of the cultivated Arab area) and 504,000 in 1984/5 (68 percent of the cultivated area). Changes in production patterns are shown in Table 3.3.

The bulk of field crop area is for winter and rain-fed crops (over 90 percent in 1980/1), and almost all of this is wheat and barley. Sugar beet and chick-peas are additional crops cultivated by Arabs. The area devoted to cultivation of wheat in 1959/60 was 153,000 and that for barley was 268,000 dunums (28 percent and 49 percent respectively of the field crop area). By 1980/1, the areas were 302,000 dunums for wheat and 172,000 dunums for barley (57 percent and 32 percent respectively of the field crop area. The areas for these crops have since fallen, to 269,000 and 114,000 dunums in 1984/5 (at 53 percent and 23 percent of the field crop area). However, this was part of a national decline in area devoted to these rainfed crops, which was more accentuated in the region.

Of the total field crop area in the region in 1980/1, most was cultivated by Beduin in the Negev: 214,000 and 147,000 dunums of wheat and barley respectively (constituting 71 percent and 85 percent of the regional total for those crops). In the early 1960s, when Israeli industry was attempting to establish a local sugar refining capacity, Arab cultivation of sugar beet, grew to 15,000 dunums in 1964/5 (Israel 1966: 359). By 1980/1, this crop was hardly grown anymore.

Summer field crop area is cultivated mainly with sunflowers, groundnuts, tobacco and sesame, in that order. However, the prominence of these crops has fallen significantly: whereas 35,000 dunums were cultivated with tobacco in 1959/60, there were less than 5,000 dunums by 1980/1. A similar fall occurred

Agriculture: A Reserve for Regional Growth

in sesame cultivation, from 35,000 dunums to 4,000 dunums in the same period. Some of this area was turned over to sunflower cultivation, which rose from 3,000 dunums to 21,000 dunums between 1959/60 and 1980/1. This shift seems to reflect changes in national demand for these industrial field crops. Arab farmers grow the bulk of the national tobacco crop which must be sold to the national cigarette monopoly.

There are few examples of Arab cultivation of other, new field crops. Cotton, for instance, is one of the more successful innovations in Israeli agriculture, yet it is almost unknown in the Arab region. Therefore, neither the region's cultivation of wheat nor of field crops in general has decreased in prominence. Until the beginning of the 1980s, total cultivation of these crops was growing in the region and their proportion of total area had decreased only minimally. Instead, there has occurred a certain shift between different field crops, reflecting more a change in the structure of national demand for industrial field crops than any move away from subsistence agriculture.

Vegetables, Fruits and Olives

There has been a notable increase in the area cultivated by other crops in the past 20 years, though there is no clear evidence that this has been as an alternative to field crop cultivation. Only 55,000 dunums were devoted to vegetables, potatoes and melons (VPM) in 1959/60, the area grew to 65,000 dunums by 1980/1, and has increased sharply since, reaching 81,000 dunums in 1984/5. This branch accounted for 7 percent, 9 percent and 11 percent (respectively in those years) of total Arab cultivated area.[36] Most of VPM area in 1984/5 was devoted to melon cultivation, some 33,000 dunums, or 41 percent of the regional VPM area.

The two other major vegetables cultivated in the region in 1984/5 were cucumbers (11,800 dunums), and tomatoes (6,400 dunums) with some of the latter destined for industrial processing. At different periods, the distribution of land cultivated by these vegetables has altered sharply: for example, in 1974/5, 32,000 Arab dunums were planted with tomatoes; crops once grown by Arab farmers, such as peas, have been abandoned. Other vegetables whose cultivation has increased are marrows, strawberries, peppers, cabbage, haricot beans and eggplants.

Agriculture: A Reserve for Regional Growth

Table 3.3: Arab and Total Cultivated Area in Israel, by Branch and Selected Crops, Selected Years
(Thousand dunums)

BRANCH/CROP	1959/1960	1964/1965	1969/1970	1974/1975	1980/1981	1981/1982	1982/1983	1984/1985[a]
VEGETABLES AND MELONS	57.8	76.4	79.2	72.5	65.3	78.5	80.3	80.6
Tomatoes	7.2	9.1	11.2	11.9	8.4	11.2	9.4	6.4
Cucumbers	6.6	6.6	6.9	8.7	7.6	9.6	8.7	11.8
Dry Onions	4.9	5.8	10.2	11.1	4.8	7.4	7.8	3.4
Potatoes	1.2	1.1	1.1	0.6	0.2	0.5	0.6	0.3
Melons	18.8	34.4	26.8	31.9	30.0	28.9	32.6	32.9
Miscellaneous	19.1	19.4	24.3	8.3	14.3	20.9	21.2	25.8
FIELD CROPS	548.8	624.9	525.5	619.6	533.5	514.4	476.4	504.0
Wheat	152.9	172.5	284.4	311.8	302.0	254.7	279.7	269.1
Barley	268.5	334.3	128.0	234.2	171.7	188.4	125.4	114.0
Pulses for grain	28.0	17.7	12.4	6.1	4.2	7.2	13.6	...
Sesame	34.7	15.7	9.2	2.6	0.4	...	...	...
Tobacco	35.3	30.6	25.1	8.5	0.5	...	...	...
Peas for canning	1.3	1.8	0.2	0.1	-	0.2	0.2	-
Sugarbeet	-	14.7	11.7	1.1	0.1	-	-	-
Sunflowers	2.7	9.3	13.8	27.8	20.6	22.1	19.0	7.6
Other	25.4	28.3	40.7	27.4	34.0	42.0	38.5	113.3
PLANTATIONS[b]	123	127	130	132	130	158	162	148
Citrus	4	5	5	3	2	2	2	2
Apples/Pears Plums, Cherries	1	1	1	1	1	11	9	8
Almonds, Pecans	1	14	12	18	17	17	18	16
Grapes	13	15	19	1	10	16	13	12
Olives	83	82	82	83	94	106	115	99
Miscellaneous	11	10	11	12	6	6	5	11
CROP AREA[c]								
ARAB	729	828	734	824	728	751	719	733
NATIONAL	3437	3769	3704	3924	3824	3700	3766	3767
ARAB AS % OF NATIONAL	21	22	20	2	19	20	19	19

NOTES: (...) denotes unavailable data.; a. Provisional figures; b. Rounded figures; c. Crop area denotes area actually cultivated with the three specified branches, and does not include all cultivated area (i.e. including flowers, afforested area, fishponds and other non-specified area).
SOURCES: For 1959/60, from (Israel 1961: 172-3; 176); For 1964/5, from (Israel 1966: 356-7; 359); For 1969/70, from (Israel 1970: 309-10) and (Israel 1971: 319; 32`2); For 1974/5, from (Israel 1976: 354-8); For 1980/1 field crops and vegetables, from (Israel 1983: 416-7), fruit plantations from (Israel 1983a: 35-41; For 1981/2, from (Israel 1983b: 416-7); For 1982/3, from (Israel 1984: 394-5); For 1984/5, from (Israel 1986: 352-3).

Agriculture: A Reserve for Regional Growth

Concomitant with the increased cultivation of VPM was the growth in Arab orchard area. In 1959/60, fruit trees covered 122,000 dunums (17 percent of the region's total cultivated area), increasing only slightly to 130,000 by 1980/1 (18 percent of the total area) and rising to 148,000 in 1984/5 (20 percent of the total area). Arab farms cultivate a variety of fruits but hardly any citrus: some 2,000 dunums are devoted to citrus fruit. The bulk of Palestinian citrus orchards in the coastal plain were confiscated by the state after 1948. The world-famous Jaffa orange, originally cultivated and developed by Palestinian Arabs, is now almost exclusively produced by Israeli Jewish farmers.

Olives are the main Arab crop, covering approximately 70 percent of the total. Total olive area has risen from 83,000 dunums in 1960/1 to 94,000 in 1980/1, and peaked at 115,000 dunums in 1983/4, only to fall back to 93,000 dunums in 1984/5, a low season. The substantial growth in plantation area, though primarily due to increased olive cultivation, also reflects the inclusion of 8,000 dunums of apple area from the annexed Golan Heights. Certain fruit tree crops, notably almonds, have expanded and new varieties, such as peaches, apricots, plums, cherries, bananas and avocados have appeared on a small scale.

The significant increase in olive area has in recent years acquired a political significance, though it is mainly a consequence of Arab farm economics:[37]

> As the olive tree does not provide a fixed income at the best of times, and the return on a work day for this branch is not especially high, what is the cause for its continued cultivation? The answer is found in the type of soil in which olive trees are planted, which is mostly hilly, not very deep, and at times inclined or in narrow valleys between hills. Marginal soil such as this is unsuitable for most fruit trees... (Abu Kishk 1984: 154).

Livestock, An Arab Tradition

Livestock breeding occupies a more or less stable position in Arab agriculture, and there has not been the degree of innovation see in this branch in Jewish areas. The two most numerous types of livestock nationally are cattle (especially dairy cattle) and poultry. Regionally, however, the number of cattle has fallen steadily from 44,000 in 1959/60 to 26,000 in 1984/5. The number of poultry has been constant since the 1960s, at an estimated level of 250,000, all of them home/farm hens. The reason for the relative non-participation of Arab agriculture in the

Agriculture: A Reserve for Regional Growth

branches of poultry and dairy cattle is that these branches are subject to a system of quotas whereby no farmer can establish a dairy cattle or poultry broiler farm before obtaining a license; no Arab farmer has to date received such a license and the branch is effectively closed to Arab farming (*Ibid:* 156).

Arab farmers, especially in the Negev, breed a relatively large number of sheep and goats - some 120,000 and 99,000 heads respectively in 1984/5. Building on their historic skills in sheep and goat breeding and herding, the Beduin have excelled in breeding new goat varieties, increasing both fertility and milk production. The milk is either consumed or used to produce clarified butter (*samna*) and traditional cheeses for local consumption. Successful breeding requires a relatively high level of capital and investment, and it is therefore not surprising that its advance has been slow in the Arab region. Despite Arab specialisation in sheep and goat related production, Jewish predominance in cattle breeding, new sheep varieties and poultry, has kept Arab participation in the livestock branch at a relatively low level.

The Rationale of Arab Production Shifts

As shown in the preceding review of the pattern of Arab cultivation, there have been shifts into crops more amenable to labour intensity, especially vegetables and certain fruits. This process has been influenced by a variety of factors, with available and relatively inexpensive inputs prominent among them. Often there is not a clearcut profit seeking motive in such shifts. In Israel at least, the imperative of continuing to cultivate a piece of land, even at a loss as with olives, is peculiar to Arab agriculture. This manifests an attachment to land and a certain 'way of life' that transcends much conventional economic logic.

Of course, adherence to the rationale of market signals and forces has helped to guide Arab farmers from subsistence into cash crops. But these factors reached Arab farmers through the intermediation of the prerequisites of Jewish development and the corresponding expropriations, restrictions, quotas and incentives directed at Arab farming. The most obvious aspect of developments in Arab agricultural production is that it has adapted to a range of conditions dictated both by the impetus of the internal dynamics of development and the external pressures and constraints generated by a highly capitalised, organised and competitive national economy. Consequently, while Arab agriculture has not thrived in absolute terms, it has survived and established its place nationally.

Agriculture: A Reserve for Regional Growth

This is examined in detail in the section after next, through reference to data of differential volume and value productivity data for the region and nationally. But first, it will be useful to discuss the system whereby Arab farm output is marketed. As shall be seen, much of the region's potential value added through agriculture is reduced because of its unequal access to local and export markets.

PRICING, PROCESSING AND MARKETING: REGIONAL FRAGMENTATION[38]

The marketing of Arab agricultural produce is carried out through seasonal contracting to national agencies which set a price growers usually have to accept. Whatever surplus remains is sold locally, though this is generally small due to the lack of any organised Arab regional marketing. This system is not mandatory but farmers deal with these agencies in the absence of any alternative local or export marketing arrangements. The absence of Arab cold storage facilities, quality control and other ancillary establishments increases dependency on national agricultural institutions. Certain Arab produce, especially vegetables, are exported through national agencies.

Marketing Boards and Export Channels

Most Israeli agricultural marketing is organised within the cooperative sector through local and regional groupings linked to *Tnuva*, the Histadrut owned national cooperative for wholesaling, processing and distribution. *Tnuva* handles some 75 percent of all farm output: "With much of the trade monopolised by statutory or quasi-statutory bodies there is little room for alternative channels to become established and growers must, perforce, use the existing facilities" (Hunt 1974: 20). Though the regulation of agriculture has eased in past years, it is still the rule rather than the exception.

The cooperative basis of most Israeli agricultural production is crucial to the effective and fair working of the regulated marketing system:

> Although some of the actual trading is done by entrepreneurs operating from wherever happens to be convenient, much trading is done by and all operations are supervised by a series of elected bodies operating from central and regional offices. There are two major elements in the situation. Firstly the system of statutory production and marketing boards

which oversee the trade in all commodities and secondly the existance of large producer cooperatives (*Ibid:* 19).

The production and marketing boards include representatives of all branches of production and distribution in all regions as well as consumer interests. Producers are represented either through Jewish *moshavim* and *kibbutzim* federations, or the Histadrut Farmers' Union. Arab farmers are not represented in the former group, and it was only in 1985, some 40 years after the establishment of Israel, that they were admitted to the latter.

Cooperative efforts have been largely unsuccessful in the Arab region. There were a number of Arab marketing cooperatives in the early 1950s, but these had all ceased to operate by 1958.[39] The 34 production cooperatives that existed in 1951 have since been reduced to two. By the end of the 1970s there was only one active Arab agricultural credit cooperative and 13 for general agricultural purposes. The most notable Arab cooperative effort has been in obtaining and distributing irrigation and drinking water.

The marketing boards advise the government and communicate to producers what they consider should be the total area of particular crops, based on an analysis of market preferences. Against this background, applications from individual producers are made to plant crops. In the past, the Ministry of Agriculture would coordinate this process and determine the amounts of crops planted, by village, according to national priorities. But now there are much more flexible guidelines and farmers, including Arabs, are more or less free to apply to grow what they want. Certain cash crops, such as tomatoes, cucumbers and strawberries are still subject to strict area quotas. With most crops, farmers now know roughly how much they will be able to sell and therefore plant accordingly. However, some branches such as poultry, dairy farming and numerous fruit trees have remained effectively closed to the Arab farmer through continued state refusal to grant cultivation permits, or other factors (e.g. land, input provision, or capital investment requirements).

Determination of export crops is the responsibility of the export company, Agrexco, which is owned jointly by the government and the boards. Agrexco is not always responsible for harvesting decisions as the precise arrangements and degree of prior involvement with the producers varies from crop to crop. With most fruit and flowers, Agrexco only advises the boards; for vegetables, it contracts directly with individual growers and packhouses or makes marketing contracts with individual growers or packhouses. Israeli officials consider that the

Agriculture: A Reserve for Regional Growth

successful balance struck between export and local marketing is a result of:

> ...the underlying philosophy of that development, namely that marketing abroad should be handled by one channel, by one hand. The marketing abroad through one hand allows to concentrate the resources for the necessary activities which otherwise would be fragmentised. It allows to build an infrastructure that otherwise would be uneconomic for small exports. Exporting through one hand also enables to avoid competition abroad among many Israeli exporters selling identical items. It allows to plan and to carry out a comprehensive marketing strategy... (Shehory 1980/1: 20).

Grading, Packing, Pricing and Transport to Market

The prerequisite of any successful marketing effort is a quality grading and packing process. Quality control takes place at producer/owner packhouse and later by ministry inspectors at exporting points. Grading, packing and quality control facilities differ from crop to crop. Some crops, such as avocados, are more amenable to centralisation of packing house facilities. Vegetables, however, which are more perishable and grown in a less centralised fashion (i.e. much of it by small-holders) are packed by the farmers themselves, though usually in facilities belonging to Jewish settlements. Exports are checked through transit stations managed by the boards or Agrexco. Such arrangements do not exist in the Arab region and Arab farmers deal with the nearest station, usually part of the local Jewish settlement, which grades produce and then distributes the villages' output between the three main markets in Haifa, Jerusalem, and Tel Aviv. Arab farmers sometimes grade their produce in a crude way, taking it to the markets themselves.

The boards issue licenses for the movement of wholesale produce to market, with the power to regulate quality and standards and prevent price competition. The licensing of merchants also restricts distribution to existing channels and reduces the number of new and competing businesses being set up. The price paid to the farmer by local packhouses is the average between the prices for which all produce is sold in the three main markets. In addition to selling to the packhouses, some Arab farmers sell to buyers who come to the villages; others occasionally wholesale or retail directly. Farmers can now theoretically sell their output wherever they wish. There are strict controls on unorganised marketing by Arab farmers, with road checkpoints established by the Ministry of Agriculture to ensure that farmers do not 'smuggle' goods to market.

Prices for locally sold produce are established in the local retail markets and in the three or four wholesale markets - farmers can sell at any price they can get. Sometimes minimum price guarantees are underwritten by the government. This does not apply to export crops which move through Agrexco. It determines the price at which it will eventually buy before planting and seasonally contracts quantities. The farmer can choose to accept the price or not. In recent years, prices have been usually set in dollars and translated into Israeli currency at the official rate at time of sale, thus protecting growers against the effects of inflation.

The field survey of two Arab villages in the Galilee and Triangle confirmed much of the above (Khalidi and Sabbagh 1985a). Some 75 percent of farmers sampled indicated that pricing takes place after harvest, with a few reporting pre-planting arrangements. This would appear to indicate that in the area of these villages at least, there is a degree of marketing outside regulatory or export channels. In most cases (60 percent of responses), it is the farmer who decides the crops to be planted, with some 35 percent recording that marketing agencies determine the crop (i.e. on the basis of marketing contracts). Farmers indicated a variety of marketing channels: some 50 percent marketed through the boards, 5 percent through Agrexco, and a large proportion through individual Arab wholesalers or local retailers (30 percent and 5 percent respectively).

According to this survey, marketing was largely outside the village (75 percent to national markets), with a small amount sold locally or for export (10 percent and 5 percent respectively). The isolation of Arab producers from marketing facilities is exhibited in the small proportion (under 10 percent) who benefit from storage or cold storage facilities. All farmers surveyed used some sort of transport to deliver their produce to market, with costs borne mostly by themselves.

The existing marketing arrangements bind Arab farmers to a system within which they have no influence, either through the regulatory agencies or the market. While the statutory nature of these arrangements have loosened recently, this will probably only lead to further fragmentation and isolation of individual Arab producers within the market. As indicated earlier, limited Arab access to marketing or export credit schemes further restricts the possibilities of significant agricultural development. Thus are Arab farmers further handicapped and their potential bargaining power broken as a result of their exclusion from the complex and effective marketing system that Israeli agriculture has developed.

REGIONAL AGRICULTURE IN THE NATIONAL ECONOMY: SPECIALISATION AND PRODUCTIVITY DIFFERENTIALS

It is clear from the above that Arab agriculture occupies a unique position in the region and in the national economy. Most advocates of Zionist political economy have emphasised the extent of 'modernisation' and development in Arab agriculture. Such a characterisation has been shown to be deficient insofar as it implies the existence of a modernisation process that began after 1948 or one that has been engineered by the state of Israel. Further, clear disparities in most aspects of access to and use of resources have been shown between Arab and Jewish agriculture. If, as many observers suggest, Arab development is to be measured in the absolute terms of positive indices of production, number of tractors, etc., then there has indeed been agricultural development. However, to divorce such figures from the national context is misleading.

When Arab agricultural development is viewed in its overall Israeli framework, two observations become pertinent. First, differentials in almost all branches are glaring and indicate definite disparities in development. Secondly, and in light of that, it is surprising that Arab agriculture continues to hold its own. There are two 'macro' statistical angles to the analysis of the national role and status of the Arab agricultural economy. Data on regional-national differentials in value of production, value added, and different productivity indices illustrates the first approach, and are discussed below. Before that, however, it is instructive to highlight the extent to which Arab agriculture has been forced to concentrate on specific branches in order to maintain its position.

Regional Specialisation

A simple but useful ratio applied in regional analysis, the location quotient (LQ), highlights the degree to which the region has specialised in certain branches and crops, helping it to withstand the negative impact of productivity differentials. The LQ elucidates the second assertion made above and indicates the areas in which regional agriculture maintains significant national linkages.[40] An LQ greater than one shows regional over-specialisation; an LQ close to one indicates a regional-national balance; an LQ less than one means the region is under-specialised in the branch being investigated.

Agriculture: A Reserve for Regional Growth

Location quotients have been calculated for the main Arab branches and crops in Israel for two agricultural years, 1980/81 and 1983/4.[41] A significant aspect of the calculations is that they show a clear regional identity of Arab agriculture. There are few crops in which the region appears to be well or stably integrated into the national economy. The LQ range is polarised: most crops either have high and rising LQs or very low and stable ones. Only a few approach one, confirming the strong imbalances noted in the regional-national relation.

Regional fruit plantations as a whole are relatively under-specialised, though less so recently, with their LQ rising from 0.75 to 0.97. This is primarily due to increased Arab specialisation in three main crops. The LQ of these rose in the period: grape vines (from 0.88 to 1.17); olives (from 4.12 to 4.35) and almonds (from 1.99 to 2.1). As noted, the region is comparatively weak in cultivation of the important Israeli export crops of citrus and avocados. The LQs for both are low. Only in pome/stone fruit trees such as plums and cherries has the region strengthened its overall weak position with an LQ rising from 0.40 to 0.68.

Regional cultivation of vegetables and melons exhibits similar polarisation. Overall, the region is increasing its specialisation in this branch, though at levels above the national pattern: the LQ for the branch as a whole increased from 1.01 to 1.29. This was shown in the the growing LQ in the labour intensive crops: cucumbers (from 2.12 to 2.84); melons (from 1.73 to 2.25) and onions (from 0.77 to 1.80). Other crops with high LQs in 1980/1 were strawberries (3.50), beans (1.80) and marrows (1.51). An interesting development in this branch is the region's move away from tomato cultivation, a mainstay of the region in the 1970s: the LQ for this crop fell from 0.94 to 0.74.[42] The LQ for other vegetables was well below one.

Regional specialisation in field crops appears to be decreasing. The branch LQ fell from 1.09 to 0.96. This decline is a good example of how the overall national contraction in cultivation of field crops affected the Arab region more strongly than it did national cultivation. However, Arab cultivation of its four major field crops remains high. The LQs for wheat and barley fell from 1.51 to 1.47 and from 4.01 to 3.71 respectively. In 1980/1, regional specialisation was especially high in tobacco and sesame, with LQs of 5.00 and 5.10 respectively. Arab cultivation of all other field crops was underspecialised, with LQs falling to below 0.50 in 1983/4. The fall in Arab field crop cultivation in the period was strongest in those 'marginal' crops which are apparently least essential to the regional economy (maize, cotton, groundnuts, sunflowers and fodder).

Agriculture: A Reserve for Regional Growth

Location quotient calculations in terms of value of production for 1981/2 confirm the above pattern and indicate further those branches crucial to regional agricultural income. Location quotients were highest for vegetables and non-citrus fruit (2.97 and 2.20 respectively), and below one for all other branches: field crops (0.52), citrus (0.17), egg production (0.09) and fish (0.52). Only in meat and milk production was the degree of regional specialisation close to the national level, at 0.87 and 0.96 respectively.[43]

Productivity Differentials

Regional specialisation has arisen because of and despite the productivity differentials between regional and national agriculture. Due to its low level of capitalisation, Arab agriculture has not been able to contribute to national economic growth to the same degree as national agriculture. Data on the change in value added in agriculture between 1971 and 1981 indicate that while national agriculture increased gross value added by 186.8 index points, the region lagged behind at 170.3 (Israel 1985: 412-13). The differential was greatest in field crops (362.2 national to 157.6 regional) and poultry (108.6 to 53.6) and least in vegetables and melons (179.4 to 160.9). Only in those branches in which Arab agriculture either recently entered or which account for a small share (flowers and plantations) did regional value added grow by more than the national rate. This can be seen in Table 3.4. below.

The region was responsible in 1980/1 for producing 8 percent of the total national value of production and 6 percent of gross value added in agriculture. This low level is not surprising given its relatively small share of most other resources. However, these figures are particularly revealing in light of the fact that in 1980/1 the region worked 19 percent of national cultivated area and provided 11 percent of total man-years in agriculture. Arab and national labour productivity figures (in terms of value added per man year) show that in 1980/1, Arab labour was 58 percent as productive as the national level. This lower degree of Arab labour productivity is attributed to the two major factors already noted: differentials in available resources (land and water) and use of complementary (capital and other) inputs.

Agriculture: A Reserve for Regional Growth

Table 3.4: Growers and Value Added, Change Indices
1971-1981
BASE 1971 = 100.0

Type of Locality	Value Added (at 1971 prices)							Growers
	Total	Plantations	Field Crops	Vegetables	Poultry	Cattle/livestock	Other	
National	186.8	151.0	362.2	179.4	108.6	138.9	156.6	102.0
Arab	170.3	233.0	157.6	160.9	53.6	125.9	153.4	104.0
Small Villages	159.0	297.8	81.3	182.9	751.3	115.8	142.4	152.9
Large Localities	174.5	221.6	160.3	166.8	350.5	134.8	141.2	77.6
Bedouin in the Negev	164.6	459.7	201.6	..	138.0	174.3	-	..

(..) Denotes unavailable data
SOURCE: From (Israel 1985: 412-413).

In all branches, the productivity of Arab land (in terms of value of production or value added per cultivated dunum) is much poorer than national land (see Tables 3.5 and 3.6 below). For all crops in 1981/2, the Arab value of output per dunum was 28 percent of the national level; this figure was lowest, as expected, in field crop cultivation, at 13 percent; for fruit tree cultivation, Arab land was 39 percent as productive as the national level; Arab productivity in vegetables and melons approached the national level and was 63 percent as productive. Only in the regional citrus sector was Arab cultivation more productive (156 percent) than nationally. Volume productivity figures tell much the same story: Arab output per dunum in 1981/2 was 15 percent of the national level in field crops, 26 percent of the national level in fruit output and 50 percent as productive in vegetables and melon output.

However, due to the region's specialisation in those crops in the fruit and vegetable and melons branch which provide among the highest returns in the country, it is relatively more productive in value/volume terms in those branches than is national agriculture. Thus, in 1981/2, Arab fruit trees produced 124 percent as much income per ton than did national agriculture; Arab vegetables and melons fetched 125 percent as much income per ton than did national output. Arab field crops, however, were only 32 percent as profitable per ton as national cultivation. Therefore, despite the lower overall labour productivity of Arab

Agriculture: A Reserve for Regional Growth

agricultural labour and land, it has concentrated on those areas where it can be assured high returns on those inputs it can provide - mainly back-breaking and tedious labour.

Table 3.5: Value of Arab Agricultural Production in Israel, Selected Crops, Selected Years
(Million current Israeli shekels)

MAIN GROUP[b]	Value of Arab Production			Arab % of National Production		
	1959/ 1960	1969/ 1970	1981/ 1982[a]	1959/ 1960	1969/ 1970	1981/ 1982[a]
GRAND TOTAL	3.86	9.72	2391.7	5.15	4.87	4.99
CROPS	1.86	6.16	1743.3	4.89	5.41	5.80
FIELD CROPS	0.75	2.36	299.8	6.41	8.45	2.60
VEGETABLES/ MELONS	0.53	2.33	664.7	7.79	9.87	14.84
CITRUS	0.13	0.42	55.8	1.17	1.09	1.00
OTHER FRUIT	0.45	1.05	718.0	5.69	5.07	11.00
LIVESTOCK & PRODUCTS	2.02	3.56	648.4	5.47	4.16	3.64
LIVESTOCK (FOR MEAT)	1.27	2.02	346.7	8.35	5.14	4.35
MILK	0.36	1.07	235.1	4.23	4.97	4.79
EGGS	0.07	0.11	16.8	0.74	0.64	0.47
FISH	0.06	0.13	19.7	3.16	2.83	2.62

Notes: a. Last year for which data are available on value of Arab production.
b. Certain minor groups which are insignificant to Arab production are not included here; thus the sum of the sub-groups do not all equal the total of the main group.
SOURCES: Data on Arab value of production: for 1959/60, from (Israel 1961: 200); For 1969/70, from (Israel 1971: 327). Data on national value of production for 1959/60 and 1969/70 and all data for 1981/2, from (Israel 1983b: 419).

If only in that sense, Arab labour can be considered relatively more productive than national labour. In terms of labour's essential role in maintaining a national position for the Arab agricultural base, it is highly productive. Productive labour input in fruit trees and vegetables allows for a continued, though apparently necessary, lower labour productivity in field crops. It would be interesting to speculate on how that labour would perform given equal access to natural resources and inputs. However, the region remains burdened with the country's more

Agriculture: A Reserve for Regional Growth

marginal land, and is barred from compensating for that and other handicaps with the sort of alternative resources available to other Israeli farmers.

The regional specialisation noted is not in itself undesirable; such a regional division of labour exists in most countries, especially in developing economies. Yet, it is undesirable for this region and constitutes a long-term obstacle to its development because of the enforced and inequitable distribution of resources which has given rise to this particular allocation. In such circumstances, the usual forces of market equilibrium have not been observed and therefore cannot be invoked to evaluate, and much less to justify, regional-national disparities.

Table 3.6. Volume of Arab Agricultural Production in Israel, Selected Crops, Selected Years
(Thousand tons unless otherwise specified)

BRANCH/CROP	1959/ 1960	1964/ 1965	1969/ 1970	1974/ 1975	1981/ 1982[a]	Arab % of National Production 1981/82
VEGETABLES/						
POTATOES	29.5	42.7	64.4	99.5	106.3	9.7
MELONS	9.1	37.5	30.1	29.9	23.4	19.8
FIELD CROPS						
Wheat	6.2	17.2	9.0	15.1	20.5	13.9
Barley	5.6	27.7	5.5	9.6	3.0	23.1
Pulses for grain	8.5	1.0	-	0.9	0.9	2.1
Groundnuts	0.6	0.4	1.5	2.4	2.3	8.9
Tobacco	1.5	1.6	1.3	2.2	0.5	100.0
Sunflowers	0.1	0.7	1.3	2.2	1.8	19.3
Hay	9.4	32.0	10.4	17.5	17.4	15.1
CITRUS	6.8	9.9	13.9	15.1	17.9	1.0
NON-CITRUS	12.6	38.2	16.1	14.4	36.5	7.8
Table Grapes	3.0	5.2	4.1	4.0	3.5	8.0
Olives	5.2	7.0	3.4	0.7	24.1	64.8
Other Fruit	4.4	26.0	8.6	9.7	8.9	2.3
MILK (mill. litres)	19.2	21.7	26.4	32.7	35.5	4.5
LIVESTOCK (for meat)	6.8	6.5	7.2	7.9	8.9	3.1
EGGS (millions)	12.5	13.0	13.5	15.0	15.0	9.7

NOTES: a. Last year for which data are available on volume of Arab production.
SOURCES: For 1959/60, from (Israel 1961: 193); For 1964/5, from (Israel 1966: 369); For 1969/70, from (Israel 1971: 326); For 1974/5, from (Israel 1976: 362); For 1981/2, from (Israel 1983b: 420-421).

Agriculture: A Reserve for Regional Growth

NOTES

1. For example, the Israeli private sector policy of investment in subcontracting (female) labour intensive processes such as clothing manufacture to Arab villages provides opportunities for small-scale entrepreneurs or middlemen. On the other hand, Arab agricultural skills can remain unexploited due to price, licensing and marketing controls or quotas which favour Jewish farmers.

2. This is not surprising given the relatively small land area of 27,027 square kilometers (in Hadawi 1970: 19) which constitutes historic Palestine, and over which two peoples lay claim. Israel itself covers an area of 20,325 square kilometers, excluding the annexed Golan sub-district but including East Jerusalem (Israel 1985: 16).

3. Generally, my analysis cannot discuss the many interesting issues of national economic development, except insofar as they provide the context for Arab economic activity and when comparison helps to highlight specific aspects of that. However, there is a vast literature on all aspects of Israeli agriculture, as well as in-depth reporting available in the Ministry of Agriculture's periodical, *Agriculture in Israel*.

4. Regardless of the extent to which Israel did or did not 'make the desert bloom' (though Israel has conducted some notable reclamation efforts in the Negev Desert, not unlike those Egypt was able to undertake once the capital was available), most of the increase in Jewish cultivated area between the pre- and post-1948 period was the result of acquisition of already cultivated land.

5. One dunum equals 1000 square metres. It is not clear how much of the 400,000 dunums added to Jewish cultivated area between 1960 and 1984, from 3.3 to 3.7 million dunums (Israel 1966; Israel 1985) was expropriated in that period.

6. See (Kislev 1976) for a well researched account of this period for which he quotes Israel Land Authority figures of over 100,000 dunums expropriated. (Jiryis 1973) provides an authoritative review of the legal framework for expropriation until the 1960s.

7. See (Abu Kishk 1981) for a overview of the problems created by land shortage.

8. The first organised effort to provide aid to the Arab sector began fourteen years after the establishment of the state, as discussed below.

9. Palestinian refugees in South Lebanon are renown until today for having introduced and developed citriculture into Lebanon. See (TEAM 1983) for an account of the contribution of the Palestinian refugee labour force in the Lebanese economy.

10. This analysis is very much in the tradition of dual sector development popularised in the Lewis and Ranis and Fei models.

11. There is actually not a great deal of evidence that Extension Services, rather than accumulated skills and 'peasant rationality' in confronting and adapting to circumstances, was the major factor behind Arab technological application and innovation, as claimed by some Zionist political economists. The most detailed evidence on this subject, though by no means conclusive can be found in (Arnon and Raviv 1980). It should be noted as well that those areas where Arab farmers have made significant

Agriculture: A Reserve for Regional Growth

advances (the Triangle especially) are not newly prosperous.

12. Figures on the pre-1966 period come from tables in (Israel 1966).

13. The only exception to this is in the extent to which traditional inheritance methods created increasingly unviable plots (see, e.g. Flapan 1963). Additionally, despite much debate in agricultural development theory, it has not been substantiated that family farming units in themselves, as opposed to larger scale collective or consolidated units, are inefficient or barriers to development.

14. IL 55 million, calculated according to exchange rates in (Israel 1985: 254).

15. According to a former official in the Ministry of Agriculture involved in these efforts, the total forecasted investment was not realised (Abu Kishk 1985).

16. Unless otherwise mentioned, agricultural data refers to the agricultural year 1980/1, the year with the fullest available data from the Census of Agriculture undertaken in 1981. Census data quoted here on area are calculated from (Israel 1983a), data on volume and value are from (Israel 1983b: 419-21), data on value added from (Israel 1985: 412-15).

17. Excluding the Negev Beduin from this calculation helps to focus upon the main section of the Arab producing region. It is necessary to include Jewish cultivated Negev, since it is relatively productive and well integrated into the national agricultural sector. In most other calculations in this sector, it is not possible to exclude the Negev Beduin areas.

18. Haifa and its immediate surroundings constitute the Haifa subdistrict, which, together with the Hadera subdistrict, constitute the Haifa district.

19. See Appendix 1 for details of design and implementation of the surveys undertaken.

20. Whereas Jewish farming is almost totally organised within cooperative or collective production units (*moshavim* and *kibbutzim*), there have been to date no successful Arab examples of production cooperatives. This has been the technical reason to date for the exclusion of Arab farmers from the national Histadrut affiliated Farmers Union, which plays a central role in representing farmers interests at the national level.

21. However, this is becoming less of a problem as fewer of those who inherit land are farmers or willing to farm it; if the land is not leased out, it can be kept within the immediate family if one of the inheriting children is a cultivator and can manage all the parcels.

22. The concept of 'lot viable' estimated at 30 dunums or more was introduced into Palestine by British Mandatory officials and also considered a valid criterion by Israeli agricultural planners in their 1963 Plan for Arab agriculture, discussed above.

23. 1972 figures from (Abu Kishk 1984: 166-9).

24. This would appear to indicate a rational and very 'untraditional' type of economic behaviour - yet another reason to reject the all too easily perpetuated characterisations of the character of Arab agriculture made by many Israeli authors.

25. Of the sampled farms in the two surveyed villages in the Galilee and Triangle, 80% of those using irrigation reported that *Mekorot* provided their irrigation water (Khalidi and Sabbagh 1985a). All the water in the

Agriculture: A Reserve for Regional Growth

Triangle farms came from *Mekorot*, while 26% of surveyed Galilee farms obtained their water from springs or artesian wells.

26. Sampled farms in the two surveyed villages in the Galilee and the Triangle exhibited similar proportions of irrigated area: all farms surveyed in the Triangle irrigated more than 50% of their land, while 60% sampled in the Galilee irrigated less than 50%, and half of these under 25%. (Khalidi and Sabbagh 1985a).

27. The mean year of introduction of irrigation was 1970.

28. Throughout, the authors carefully avoid discussing the role of expropriation in this process: "As the population of the villages increased sharply and the areas of land remained, at best, unchanged, the time came inevitably when agriculture was no longer capable of providing work for the entire labour force of the village" (Arnon and Raviv 1980: 154). In their discussion of the reasons for land shortage, the main factor cited by the authors is fragmentation, caused through inheritance, splitting land of Triangle villages after the 1949 armistice and ceasing to cultivate marginal lands.

29. In fact, as indicated in Chapter Two, labour opportunities in urban areas in the Palestinian Mandatory economy were not generally limited.

30. Figures on the overall Arab labour force in agriculture are from (Israel 1975; 1983b; 1986). Data quoted later in this section on employment in Arab agriculture are from (Israel 1985: 342) and (Israel 1986: 354), except for 1966 figures which come from (Israel 1967).

31. This was also confirmed by survey results in (Khalidi and Sabbagh 1985a), where only 30% of sampled farmers specified that they employed wage labour, and mostly in labour intensive production stages, such as harvesting. This phenomenon was more evident in the Triangle (i.e. those who used a greater degree of irrigation) than the Galilee. Also, see (Arnon and Raviv 1980: 173).

32. The preceding argument not only involves refutation of the major premise advanced by Zionist political economy to explain Arab agricultural development, but also a complete reorganisation of the standard statistical data on Arab labour in agriculture.

33. Unless otherwise specified these and following figures on the rural population are calculated from (Israel 1985b: 109-16)

34. This does not necessarily contradict above indications and figures of a higher rate of Arab agricultural wage employment because of rural-urban differences mentioned. And, even if the total number of wage labour in Arab agriculture is smaller than the figure of 2,000 suggested, the total calculation might change, but the degree of labour loss in Arab agriculture would be the same.

35. Figures on area for 1959/60 and 1960/1 are calculated from (Israel 1961: 172-6); for 1969/70 from (Israel 1970: 309-10) and (Israel 1971: 319-22); for 1974/5 from (Israel 1976: 357); for 1980/1 are from (Israel 1983a); for 1983/4 from (Israel 1985: 396-7); for 1984/5 are from (Israel 1986: 352-3). Figures on livestock are from (Israel 1986: 365).

36. The fall in field crop area being responsible for this change in the proportion of VPM area from the total.

37. It was reported (in *Jerusalem Post*, 15 May 1986) that Arab owned lands in the central and northern Galilee previously left uncultivated have in

recent years been planted extensively with olive trees to prevent their possible expropriation due to non-cultivation for more than a few years.

38. Unless otherwise mentioned, information in this section is drawn primarily from (Hunt 1984), (Shehory 1980/1) and (Abu Kishk 1985).

39. The Arab cooperative experience is discussed further in Chapter Five. Data presented here on cooperatives is from (Daniel 1976: 290), and (Weigart 1977: 30).

40. The location quotient, (LQ), is in effect the ratio of two ratios. The first ratio is that between the datum being investigated for the region and the same datum for the national economy. The second ratio is that between a regional reference variable and a similar reference variable for the national economy. The ratio of the former to the latter provides a third ratio, the LQ, which indicates the degree to which the region is over or under specialised in comparison to the national economy as a whole. Comparison of LQs for different years helps determine regional trends. The data investigated here are areas cultivated with different crops in 1981, regionally and nationally. The reference variables are total regional and national cultivated area. A further LQ is calculated for main branches of production according to value of production, regionally and nationally. For a useful introduction to this and other methods of regional economic analysis, see (Bendavid-Val 1983).

41. Figures quoted below for 1980/1 are calculated from (Israel 1983a); 1981/2 figures are from (Israel 1983b); figures for 1983/4 are from (Israel 1985).

42. Farmers surveyed in two villages in 1985 (Khalidi and Sabbagh 1985a) complained about recent low returns on tomatos.

43. These last two figures possibly reflect the cultural and nutritional preferences of the Arab and Jewish populations.

Four

ARAB LABOUR IN ISRAEL: THE REGION SUBSERVIENT

There are several dynamics operative within the regional-national relationship which belie the oversimplified and therefore misleading characterisations of Arab economic development in Israel encountered in both Zionist and non-Zionist political economy. One is that analysed in the preceding chapter, whereby despite handicaps and barriers, a growth base has been created in Arab agriculture, determined both from within and outside the region. Arab industrial and commercial activity, while less autonomous, can also be seen to have a distinct pattern of its own, influenced by local capacities and traditions. However, the weak resource and capital base of Arab industry has dictated an integration into national production processes within a context that has maintained a strong degree of dependency on external sources of economic power.

A third dynamic, perhaps the one most prominent in Arab economic development in Israel since 1948, characterises the relation between Arab labour and the national economy. The evolution of the Arab labour force in Israel has been overwhelmingly determined by national prerequisites. The features of that labour force respond to external demand factors while regional interests have had little impact on labour force development. Though this has not precluded the acquisition through the work process of skills and experiences which benefit the region, to date such advantages have been, at best, only indirectly realised. Instead, Arab labour remains subservient to national growth interests as the regional growth potential of the Arab labour force continues to be channelled outside the region.

The transformations witnessed in Arab agriculture since 1948 produced a definite surplus of labour which had previously been employed or 'employable' in farming activities. As has been seen in the preceding discussion, not all of the labour 'released' from the rural sector was necessarily underemployed. While the process of agricultural transformation in most developing economies results in similar labour surplus creation, this process was both accelerated and in a sense, distorted, in the Arab experience in Israel. Accelerated, because of the context of land loss and marginalisation of Arab agriculture determining the process; and distorted, because the regional economy had no chance to manage this process or benefit from it by redirecting labour to local requirements.

The various characteristics of Arab labour and the phenomena which manifest its national position therefore reflect both its origin and the external market which it supplies. It is instructive to analyse its position at this particular stage in the discussion of the Arab regional economy for that reason. On the one hand, the gradual attrition of the traditional (rural/agricultural) Arab economy has played an important role in creating the particular regional labour force. Equally influential in shaping this labour force has been the changing nature of national demand for labour, and the degree to which Arab manpower has responded to that. Also significant to the process is the weakness of local non-agricultural alternatives available to Arab labour, discussed in Chapter Five.

In most aspects, the composition and characteristics of the Arab labour force in Israel altered dramatically since the 1950s. Developments have been affected by a regional-national dynamic with several facets. On the one hand, the general decline of Arab agriculture, combined with a weak local economic infrastructure, forced the existing labour force and new entrants to search for employment outside the region. At the same time, Israeli economic development demanded a range of labour inputs, especially in construction and unskilled work in agriculture and industry, which the region could readily provide.

While this latter influence might be expected to have encouraged the convergence of regional and national labour force characteristics, a third influence has tempered such a process. The internal dynamics of Arab demographic and social processes have retarded regional/national convergence on a number of levels. Furthermore, the absence of any active state inspired or other encouragement of the narrowing of disparities has allowed the maintenance of certain distinctive features in the Arab labour force. These include comparative regional/national labour force participation and unemployment rates, sectoral composition, occupational distribution, the degree of physical mobility and income distribution.

Arab Labour in Israel: The Region Subservient

The following discussion commences by reviewing the demographic, sectoral and occupational features of the Arab labour force. Subsequently, the distinctively Arab phenomenon of high physical mobility of labour is examined, followed by a discussion of differential (Arab/national) income, expenditure and savings patterns. Finally, the overall role of Arab labour in the national economy is highlighted through recourse to some tools of regional economic analysis.

LOW ARAB PARTICIPATION IN LABOUR FORCE[1]

Since 1948, the rate of participation of the Arab population (aged fourteen and over) in the labour force has gradually grown, though it still remains lower than the national rate. Developments in Arab participation rates would appear to be a function of two factors, one a long-term trend affected by social factors, and the other related to short-term economic fluctuations. Over thirty years, changes have taken place in social attitudes whereby women have become increasingly willing and able to enter the labour force. However, the degree of Arab female participation remains lower than the level of participation of Jewish women, and this disparity keeps overall Arab rates lower than national ones. Those same social attitudes also condition the degree and direction of female occupational mobility. Therefore, much of Arab female labour is concentrated in family agriculture and other labour intensive processes which can be practiced by women close to their homes. This labour mode is among the most readily capable of expanding and contracting in response to the effects on the male labour force in periods of economic boom or recession.

From a rate of 44 percent in 1954, Arab labour force participation had risen to 46 percent by 1964, while the national rate rose in the same period from 49 percent to 53 percent. For Arab women, the rate of participation was higher in 1954 than in 1966: 11.6 percent compared to 9.3 percent. This is possibly a manifestation of the greater degree of reliance on local agricultural activity in the 1950s and the consequently greater opportunities and necessity for women to work. In periods of economic growth, such as in 1964 and 1974, there were more opportunities for the male work-force to obtain non-farm employment. Consequently, it is not surprising that female participation rates fall: in 1974, this rate was back down to 9.4 percent. However, in times of general economic recession, such as 1954 and 1984, more women enter the labour force to help safeguard family subsistence. Table 4.1 exhibits major trends in the Arab labour force.

Table 4.1: Arab Civilian Labour Force Characteristics in Israel, Selected Years
(Thousands and Percentages)

Characteristics	1954	1964	1966	1974	1984	1985
Population (14 yrs+)	98.3	148.0	159.6	269.1	411.3	428.0
Civilian Labour Force	43.3	68.2	73.8	107.7	158.9	171.0
% of Popun.14 yrs+	44.0	46.1	46.3	40.0	38.6	40.0
Arab labour force % of national labour force	7.7	7.7	7.8	9.5	11.0	11.7
Females as % of Arab labour force	12.5	9.9	10.2	11.6	14.6	15.7
Unemployed	5.0	2.0	8.2	3.0	10.5	16.2
% of Civilian Labour Force	11.5	2.9	11.2	2.8	6.6	9.5
Employed	38.3[a]	66.2	65.6	104.7	148.4	154.8
% Empl. away from locality of residence	...	...	47.5	49.8	52.7	46.6
Sector			(Thousands)			
Agriculture	22.7	25.8	25.6	14.8	13.4	16.3
Industry/mining	4.0	10.3	9.8	18.3	31.9	32.8
Electricity/water	0.3	0.5	0.5	0.5	0.9	0.6
Construction	3.3	14.0	12.9	23.6	31.0	30.0
Commerce[b]	2.5	5.1	4.8	12.6	19.9	20.0
Transportation	1.0	3.1	4.0	7.1	9.3	8.7
Finance/business services	-	-	-	1.5	5.0	4.8
Public services	5.4[c]	5.1	5.4	16.9	26.0	29.4
Personal Services	...	2.2	2.6	7.1	11.1	12.2
			(Percentages)			
Total Employed	100.0	100.0	100.0	100.0	100.0	100.0
Agriculture	57.9	40.0	39.1	14.5	9.0	10.5
Industry/mining	10.2	15.6	14.9	17.9	21.5	21.2
Electricity/water	0.8	0.7	0.8	0.5	0.6	0.4
Construction	8.4	21.1	19.6	23.0	20.9	19.4
Commerce	6.4	7.7	7.4	12.3	13.4	12.9
Transportation	2.6	4.7	6.0	6.9	6.3	5.6
Finance/business services	-	-	8.2	1.5	3.4	3.1
Public services	13.7	7.7	8.2	16.5	17.5	19.0
Personal Services	-	3.3	4.0	6.9	7.5	7.9

Notes: (...) Denotes unavailable data. a. The total figure for employed in 1954 is smaller than the sum of the different sectors as those registered as 'unemployed' are included in the sectoral figures. b. Includes finance in 1954, 1964 and 1966. c. Includes personal services for 1954.
SOURCES: For 1954, from (Israel 1954: 116-8); For 1964, from (Israel 1964: 294-7; 306-9); For 1966, from (Israel 1966: 259); For 1974, from (Israel 1974: 289; 301; For 1984, from (Israel 1984: 325; 340); For 1985, from (Israel 1986: 293; 312).

Arab Labour in Israel: The Region Subservient

The inclusion of the labour force of East Jerusalem in post-1967 figures poses certain problems as different social and demographic factors influence participation rates there. Among these are the fact that Arab urban women are less likely to find socially acceptable employment opportunities than are rural women. Also significant is the different demographic structure of this population which since 1948 had been isolated from the influences of the 'modern values' of Israeli society. On the other hand, it should be noted that an urban climate can promote greater female employment. In addition, until the early 1980s there was a high level of emigration to the Arab states by families from the occupied territories (and East Jerusalem), including women of working age. This engendered a greater degree of dependence on remittances for subsistence of those remaining. These factors are likely to have distorted some of the characteristics of the Arab Jerusalem labour force.

Consequently, the overall Arab labour force participation rate began to fall in the 1970s, to 40 percent in 1974 and stabilised in the early 1980s at between 38-39 percent. Nationally, the trend was upwards, from a rate of 48 percent in 1974 to 50 percent in 1984 (though still lower than the rates prevailing until the 1960s). However, in the same period, female labour force participation began to rise, reaching 11 percent in 1984. This would appear to reflect the effects of the long-term social trend mentioned above, as well as that short-term effect related to the recessionary forces operative in recent years in the Israeli economy.

The differential rates of regional and national labour force participation are manifested in another series of figures. A comparison of the respective Arab proportions of the national labour force and of total population underlines the situation described above. From 1954 to 1984, the size of the Arab labour force grew from 43,000 to 159,000, an increase of 270 percent, or an average annual increase of some 9 percent. The national labour force grew in the same period from 561,000 to 1.444 million, an increase of 157 percent, or an average annual increase of some 5 percent.

While the region constituted 7.7 percent of the national labour force in 1954, it was some 13 percent of total population in that year. In 1964, the proportions were 7.7 percent and 11 percent respectively; in 1974, with the inclusion of the East Jerusalem population and Arab demographic growth, the percentages had risen to 9.6 percent and 15 percent. In 1984, they stood at 11 percent and 17 percent. While the weight of the Arab labour force in the national economy has grown in thirty years, this has not outstripped the increase in Arab demographic significance, and in fact has followed it. The ratio of the two percentages (Arab proportion of labour force to Arab proportion of population) has stayed around 0.64 since 1954, except for a small rise in the early 1960s. Therefore, whatever strategic significance Arab demographic growth might have for the future of the Jewish state, it is not as readily or strongly manifested in Arab labour force growth.

ARAB UNEMPLOYMENT CUSHIONS ISRAELI RECESSION

Generally, unemployment is more prevalent among Arabs and affects the Arab labour force more strongly. When national unemployment rates are low, the Arab rate is close to, or lower than, the national level. Yet invariably, high national unemployment rates are accompanied by higher Arab rates. This reflects a greater 'dispensability' of Arab labour as compared to Jewish labour, its generally more insecure occupational status and greater geographic and inter-sectoral mobility.

In 1954, when the Arab region was still under military rule, the Arab unemployment rate stood at 11.5 percent, compared to 8.5 percent nationally (see Table 4.1 above).[2] In the relatively prosperous early 1960s, the low national rate of 3.3 percent was accompanied by a lower Arab rate of 2.9 percent (in 1964). The period of severe economic crisis in Israel in the mid-1960s, however, sent Arab unemployment rates soaring to 11.2 percent and 17.7 percent in 1966 and 1967 respectively, while national unemployment was much lower, at 7.4 percent and 10.4 percent. By 1974, in the period of the post-1967 Israeli economic boom, both regional and national unemployment stood at 3 percent. However, by 1984, as the Israeli recession began to be felt, Arab unemployment had again risen above the national rate, to 6.6 percent, compared to 5.8 percent. In 1985, Arab unemployment had reached 9.5 percent, a level not witnessed since the 1960s. The national rate was still lower, at 6.7 percent.

The national rise in the number of unemployed between 1979 and 1985 of 165 percent (from 37,000 to 98,500) was disproportionately borne by the Arab region, where unemployment increased by 550 percent (from 2,500 to 16,200). Arabs formed 11.7 percent of the labour force in 1985 but over 16 percent of the unemployed in that year. Throughout 1985, and into 1986, as national unemployment rates continued to rise, the region was hit particularly hard, with labour exchanges in Nazareth reporting unemployment rates well above the worst experienced in Jewish localities.

There is no single or definitive cause for this phenomenon. Job insecurity for Arabs in Israel is a function of several factors which do not apply to Israeli Jews. An important determinant is differential sectoral demand, whereby Arabs are particularly affected by expansion or contraction in certain sectors. Because of the specific nature of Arab sectoral concentration, the regional labour force as a whole is more vulnerable to economic fluctuations than is the national labour force. Further, Arab occupational distribution and the related characteristics of Arab labour tenure status also determine their expendability in times of employment cuts. The special provision for the job security of Jewish workers by state and affiliated bodies in recessionary periods adds to the instability of Arab labour in the national economy. Weak and disorganised Arab representation in the national trade union system also contributes to preventing effective defence of job rights. These factors, operating differentially on the temporal, geographical and sectoral levels, combine to increase the likelihood that Arabs will be among the first to be dismissed in times of economic slump and will find it more difficult to obtain new jobs during such periods.

SECTORAL STRUCTURE: AGRICULTURE GIVES WAY TO CONSTRUCTION AND INDUSTRY

The sectoral structure of the employed Arab labour force has altered radically since 1948. The relative importance of certain sectors to the regional and national economies have been transformed. Clear long-term trends can be distinguished in the national labour force, with some sectors gaining in importance, others decreasing and others remaining more or less the same. However, regional employment patterns have followed less definite and consistent paths, with most trends more short term and reversible. This would suggest that in large part, regional employment patterns are determined externally and respond to changes in national demand differently than is the case with Jewish labour.

Divergent National and Regional Trends

The main exception to this dynamic is the course of developments in Arab agricultural employment, which have been consistent with a national decline.[3] Until the 1960s, agriculture was the main employer of Arab labour. However, the share of agriculture in total Arab employment was falling, from 58 percent in 1954 to 39 percent in 1964. Subsequently, it became an increasingly smaller sector, constituting 14 percent of Arabs employed in 1974 and only 9 percent by 1984. Agriculture, however, slightly regained its share of the Arab labour force in 1985, when it stood at 10.5 percent. Nationally, the trend was similar, with agriculture accounting for 18 percent, 13 percent, 6 percent and 5 percent of national employment in 1954, 1964, 1974 and 1984 respectively. These developments are traced in Table 4.1 above.

In most other sectors, regional trends have differed from those in the national labour force. This has been most notable in construction, where there has been no single regional trend, unlike the general national trend. The 1970s were marked by the prominence of construction employment among the Arab labour force. Whereas its share of Arab employment was only 8 percent in 1954, construction had by 1964 become the second largest sector for regional employment. By 1974, with the expansion of Israeli building activity in the post-1967 period, construction took the lead, absorbing 24 percent of the employed Arab labour force. However, in the early 1980s construction employment contracted, and by 1984 accounted for just under 21 percent of Arab employment. The share fell further in 1985, to 19 percent. National employment in construction has been constantly declining, from 10 percent of all employed in 1954 and 1964, to 8 percent in 1974 and 6 percent in 1984. It is difficult to guage from available data the extent to which construction employment is in the regional or the national economy.[4]

The falling national and regional shares of construction is due to two factors. Over the long term, it can be ascribed to the construction requirements of the Jewish state until the 1960s which have diminished somewhat, especially since the economic slowdown in Israel began to take its toll of construction activity as of 1983. Of more recent influence is the newly acquired prominence of industrial employment among the Arab labour force, the culmination of a process which began in the 1970s. In industry, as with construction, regional and national patterns differ.

Industrial employment (including electricity and water) has absorbed a consistent 23 percent to 25 percent of the national labour force since the 1950s. However, industry accounted for only 10 percent of Arab labour in 1954, 16 percent in 1964, and 18 percent in 1974. It was in the 1980s that industry became preeminent for Arab labour in Israel. By 1985 the sector was employing the greatest proportion of the regional labour force, just under 22 percent.[5]

Detailed figures for 1983 show the Arab industrial labour force of some 27,000 to be concentrated primarily in textiles and clothing manufacture (26 percent of the Arab industrial workforce). Basic metal and metal products manufacture accounted for 18 percent of Arab industrial employment, while the food, beverages and tobacco industries shared 16 percent. Chemicals and plastics accounted for 6 percent of regional industrial labour, and the share of paper and printing was 4 percent. Significantly, there is minimal Arab employment in manufacture of diamonds, heavy machinery, and electrical, electronic, transport or military equipment. These strategic branches, which employ only 6 percent of Arab industrial labour, account for 33 percent of the national industrial labour force. In other sectors, national and regional trends have also differed. Transport and communications have always absorbed between 6 and 8 percent of national employment, while regionally, the share of this sector has fluctuated more strongly and widely.

Transport employed 3 percent of employed Arabs in 1954, 5 percent in 1964, 7 percent in 1974, falling to 6 percent in 1984. Similarly, while the share of personal services in employment has steadily decreased nationally since the 1950s, it has been less stable regionally, from 10 percent in 1954, to 3 percent in 1964, and steadying at around 7 percent since 1974. In 1983, some 75 percent of Arabs employed in this sector were to be found in bus, taxi and truck transport, compared to only 40 percent nationally.

There are two sectors in which, as with agriculture, regional employment trends have been similar to national ones, though not necessarily influenced by the same factors. Public service employment in the region, primarily a function of local demand conditions and the level of state investment in regional education, health and other services, has absorbed an increasing proportion of the Arab labour force, doubling every ten years. In 1954 this figure stood at 4 percent, rising to 8 percent by 1964 and reaching 16 percent in 1974. This increasing trend was similar to national developments. However since 1982, when it had reached 19 percent, the share of regional public service employment declined somewhat, reflecting public sector cutbacks in the region. By 1984, this share had fallen to 17.5 percent of the employed Arab labour force, rising to 19 percent in 1985; nationally the 1978 level of 29 percent was maintained.

This difference is not surprising in light of the range of national public sector jobs, especially those related to the military and government, in which Arab employment is restricted. While in 1983, 14 percent of Arabs in public services were in government administration, only 4.4 percent of all Israeli government administration employees were Arab. In that year, most Arab public service employees were found in education (48 percent) and health (16 percent), with a smaller proportion in local authorities (9 percent).

Commercial activity has absorbed a growing proportion of the regional labour force. Much Arab commercial activity is

Arab Labour in Israel: The Region Subservient

informally organised, and takes place inside and outside the region, as well as between the regional and national economies. The level of Arab commercial activity is to a great extent determined by the willingness, need and ability of entrepreneurs to enter into such business. As such, labour supply in this sector is relatively elastic, insofar as there are many and regular openings for 'middleman' activities between the region and the national economy. This is discussed further in Chapter Five.

The share of commerce and finance grew from 6 percent in 1954 to 13 percent by 1974, and rose to 16 percent in 1985. Growth in national employment in these sectors has similarly grown steadily from 11 percent in 1954 to 22 percent in 1985. The largest proportion of Arabs in commercial employment were, in 1983, to be found in restaurants, cafes and hotels. Both retail food and other retail branches (clothing, household goods, food and household goods, restaurants, etc.) each accounted for 24 percent of the sector's work-force, while wholesale activity absorbed 10 percent of the sector's Arab workers. Employment in finance has grown recently, absorbing 3 percent of Arab employed in 1984. Most of those Arabs employed in this sector in 1983 were in legal and business services (60 percent), with employment in banks and financial institutions accounting for most of the rest (30 percent).

Labour Demand: Structural Patterns and Transitory Deviations

The nature of demand for Arab labour in the Israeli economy has been analysed by Najwa Makhoul in terms of two types of demand, manifested in different periods. Prior to 1967, Makhoul argues, demand for Arab wage labour was a "transitory phenomenon, (in response to a temporary demand generated by the construction boom), ending with the recession of the mid-sixties when they were massively laid off and absorbed back into agriculture" (1982: 84). Demand for Arab labour in the national production process since 1967 has,

> ...emerged as structural in character following from a basic transformation in the labour market in response to the restructuring of the Israeli economy which involved, among other things, a shift into export-oriented military and related industrialisation, and the consequent development of a dual labour market: a primary labour market connected with the more strategic military industry open only to Jewish citizens, and a secondary labour market connected with the consumer goods industry open also to Arab citizens. This structural

transformation in the labour market which allowed for Jewish labour mobility also affected the kind of labour in demand within the secondary labour market, and hence the entry of Palestinian Arab workers...*(Ibid)*

While this analysis highlights the important national determinant of the structure of the regional labour force, industry is not the only sector to reflect that. In fact, the intra-sectoral distribution in industry suggests a lesser degree of integration into Israeli industry than might be assumed.[6] It has been noted that there exists a national-regional demand relation in other sectors as well. For example, Arab employment in construction is primarily in the Jewish sector, while regional personal service activity and a certain part of commercial activity is also very much determined by external (national) demand for that labour. Personal services include several sub-branches prevalent in the region, such as garages and other repair services, and domestic services, all of which have established Jewish customers. Commerce includes work in hotels, restaurants and cafes, and retail trade, areas in which Arab labour finds employment in Jewish cities and towns. Most of the employment in finance takes place inside the region in externally owned banks, insurance, accounting and legal firms.

Further, the claim that the post-1967 situation has not also been characterised by 'transitory demand' for Arab labour is questionable. Construction employment, for instance, has followed to a greater degree than has been the case nationally, the booms and slumps in construction activity. 'Transitory demand' can also be discerned in the case of Arab employment in Jewish agriculture, which can easily dispense with Arab labour from Israel when necessary, either through overall cutbacks, or through increased employment of workers from the occupied West Bank and Gaza Strip.

As stated at the outset, a specific pattern of national-regional demand has developed. The emerging profile of the Arab labour force, therefore, indicates a sectoral structure geared to, though not absolutely determined by, changes in national demand for particular labour processes. This has been succinctly expressed by Makhoul who noticed that "the obvious rule of the transformation is that of agriculture giving the lead to construction in the 1970s, and construction giving the lead to industry in the beginning of the 1980s" *(Ibid: 87)*.

Table 4.2: Arab Employed Persons Aged 25 and Over in Annual Labour Force Who Worked in Israel in 1978 and 1983 By Sector, 4 VI 1983
(Thousands and Percentages)

Economic Sector in 1978	Economic Sector in 1983								
	Personal and Other Services	Public and Community Services	Financing and Business Services	Transport storage & Communication	Commerce, restaurants & hotels	Construction (building & public works)	Electricity & water	Industry (mining & manufacture)	Agriculture forestry & fishing	TOTAL
Code	9	8	7	6	5	4	3	1-2	0	
Total -thousands	3.9	18.0	2.2	5.8	8.2	14.9	0.6	13.2	4.1	76.3ᵃ
-percentagesᵇ	5.5	25.4	3.1	8.2	11.6	21.2	0.8	18.5	5.8	100.0
-percentagesᵇ	100.0	100.0	100.0	100.0	100.0	100.0	100.0	100.0	100.0	
Agriculture, fishing	0.5	0.4	0.7	1.2	0.9	1.3	3.7	1.3	90.2	6.2
Industry	3.0	2.4	6.0	4.9	4.4	3.6	1.9	89.7	2.4	19.5
Electricity, water	-	0.1	-	-	0.3	0.4	88.9	0.1	-	0.9
Construction	2.4	2.0	3.7	4.5	4.0	90.9	1.9	3.2	3.7	21.4
Commerce	2.1	1.3	0.9	2.6	85.0	1.5	-	2.1	1.4	11.3
Transport, storage	1.2	0.3	0.5	84.5	0.9	0.9	0.9	1.1	1.1	7.6
Financing, business services	-	0.3	80.7	0.1	0.2	0.2	-	0.5	-	2.8
Public, community services	0.9	92.7	7.4	0.9	2.5	0.9	2.8	1.1	1.0	24.7
Personal, other services	89.8	0.5	-	1.2	1.8	0.4	-	0.8	0.2	5.6

Notes: a. Includes 5,400 employed persons in sectors unknown at the time of the census; b. Percentages are computed from employed persons in known sectors only.
Source: From (Israel 1985: 366).

Recently available data allows us to trace the direction of inter-sectoral mobility of Arab workers aged over 25 in 1983, according to their sectoral distribution in 1978 (see Table 4.2). These indicate a higher degree of stability of employment between 1978 and 1983 in the primary and secondary sectors, and in public and personal services, than is the case in the other tertiary sectors. Between 89 percent and 93 percent of those employed in agriculture, industry, construction and services in 1983 were employed in the same sector in 1978. In finance, transport and commerce, the proportions were between 81 percent and 85 percent. Further, it is indicated that contraction in agricultural employment after 1978 directed most labour into construction and industry. Over the period, industry 'graduated' labour into all sectors, but mostly into construction, public services, commerce and transport. Of those employed in construction in 1978, the greatest number employed elsewhere in 1983 were to be found in industry, with relatively large proportions working in public services, commerce and transport.

Overall, those sectors which had by 1983 absorbed the largest numbers employed in other sectors in 1978 were industry, construction, public services and commerce, each with over 1200 new entrants from other sectors. The degree of articulation between the primary and secondary sectors in the region is therefore significant, though it does not appear to be any more stronger than is the case nationally. However, it is relevant to the overall analysis, insofar as it further illustrates the degree of complexity and dynamism in the region. This pattern is somewhat unique as compared to the national economy, contrasting with the static and deterministic structure ('modernised' or 'colonised') which some analyses have portrayed.

OCCUPATIONAL RIGIDITIES
AND THE DE-SKILLING PROCESS

There are three outstanding aspects of the occupational structure of the Arab regional labour force which arise from an examination of trends and most recent data. Though there has been a transformation since the 1950s whereby Arab labour has acquired new and more advanced skills, this process has been slow and minimal, especially in comparison to the non-Arab labour force. A second observation pertains to the extent to which the Arab labour force is over-concentrated (compared to the national distribution) in manual, relatively low-skilled and productive occupations. Finally, data from the 1983 Census of Population indicate that the acquisition of skills is not necessarily a path to long-term job advancement or security for Arabs, and that a type of occupational 'de-skilling' has appeared among Arab labourers.

An examination of these issues will shed further light on the process whereby the Arab labour force has come to fulfil a specific role in the national economy. This has been characterised by relatively low skilled, manual and productive tasks performed by a geographically and sectorally mobile labour force. It has served as a sort of cushion for the national economy, absorbing the fluctuations and filling the gaps created in the labour market by the particular structure of the Jewish labour force and the development of the national economy.

Slow Acquisition of Skills

The occupational characteristics of the Arab labour force are very much determined by the changing structure of demand in the national economy, with regional prerequisites having minimal effect. In itself, as with Arab agricultural activity, this is not necessarily detrimental to regional development. However, given the absence of a regional authority or economic power which might have otherwise regulated human resource development and ensured an optimal allocation of skills, few local benefits appear to arise from the process.

Standard occupational strata can be combined into two major groups.[7] The *white collar* category includes scientific/academic, professional/technical, administrative/managerial, clerical and sales workers. At the lower end of the occupational spectrum, the *blue collar* category covers service, agricultural, and both skilled and unskilled production workers. Over the past thirty years, there has been a clear shift in the distribution of the Arab labour force between these two major groupings.

In 1954, only 16 percent of employed Arabs were white collar; sales and scientific/professional workers constituted most of these (7 percent and 5 percent respectively of total employed - also see Table 4.3).[8] In that year, 50 percent of Arab employed were blue collar agricultural workers while 30 percent of employed Arabs were skilled and unskilled workers in production: industry, mining, transport and construction. By 1974, 21 percent of employed Arabs were white-collar, mostly in the professional/technical and sales categories (9 percent and 7 percent respectively of total employed). With the shift of labour out of agriculture by this period, 38 percent of Arab blue collar labour was classified in the 'skilled production' workers category, with some 15 percent in each of the 'agricultural' and

Arab Labour in Israel: The Region Subservient

'unskilled production' workers categories. Service workers, who had constituted 5 percent of employed in 1954, accounted for 9 percent of Arab employment by 1974. The move of Arabs into white collar occupations has continued, and 26 percent of employed Arabs were in these categories in 1984. In that year, 40 percent of employed Arabs were skilled production workers, 14 percent were unskilled production workers, and 11 percent were service workers.

Therefore, the distribution of Arab labour between white collar and blue collar occupations has shifted from 16 percent and 84 percent respectively in 1954 to 26 percent and 74 percent in 1984. While this indicates a certain degree of overall human resource development, in comparison to national labour force advancement, the Arab transformation has been both slow and limited. The distribution of the national labour force among white collar and blue collar occupations has changed from 37 percent and 63 percent respectively in 1954 to 54 percent and 46 percent in 1984. While only one-quarter of Arab workers are white collar, over half of the national employed (and more of Jewish employed) are in these categories. Most noticeable is the fact that under one-third of national employed in 1984 were engaged in production related occupations, whereas over half of Arab workers were thus employed. In these terms alone, the less advanced and largely productive role of Arab labour in the national economy is clear.

Concentration in Low-skilled Occupations

It is possible to identify those occupational categories in which Arab representation is relatively significant compared to national labour force structure. This can be done through reference to figures for the Arab proportion of different occupations in 1983, bearing in mind that overall, Arabs constituted 10 percent of the national labour force. In 1983, Arabs accounted for 33 percent of all Israeli unskilled production workers, 15 percent of the country's skilled production workers, and 14 percent of agricultural workers. In all other major occupational categories, Arab representation was below 9 percent; the proportion was lowest among administrative/managerial, scientific/academic, and clerical grades.

Table 4.3: Employed Arab Labour Force in Israel, by Occupational Characteristics and Status at Work, Selected Years

Code/Category		1955	1963	1974	1984	1985
		(Thousands)				
Total Employed		43.4	68.2	104.7	148.4	154.8
Occupation						
0	Scientific & academic workers	}2.0	}2.9	1.2	3.6	3.9
1	Other professional, & technical workers	}	}	9.2	13.7	14.1
2	Administrators, Managers	0.3	}0.4	0.4	2.5	2.9
3	Clerical & related workers	1.2	}	3.7	9.3	9.3
4	Sales workers	3.1	2.6	7.6	11.0	11.0
5	Service workers	2.0	2.9	9.4	15.9	17.5
6	Agricultural workers	21.8	24.7	15.5	13.1	16.0
7-8	Skilled production workers	5.6	9.9	38.6	58.9	59.8
9	Other production & unskilled workers	7.4	23.5	16.0	20.4	20.3
	Not known	-	1.3	3.2	-	-
Status at work						
	Employees	...	...	78.8	115.3	122.0
	Employers, self employed	...	...	22.0	29.3	29.0
	Cooperative/kibbutz members	...	...	0.6	1.3	1.1
	Unpaid family members	...	...	3.3	2.5	2.8
		(Percentages)				
Total Employed		100.0	100.0	100.0	100.0	100.0
0	Scientific & academic workers	}4.6	}4.2	1.1	2.4	2.5
1	Other professional, & technical workers	}	}	8.8	9.3	9.1
2	Administrators, Managers	0.7	}0.6	0.4	1.7	1.9
3	Clerical & related workers	2.8	}	3.5	6.3	6.0
4	Sales workers	7.1	3.9	7.2	7.4	7.1
5	Service workers	4.6	4.2	9.0	10.7	11.3
6	Agricultural workers	50.3	36.2	14.8	8.8	10.3
7-8	Skilled production workers	12.9	14.5	36.9	39.7	38.6
9	Other production & unskilled workers	17.0	34.5	15.3	13.7	13.1
	Not known	-	1.9	3.0	-	-
Status at work						
	Employees	...	...	75.2	77.7	78.8
	Employers, self employed	...	...	21.0	19.7	18.7
	Cooperative/kibbutz members	...	...	0.6	0.9	0.7
	Unpaid family members	...	...	3.2	1.7	1.8

Notes: (...) Denotes unavailable data.
SOURCES: For 1955, from (Israel 1955: 189); For 1963, from (Israel 1964: 317-9); For 1974, from (Israel 1974: 289); For 1984 and 1985, from (Israel 1986: 312).

Arab Labour in Israel: The Region Subservient

On a further level of disaggregation, it is useful to note the specific occupations in which Arab employed are relatively 'over-concentrated'. In the three above-mentioned major categories in which Arabs are over-represented, there are a large number of occupations with 10,000 workers or more which employ a disproportionately large amount of Arab labour.[9] The minor category with the greatest proportion of Arab workers is that of unskilled production workers whose sectoral position is unspecified (57 percent of the national total of 20,000 workers in 1983). This is followed by building workers (29 percent of the total of 25,000), woodworkers and carpenters (26 percent of the total of 23,000), textile spinning, weaving and finishing workers (23 percent of the total of 10,500), drivers (18 percent of the total of 49,000), skilled farm workers (15 percent of the total of 23,000), machinery assemblers, installers, repairers (15 percent of the total of 25,000), tailors and dressmakers (13. 5 percent of the total of 25,000) and blacksmiths and welders (13 percent of the total of 50,000).

This relative 'over-concentration' of regional labour can also be noticed in a few of the other major occupational categories where Arab labour constitutes less than 10 percent of the total. For example, of the 23,000 Israeli policemen, watchmen and related workers, some 13 percent are Arab. Of the 32,000 proprietor retailers in the country, almost 11 percent are Arab. Similarly, of the national total of 75,000 kindergarten, primary and secondary school teachers and workers, 13 percent are Arab.

This latter figure provides an interesting example of the imbalance in regional-national labour force structure. While this minor occupational category is the second largest profession in the country after accountants (who number 85,000), it is also the second largest Arab profession, numbering 9,800. However, unlike the national labour force, the largest single occupational category for Arabs is 'non-specified unskilled workers', i.e., those unskilled workers who are not employed in any defined or single sector. In such a distorted fashion does regional labour force structure reflect certain basic national trends while also accomodating other requirements of national demand.

The similarities and differences in regional and national labour force trends can also be seen in data on the growth of wage labour (employee) status (see Table 4.3 above). In 1966, 33 percent of Arab employed were still either self-employed, employers or unpaid family labourers. This reflected the continued significance of agriculture in the regional economy, the still limited articulation between the Arab and national economies, and the serious recessionary climate of the period. In 1966 and 1967, Arab unemployment was particularly high. It is likely that these factors necessitated a greater degree of local 'self-reliance' and encouraged various forms of self-employment.

However, through the 1970s, the percentage of employees among Arab employed rose gradually, along with the national growth in this proportion. In 1970, the regional and national percentages were, respectively, 72.4 percent and 73.6 percent; by 1980, they stood at 75.9 percent and 77.4 percent; in 1984, the respective proportions had reached 77.7 percent and 79 percent. While this feature of regional labour force trends has followed national developments, Arab labour remains slightly more dependent on its 'own' sources of employment, be it through family labour status in agriculture or various forms of self-employment and unpaid family labour in commerce, transport, personal services and the rest of the 'informal' sector.

It has been argued by Makhoul that recent developments in Arab labour force composition in Israel indicate the emergence of an Arab proletariat. Basing her conclusions on Arab labour's marked "concentration in skilled manual/non-supervisory/productive wage labour", she notes that this is the "most conservative criteria by which the boundaries of the working class are defined" (1982: 84-5).

> They are distinguished from non-citizen Palestinian Arab workers employed in Israel *(i.e., from the occupied territories - RK)*, who tend to be concentrated in the unskilled parts of these labour categories. They are distinguished also from Israel's Jewish citizens, who tend to be concentrated in the mental labour categories of employment, often even when they produce surplus value as in the cases of technicians and engineers *(Ibid)*.

Notwithstanding the validity of these observations, it is not clear, as argued by Makhoul, that Arab labour is "being slowly integrated into military production related labour processes" (1982: 98). While the detailed occupational distribution of the Arab labour force indicates a significant presence in some related occupations, it is not clear that this is in military industry production units. In 1983, of the 54,000 Arabs skilled production workers (occupational categories 70 - 89), 15,000 (i.e., under 30 percent) were employed in metal, machinery, electric and electronic related professions (categories 70 - 4). It is on the basis of these figures that Makhoul's analysis rests.

However, when the sectoral figures are examined at the minor level, it is found that only some 6,700 Arabs are employed in industries producing metals, machinery, electric, electronic and transport equipment and diamonds (sectoral categories 22-8).

Arab Labour in Israel: The Region Subservient

While these categories account for 25 percent of the Arab industrial labour work-force, Arab workers constitute only 5 percent of the total therein employed. The remainder of the 15,000 Arab production workers can be expected to be found in construction and personal services (vehicle and other repairs) sectors.

An additional figure provides a good indication of the extent to which Arabs are excluded from 'strategic' employment locations. Of the 16,000 workers employed in military industries not specified under the above-mentioned minor sectoral categories, under 20 were Arab, or 0.1 percent of the total. Whatever proletarianisation might have occurred among Arab workers, it is doubtful that it has been concentrated in 'strategic' locations as suggested.

The 'De-skilling' of Arab Labour in Israel

In fact, there is startling new evidence of a 'de-skilling' process at work in the region's labour force. Of the 9,900 unskilled and other production workers in 1983, almost 10 percent had been classified as skilled in 1978 (see Table 4.4). Other entrants into the unskilled category came primarily from agriculture, services and commerce. A small number of unskilled in 1983 (0.7 percent) had been scientific, academic, professional or technical workers in 1978. Of the 27,900 skilled workers in 1983, only 5 percent were unskilled in 1978 and 1 percent came from each of agriculture, services and commerce. A relatively large proportion of service workers (8 percent), sales workers (10 percent) and clerical workers (6 percent) in 1983 had in 1978 been skilled production workers. The services and commerce occupational categories had by 1983 also absorbed a proportion of 1978 unskilled production workers.

The main inter-occupational flows appear to have been towards unskilled production, commerce, services and agricultural occupations, the categories with the highest degree of 'turnover' (in terms of the extent to which those employed in 1978 had changed their occupations by 1983). These occupations received labour primarily from the skilled and unskilled production occupational categories.

The occupations exhibiting the highest degree of 'stability' between 1978 and 1983 were professional and technical, skilled production, scientific and academic, and agricultural workers, in that order. On the whole, there appears to be minimal occupational mobility from blue collar to white collar categories except to the sales and service workers categories, which in the

Table 4.4: Arab Employed Persons Aged 25 and Over in Annual Labour Force Who Worked in Israel in 1978 and 1983, By Occupation, 4 VI 1983
(Thousands and Percentages)

Occupation in 1978		Occupation in 1983								
	Other workers in industry, building and unskilled workers	Skilled workers in industry, building, transport	Agricultural workers	Service workers	Sales workers	Clerical and related workers	Administrators and managers	Other professional, technical and related workers	Scientific and academic workers	TOTAL
Code	9	8	7	6	5	4	3	1-2	0	
Total -thousands	9.9	27.9	4.5	7.4	5.0	3.6	0.7	9.2	2.2	76.3[a]
-percentages[b]	14.1	39.7	6.4	10.5	7.1	5.1	1.0	13.1	3.1	100.0
-percentages[b]	100.0	100.0	100.0	100.0	100.0	100.0	100.0	100.0	100.0	
Scientific and academic workers	0.3	0.1	0.4	—	0.2	0.5	0.9	0.5	88.4	3.0
Other professional, technical and related workers	0.4	0.3	0.8	0.6	0.7	2.6	5.9	95.8	3.6	13.3
Administrators and managers	—	0.1	0.1	0.2	0.2	0.8	75.6	0.2	0.2	0.9
Clerical and related workers	0.6	0.4	0.3	0.5	2.7	85.1	5.0	1.2	2.2	5.1
Sales workers	1.1	0.9	0.5	1.4	80.1	1.2	0.8	0.2	0.7	6.4
Service workers	2.0	1.2	1.9	83.2	2.2	1.5	5.0	0.3	0.2	9.9
Agricultural workers	1.3	1.0	86.7	2.1	0.9	0.8	0.8	0.2	0.7	6.4
Skilled workers in industry, mining, building, transport and other skilled workers	9.6	91.1	4.9	8.0	9.9	6.0	4.2	1.4	2.9	40.1
Other workers in industry, transport, building and unskilled workers	84.7	4.8	4.4	4.1	3.1	1.7	1.7	0.2	1.0	15.0

NOTES: a. Includes 5,800 employed persons with unknown occupations at the time of the census; b. Percentages are computed from employed persons with known occupations only.
Source: From (Israel 1985: 367).

case of the Arab labour force are mostly manual labour processes anyhow. Among blue-collar workers, therefore, there is as much, if not more, evidence of downwards skill mobility (from skilled to unskilled jobs) as there is of upwards advancement (from production into services or commercial work).

INCOME DISTRIBUTION AND HOUSEHOLD EXPENDITURE

A significant, and often overlooked, aspect of regional/national divergences is that manifested by data on patterns of income distribution, family expenditure and savings. These are of interest not only in terms of the indications they provide of differentials between Arabs and Jews in Israel. Within the present analysis, this data helps to further identify those unique aspects of Arab economic structure and activity which have resulted in the emergence of an Arab region in Israel. Just as the region can be seen to fulfil a particular productive role in the national economy, so do its inhabitants manifest distinctive modes of income generation, consumption, other expenditure and savings. Available data allows for an initial examination of this feature of the regional economy.[10]

The Arab-Jewish Poverty Gap in Israel

Official sample survey data of Arab and Jewish households show clear disparities in income distribution. In 1982, gross annual income per Arab household was Israeli Shekels (IS) 144,000 (approximately $5,900), 70 percent of the average for Jewish households of IS206,000 (approximately $8,450). This divergence is even more severe when the fact that the average Arab household numbered 5.8 persons compared to 3.8 persons for Jewish households is taken into account. Considering those figures, average per capita Arab income was only 46 percent of the average per capita Jewish income (i.e. $1,020 compared to $2,220 per 'standard person'). This is the case even though the average number of earners per Jewish and Arab households was roughly the same (1.6 and 1.5 respectively)..

Net income figures, in Table 4.5, present a similar picture. Arab average annual net income per household in 1982 was only 76 percent of the Jewish average, thus raising the per capita net income figure to 50 percent. This difference between gross and net income presumably arises from differential proportions of taxes and transfers to other households paid by each group (see below). Further, the income of even the worst off ethnic groups among Jewish Israelis, the Jewish immigrants of Arab origin, is higher than that of Arabs. In 1982, the average annual net household income for these so-called 'oriental Jews' was IS140,000 compared to the Arab level of IS117,000. It therefore follows that if the claim by 'oriental Jews' that they are 'second-class citizens' is valid, Arabs should be considered as 'third class citizens'.

Data for 1982 income distribution of urban employees' households according to brackets of annual net money income per 'standard person' in the household show a concentration of Arab households at the lower levels (see Table 4.6). Whereas only 6 percent of Jewish employees' households were in the income bracket of under IS20,000 annual income per standard person, 32 percent of Arab households were in that bracket. Similarly, while 23 percent of Jewish employees' households were at income levels within the three income brackets between IS20,000 and IS35,000, 42 percent of Arab households were within those brackets. Therefore, with under 30 percent of all Jewish urban employees' households at income levels per standard person of less than $1,400, the concentration of some 75 percent of Arab households under that level testifies to the sharp inequities in income distribution corresponding to the Arab/Jewish divide.[11]

It can further be seen that in the comparative index of average gross annual money income per urban employees' household for different ethnic groups in Israel (Arabs and different Jewish groups), Arabs have consistently been at the bottom (Israel 1985: 283; also see Table 4.7). With the index for those Jews born in Europe and America at 100, the index for all Israeli Jews has been around 90 since 1970; for Arabs, the index has consistently been just over 60, rising to 65 in 1980, but falling since. By 1984, the gap had fallen to below its 1970 level - a forceful rebuttal of Israeli claims of Arab 'prosperity' in Israel.

Despite affirmation by most Israeli commentators and officials that Israeli Arabs receive the same income for the same work as Israeli Jews, both gross and net household income data for 1982 belie this (see Table 4.5). For example, whereas the average Jewish household's net annual income, where the head of the household was a professional or technical worker, was IS158,500 in 1982, for Arabs, the same figure was IS150,300. Where the head of the household was a service worker, the Jewish household's average annual net income was IS110,000 compared to the figure for Arabs of IS62,000. Disparities in other occupations is equally apparent: for skilled production and transport workers, the income level of Jewish households was IS141,000 while it was IS118,000 for Arabs; for unskilled workers, the gap was slightly narrower, at IS119,000 for Jewish

Arab Labour in Israel: The Region Subservient

households and IS95,000 for Arabs. As gross income figures exhibit the same divergences, it can be concluded that Arabs in Israel are firmly placed at the bottom of Israeli income levels, regardless of their skills, qualifications or occupations.

Table 4.5: Average Annual Net Income Per Urban Employees' Household, By Size of Household, And By Head of Household's Occupation and Years of Schooling, 1982

Characteristics	TOTAL	JEWS				ARABS
		Total	Born in Asia-Africa	Born in Europe-America	Born in Israel	
Net Income per household	151.9	153.2	140.0	164.9	153.3	117.1
Persons in Household						
1	84.7	84.8	70.7	91.6	84.2	..
2	131.5	132.0	101.1	141.3	130.5	..
3	152.6	153.4	126.9	177.7	143.7	130.7
4	171.4	173.2	149.1	196.4	172.8	103.4
5	171.1	173.0	156.0	196.1	177.8	106.9
6+	151.0	154.5	149.8	169.2	155.7	125.9
Occupation of head of household						
Scientific and academic workers	202.1	202.5	196.8	220.1	179.4	..
Other professional, technical workers	164.6	158.5	170.1	170.2	158.5	150.3
Administrators and managers	211.0	211.2	188.6	215.2	216.2	..
Clerical workers	149.3	149.6	148.4	152.6	147.5	..
Sales workers	160.7	160.3	131.9	176.9	160.3	..
Service workers	108.0	109.6	135.7	103.5	111.1	62.2
Skilled workers in industry, building, transport, etc.	139.7	140.9	133.6	149.3	141.4	118.4
Other workers in industry, building, transport and unskilled workers	115.7	118.8	126.6	117.2	105.1	95.2
Years of schooling of head of household						
1-4	106.0	108.6	121.9	96.4	99.8	96.6
5-8	153.6	123.7	124.2	125.3	114.2	113.2
9-10	137.6	138.4	132.2	145.9	138.0	99.0
11-12	157.8	157.8	159.4	166.7	141.7	148.2

SOURCE: From (Israel 1984a: 52-3).

Table 4.6: Households in Israel, By Income Groups, 1982

INCOME GROUPS			(Percent households)			
(IS)	TOTAL	JEWS	ARABS	TOTAL	JEWS	ARABS
TOTAL	100.0	96.5	3.5	100.0	100.0	100.0
Up to 19,999	100.0	84.3	15.7	7.1	6.2	32.0
20,000-24,999	100.0	92.1	7.9	6.8	6.5	15.5
25,000-29,999	100.0	94.0	6.0	8.1	7.9	14.0
30,000-34,999	100.0	95.4	4.6	9.0	8.9	12.0
35,000-39,999	100.0	96.1	3.9	7.6	7.5	8.4
40,000-49,999	100.0	98.3	1.7	15.1	15.3	7.4
50,000-59,999	100.0	98.8	1.2	12.3	12.7	}
60,000-69,999	100.0	99.8	0.2	10.8	11.2	}
70,000-79,999	100.0	99.3	0.7	7.2	7.4	} 10.7
80,000-89,999	100.0	99.0	1.0	9.3	9.5	}
100,000 +	100.0	99.1	0.9	6.7	6.9	}

SOURCE: From (Israel 1984a: 58-59).

Table 4.7: Index of Gross Annual Money Income Per Urban Employees' Household, Selected Years

	1984						
	Average per household		Households (Percent)	1984	1983	1982	1980	1970
	Earners	Persons						
Gross average income (current IS thousand)				1,790.0	513.9	203.8	37.6	1.2
TOTAL	1.6	3.8	100.0					

Indices. Base: born in Europe-America = 100.0

Origin								
Jews - total	1.6	3.7	96.4	88.7	91.6	91.2	91.5	90.0
Israel born	1.5	3.5	36.3	88.6	92.8	92.5	93.8	103.3
Asia-Africa	1.6	4.5	29.8	77.5	81.6	80.1	80.1	73.9
Europe-America	1.6	3.1	30.3	100.0	100.0	100.0	100.0	100.0
Arabs	1.5	6.0	3.6	60.4	61.1	63.9	64.9	61.1

SOURCE: From (Israel 1985: 283).

Table 4.8: Source of Income of Households - 1982

Characteristics	TOTAL	JEWS				ARABS
			Head of Household			
		Total	Born in Asia-Africa	Born in Europe-America	Born in Israel	
		Absolute figures				
Average persons per household	3.9	3.8	4.6	3.2	3.6	5.8
Average earners per household	1.6	1.6	1.6	1.6	1.6	1.5
Average age of head of household	41.9	42.0	42.8	49.1	33.6	37.2
Average years of schooling of head of household	11.3	11.4	9.6	12.1	12.4	8.2
Gross income per household (IS thous.)	203.7	205.8	180.7	255.6	208.7	144.1
Net income per household (IS thous.)	151.9	153.2	140.0	164.9	153.3	117.1
		Percentages				
INCOME TOTAL	100.0	100.0	100.0	100.0	100.0	100.0
From Employed Work	89.7	89.8	88.9	89.0	91.6	84.8
-of household head	68.8	68.9	68.9	67.5	70.6	66.5
-of wife	16.1	16.3	12.5	18.1	17.5	5.2
-of others	4.8	4.6	7.5	3.4	3.5	13.1
From Self-employment	0.9	0.9	1.0	0.9	0.8	2.2
Not from work	8.8	8.7	10.0	8.8	7.4	12.4
- from pensions	1.8	1.8	2.6	1.4	1.4	0.7
- National Insurance	5.8	5.6	7.9	4.9	4.6	10.8
From abroad	0.6	0.6	0.1	1.3	0.2	0.6

SOURCE: from (Israel 1984a: 48-9).

Also of interest in distinguishing differential income generation patterns is the data regarding the sources of income for Arab and Jewish urban employees' households. Arab households exhibit slightly less dependence than do Jewish households upon employed work (see Table 4.8). Whereas Arab households obtain 85 percent of their income from employed work, for Jewish households the proportion is 90 percent. Due to less female employment among Arabs, larger families and exclusion from military service, Arab households depend to a lesser extent than Jews upon the income of the head of the household's wife, and to a greater extent on the wages of other members of the family. A marginally larger proportion of Arab households' income originates in self-employed work than is the case among Jews.

Arab Labour in Israel: The Region Subservient

Arab households, being generally poorer and thus more eligible for state support, receive 12 percent of their total income from national insurance payments and pensions, compared to under 9 percent of Jewish households' income. Arab and Jewish households receive a similarly minimal proportion (under 1 percent) of their income from savings or from abroad.

Comparison of the preceding figures for all Arab urban families with similar data for exclusively Arab localities alone (i.e. excluding Arabs in the eight mixed urban localities) reveals an interesting disparity between the two groups within the region. The exclusion of the Arab population of the mixed cities from the sample (some 25 percent of sampled households) marginally improves the Arab comparative income position, thus slightly closing the gap with the national sample. This seems to indicate that Arab households in the mixed cities are somewhat worse off than their counterparts in Arab localities. This is not surprising, since it is likely that there is a greater dependence by Arabs in mixed cities on less renumerative wage labour, and more opportunities for 'own' income generation and family or other interdependencies in the region's 'hinterland'.

Arab Expenditure Patterns and Consumption Preferences

The differences noted above between gross and net annual income arise primarily from taxation. In this regard, while 26 percent of Jewish households' gross income in 1982 was taxed or transferred to others (family, friends), the corresponding figure for Arab households was only 19 percent. This is not indicative of preferential tax treatment for Arabs; rather it reflects the progressive taxation system in Israel whereby lower income groups are taxed at a lower rate than are higher income groups. Data for 1979/80 indicate that of the total income of Arab urban households, 17.5 percent was paid in income tax and national insurance; the national proportion (figures are not available for Jews alone) was 24 percent (see table 4.9).

Of the remaining Arab household income, 43 percent was spent upon food, compared to the national average of 23 percent. In fact, the absolute figures for Arab food expenditure exceed national figures by over 50 percent - no Jewish ethnic group spends as much relatively as do Arab households on food consumption. The breakdown of types of food consumed also reveals certain Arab/national differences, with Arabs devoting 29 percent of food consumption expenditure to vegetables and fruit, 20 percent to meat and poultry and 14 percent to bread and cereals. The corresponding national figures were 27 percent, 22 percent and 9 percent, respectively. Arabs devoted 12 percent of consumption expenditure to housing, 13 percent to housing maintenance, furniture and equipment, 9 percent to clothing and footwear, and 7 percent to transport and communication. Nationally, these proportions were 21 percent for housing, 16 percent for maintenance and furniture, only 6 percent to clothing and footwear and 12 percent to transport and communication. Other consumption expenditure items reveal similar divergences.

Naturally, some of these disparities reflect differentials in demographic structure (e.g. family size) or income levels (thus less Arab expenditure on 'luxury' items, despite high expenditure on consumer durables). However, cultural and other structural factors also exert an influence. Effectively, the regional economy exhibits certain particular consumption patterns, in addition to distinctive modes of production and labour. It is difficult to state with certainty whether, as with other differentials that have been discussed, all other things being equal, these distinctive features are more related to the 'specifically' Arab-national nature of dynamics than to 'universal' features of income determination. Nevertheless, as discussed in Chapter Two, the overall determinants of Arab economic conditions in Israel create a situation which can only be analysed in terms of its Arab (regional) specificity.

Data for income elasticities of demand for the mid-1970s also confirm the existence of particular Arab consumption modes (Israel 1979). Though the data for Arab households is subject to larger sampling errors than is the case nationally, it can be seen that the classification of goods and commodities as between 'luxuries' and 'necessities' according to these elasticities is different in most respects for the Arab and national samples. Again, while this perhaps reflects differential income distribution more than other factors, it nevertheless highlights yet another important area of regional/national divergence.

A feature of comparative income and expenditure data for 1979/80 which causes concern is the status of savings. Nationally, households saved some 4.3 percent of gross income, whereas Arab households dissaved (i.e. overspent) at a rate of -2.5 percent of gross income. This appears to stem primarily from the Arab dissaving incurred in financial saving arrangements (i.e. in commercial banking and stocks), compared to substantial national savings within this category of savings. Both nationally and regionally, real estate and business savings were positive while other savings components were negative items. Yet, while Jewish households had the financial and other means to ensure that credit outweighed debits, this was not the case for Arabs.

Table 4.9: Income, Expenditure and Savings Per Urban Household in Israel, 1979/80

Characteristics	ARABS	JEWS			TOTAL
		Head of Household Born in			
		Europe-America	Asia-Africa	Israel	
Households (thousands)	893.4	372.0	268.6	187.4	64.5
Households in sample	2,271	927	647	534	162
Average persons per household	3.4	2.5	4.0	3.3	6.2
	IS per month				
TOTAL INCOME	3,413	3,341	3,083	4,424	2,285
Thereof: imputed	391	388	307	554	201
employed work	1,995	1,843	1,878	2,734	1,234
self-employed work	510	446	460	766	343
pensions, allowances	381	424	390	235	458
NON-CONSUMPTION EXPENDITURE - TOTAL	885	868	740	1,286	430
Direct taxes, national insur.	826	787	702	1,233	402
Transfers to others	59	81	38	54	28
CONSUMPTION EXPENDITURE-TOTAL	2,309	2,135	2,259	2,853	1,972
Food	543	460	618	504	842
Thereof: vegetables, fruits	148	124	166	137	248
bread, cereals,	51	37	57	47	121
meat, poultry	122	107	151	93	173
eggs, dairy products	87	81	92	91	87
Housing	481	497	385	667	246
Dwelling maintenance	213	204	198	274	155
Furniture, household equip.	165	134	191	209	107
Clothing	112	91	130	118	146
Footwear	36	30	41	38	42
Health	98	102	90	114	64
Education, culture, entertain.	231	203	236	322	104
Transport, communication	274	274	217	406	140
Thereof: Public transport	36	30	43	32	53
Miscellaneous	156	140	153	203	126
SAVING - TOTAL	148	210	67	212	-58
Financial saving	204	271	116	273	-19
In real estate	126	67	137	254	55
Business	66	62	47	112	36
Other savings components	-85	-25	-114	-167	-75
Non-recurrent receipts	-163	-165	-119	-260	-55

SOURCE: From (Israel 1983b: 294-5).

Arab Labour in Israel: The Region Subservient

Figures on savings in exclusively Arab localities reveals a somewhat less severe position of indebtedness than when Arabs in mixed cities are included in the figures. In Arab localities, dissaving was not only at a lower absolute level, but also at a lower proportion of gross income (1.2 percent). Unlike Arabs in mixed localities, the inhabitants of exclusively Arab localities actually realised a small level of private financial savings and a greater degree of business savings while the level of dissaving in other savings components was lower. In light of the picture of poverty among the Arab citizens of Israel revealed above, and the general economic challenges that the region faces, it is hardly surprising to find Arabs as overall debtors within the national economy.

ARAB LABOUR MOBILITY: THE REGION'S 'NATIONAL SERVICE'

An aspect of Arab labour which perhaps most starkly exhibits its particular role in the national economy is its high level of physical mobility. In 1984, 78,000 Arabs regularly left their towns and villages to work elsewhere. This phenomenon, whereby almost half of all Arab employed commute to Jewish cities, settlements and work-places mainly on a daily basis, is peculiar to the Arab labour force. Most of the national labour force is able to secure employment in its place of residence. In other economies, the geographic search for employment often results in the physical relocation of workers to the locality of work. Even in developing economies, rural-urban migration is usually a process of people leaving the countryside more or less permanently for work and residence in the cities. This has not taken place in Israel, primarily due to the institutional and political barriers to Arab residence in Jewish settlements, towns and cities noted in Chapter Two.

Trends and Features of Arab Mobile Labour

Since the 1960s, when geographic mobility was no longer subject to the military government constraints, it has been an enduring characteristic of the Arab employment situation in Israel. However, the extent of mobility has fluctuated in cycles lasting several years. Between 1966 and 1968, concurrent with the recessionary climate of those years, rates of mobility (i.e. proportion of employed working away from their locality of residence) were the lowest ever, at between 40 percent and 45 percent of all employed.

Arab Labour in Israel: The Region Subservient

During the post-war boom and until 1973, mobility was higher, at between 49 percent and 52 percent. From 1974 and until 1978, steady growth in the national economy helped to establish a fairly constant proportion of Arab labour mobility, fluctuating between 47 percent and 49 percent. However, from 1979 to 1984, and mainly reflecting the building boom and economic 'liberalisation' of those years, mobility has been high, between 50 percent and the peak of 54 percent reached in 1983. In 1985, for the first time in many years, and with the sharp drop in job opportunities for Arabs in Jewish localities, the number of mobile Arab workers fell to 72,000, or just under 47 percent of the Arab labour force. Arabs readiness to move where there is work means that they are "vulnerable to any contraction of employment; the non-local Arab villager will be the first to be fired" (Waschitz 1975: 46).

This phenomenon can be compared to the prevalent process of rural-migration in developing countries. It differs, however, in several respects: its daily and commuting character; in that it is not really a rural-urban flow, the national (i.e. Arab) identity of the migratory labour force; and the fact that the migration takes place from a 'developing region' towards the employment centres of what is considered a developed market economy. However, the main tenets of migration theory appear relevant in the case of mobile Arab labour in Israel, and consequently merit attention here.

The factors which have been advanced to account for the migratory process have been analyses by several writers. The earliest was the 'reallocation of surplus labour' mechanism, popularised in the two-sector models of Lewis, Fei and Ranis and others.[12] However, such a depiction of migration as an equilibrating process between rural and urban marginal productivities could not be reconciled with the empirical evidence of increasing migration and urban unemployment. Subsequently, Todaro formulated a model based on the 'pull' of high urban wages and the 'pushback' of urban unemployment to the exclusion of factors related to the 'push' exercised by subsistence agriculture (1976). In this analysis, the decision to migrate or not is based on "...'expected' rather than nominal wage differentials, where the 'expected' differential is determined by the interaction of two variables, the nominal wage and the probability of successfully obtaining employment in the urban sector..." (Todaro 1976: 372).

Evidence collected by the Sussex University Village Studies Programme (VSP) created a much more detailed and substantially different picture (Connel et al. 1976). The focus on the village, or source, end of the migration process resulted in a re-evaluation of

Todaro's 'urban pull'. His hypothesis is countered by VSP evidence of substantial rural-rural migration, of the decision to migrate not being an individual one, and of migrants lack of access to adequate information. Most significant to the present analysis is the VSP evidence which lead to its main hypothesis, namely that "intra-rural inequality is at once the main cause, and a serious consequence, of rural emigration..." (*Ibid:* 200). This analysis also takes into account the influence of various non-economic factors: educational opportunities; kinship and family structure; demographic factors such as family size tending to push out younger members; urban contact or aspirations; and proximity of destination.

Another interesting, yet somewhat more abstract, analysis of migration is that advanced by G. Standing (1981). His approach centres on the emergence of rural capitalism, characterised by a growth of a rural proletariat, commoditisation and class differentiation. Though petty cultivation and private farming might not appear to indicate it, "these are the signs of pressure leading to class differentiation, signifying the typical agonising growth of a rural proletariat; and a rural proletariat is nothing if not mobile" (Standing, 1981). In this analysis, migrants can be an important element of the Marxist urban 'industrial reserve army': that part of the labour force which, at least temporarily, is 'super-exploitable'.

It is not possible here to further explore the interesting and important discussions initiated within the above analyses with regard to patterns of migration, migrants' characteristics, and the urban and rural impact of migration. However, in conjunction with the relevant empirical information, they help provide a useful context for better understanding the nature of the Arab migratory process in Israel, and establishing a sort of profile of the migrant/mobile labourer.

Arab labour mobility arises from four major factors. The central determinant is the decline of Arab agriculture, accompanied by landlessness on the one hand and the continued 'ejection' of labour on the other. Secondly, technological and other developments in Jewish farming have reduced the reliance on Arab labour input (from Israel, at least) while also reducing the competitiveness of Arab agriculture. Thirdly, growth in the regional non-agricultural economic infrastructure has been insufficient to provide satisfactory employment opportunities for the local labour force, reinforcing reliance on external sources. The fourth main factor is the disparity in income opportunities between rural (Arab) and urban (Jewish) regions (or between the alternatives of rural subsistence and renumerative work outside).

Mobile Arab labourers are, in general, either the landless, those no longer able to find farming work, those without the requisite skills, accumulated capital or contacts to find work in the local non-agricultural economy, those who need to supplement an existing farm income, or those whose labour skills are in relatively high demand nationally. The pattern of mobility is a daily or, in some cases, weekly commuting from those localities classified as urban or rural, but which retain their semi-agricultural character, and which are exclusively inhabited by Arabs. There is practically no mobility from the mixed localities because of the presence there of local Jewish work-places. Migrants generally work in manual jobs, often those shunned by Jews, especially in construction, personal services and some industrial processes, and job insecurity is comparatively high. While rural-urban income differentials do have a role, this is not a clear determining factor in the decision towards mobility. In fact, urban incomes appear to be used for subsistence, more conspicuous consumption (witnessed by the prevalence of consumer durables), and lastly for investment in agriculture where feasible and appropriate.

Determinants of Mobility: Urban Pull or Rural Push?

The only major attempt to statistically test hypotheses regarding Arab labour migration was undertaken by Ben Porath in his pioneering work on the Arab economy (1966). Using cross sectional data in multiple regression analysis, he first established a demand relationship between local agricultural employment (dependent) and supply of irrigated, rainfed and orchard lands, indicating an especially strong employment generation effect by irrigated land. Ben Porath subsequently attempted to explain labour mobility through reference to the same land variables, in addition to the ratio of farm-owning population to total population, overall local labour force and the proportion of Jews in the sub-district (as a proxy for closeness of employment centres). The land variables exhibited a significant negative relation to mobility, as did land and farm ownership. While a major positive influence on mobility is exercised by the size of the village labour force, Jewish/market proximity also positively affects village labour mobility.

In an attempt to analyse mobility through multiple regression of time series data (1965-79) for the whole economy, the relation explained by Ben Porath between mobile labour and availability of irrigated land was re-examined (Khalidi 1981). By introducing the further effect of productivity differentials between Arab and national agriculture (in terms of value of output per cultivated unit), a satisfactory formula emerges. Accordingly, the following determinants are associated with an increasing supply of mobile

Arab Labour in Israel: The Region Subservient

labour: increasing irrigated land (ejecting workers rather than absorbing more); a narrowing of the productivity gap between Arab and Jewish agriculture; and a shrinking rural labour force (though this partially reflects the official classification of an increasingly less proportion of the labour force as 'rural'). Neither land ownership or some status of self-employment (e.g. the ratio of farm population), nor the general availability of rainfed land and orchards appears to exercise any signiciant effect upon mobility. The strongest effect upon mobility comes from the agricultural productivity ratio, supporting the hypothesis of a distinctive 'rural push' effect in the process.

A further attempt was made (in *Ibid*) to examine Todaro's 'urban pull' as formulated in one appropriate model (Godfrey 1973). Here, also through multiple regression analysis, the hypothesis was tested that between 1968 and 1979, the difference between the size of the Arab urban and rural labour force (a proxy for migration) varied directly with the differential between urban and rural incomes and inversely with the difficulty in obtaining employment in the non-agricultural sector. The result seems to indicate a supply relationship: as more join the urban labour force, the proxy variable for unemployment in the urban, non-agricultural sector falls and the gap between urban and rural incomes narrows. Thus, while migration in this case does vary inversely with the difficulty of finding a job, it also varies inversely with the income differential. The income differential trend (downwards) does not explain the migration trend (upward) in the way that the above hypothesis assumes it will. However, it does capture the effect mentioned by Todaro, namely that "rural-urban migration in this model acts as an equilibrating force which equates rural and urban 'expected' incomes" (1976: 372). Here, increasing migration is not accompanied by a widening of the income gap.

If these formulations are correct, Todaro's hypothesis does not apply here, since migration would not appear to be responding primarily to income differentials, but to other factors, unspecified in this model, but noticed in the previously specified relationship. The mobility of Arab labour has its roots firmly in the decline of agriculture according to these results. Rather than urban factors influencing the process, it seems that whatever the mobile Arab labourer 'expects', he/she has little choice. Hemmed in from both sides, by a stagnant rural/local economy on the one hand, and a modern national economy that all but dictates the 'what', 'where', 'when' and 'how much' of employment on the other, the migrant perceives mobility as a fact of life, a necessity. Migration is thus a path to survival before it might lead to betterment.

ARAB LABOUR AND THE NATIONAL ECONOMY: A REGIONAL ECONOMIC ANALYSIS[13]

Various methods of regional analysis provide different perspectives into the way a region works. Two of those applied here view the region as a unit in relation to other regions and the country as a whole. Mix-and-share analysis addresses the question of the relative industrial composition of the region and how it changes. Location quotient analysis looks at the degree of relative specialisation of the region in selected indicators. A third method, economic base analysis, views the regional unit interacting with the country and examines the relationship between exogenous demand for the region's products and services and regional economic expansion. These methods do not reveal any previously unknown facts but use what is known to provide a more dynamic picture.

Mix-and-Share Analysis: Delineating the Regional-National Divide

The change in regional employment relative to the change in national employment over a period can be understood as the net result of three effects. The first reflects the impact on the region of change in national total employment (N): it represents how much regional sectoral employment would have changed had regional sectors grown at the same rate as overall national employment growth. The second effect stems from the sectoral mix in the region, i.e. the distribution of regional employment among higher and slower growth sectors, relative to the national sectoral mix (M). This measures the extent to which the deviations of regional sectoral growth rates from the total (multi-sectoral) national growth rate are caused by a regional sectoral composition weighted, more than is the national economy, by sectors with growth rates below the national average. The third effect relates to changing regional shares of total national employment in each sector (S). It measures the degree to which existing regional shares of national employment in different sectors determine the region's sectoral trends.

Through isolating the individual components of change in mix-and-share analysis, it is possible to comparatively analyse the differentials that have become apparent between Arab regional and national economic performance. This can help lead to a greater degree of precision in pinpointing the weaknesses and strengths in the regional structure and the links of growth generation and dependency nationally. Mix-and-share analysis, when taken further, can contribute to regional analysis in several ways. It reveals those sectors requiring further study and provides an overall picture of the role played by the region nationally. In combination with other techniques, it helps to define relationships between regional sectoral growth and overall national growth and evolve projections of future regional trends.

There are a number of important limitations in this method: focus on one variable, employment; no accounting for labour productivity increases in fast growth sectors; no consideration of unemployment; and its inability to explain reasons for different sectoral growth rates and shares or the desirability of sectoral changes. However, it remains a useful descriptive tool. Table 4.10 details the summary mix-and-share data for the Arab region in Israel for the years 1974 and 1984. The total growth in Arab regional employment of 46,700 represented a 46 percent increase on 1974 levels, compared to a national growth rate of 25 percent. This difference, largely determined by the greater regional than national population (and labour force) growth in the period, can be described as follows:

Table 4.10: Mix and Share Analysis of Arab Employment in Israel, 1974-84

Sector	Regional Change 1974-84* (000's)	(%)	National Change 1974-84 (000's)	(%)	(N) (000's)	(M)	(S)
Agriculture	-1.4	-9%	+1.4	+2%	+3.7	-3.4	-1.7
Industry, Energy	+14.0	+75%	+40.2	+14%	+4.7	-2.1	+11.4
Construction	+7.4	+31%	-8.6	-10%	+5.9	-8.3	+9.8
Commerce, Transport, Finance	+10.8	+51%	+103.9	+36%	+5.3	+2.3	+3.2
Services	+15.9	+66%	+130.1	+37%	+6.0	+2.9	+7.0
Total	46.7	+46%	+267.0	+25%	+25.6	-8.6	+29.7

NOTE: * Regional employment figures for 1974 exclude 2,600 workers whose sector was unknown
SOURCE: Calculated from (Israel 1974: 289; 301) and (Israel 1986: 294; 312)

Had each of the sectors in the region grown at the same rate as overall national employment (i.e. 25 percent), the effect would have been as shown in column (N). But the actual growth in regional employment was greater by 21,100. Thus, the net relative change of 21,100 by which the region grew faster than the nation is accounted for by the sectoral-mix (M) and the regional-share (S) effects. The sectoral-mix effect is equivalent to regional employent in each sector in 1974 multiplied by the difference between the overall national employment growth rate and the national sectoral growth rates. This effect was negative in the period, offsetting the (N) effect by 8,600 jobs in all sectors of the economy. Except for agriculture, all sectors exhibited regional growth rates higher than the national rates.

However, the relative decline nationally in construction, agriculture and industry (manifested by their falling shares of total employment) affected the region more severely than the nation as a whole. This was especially the case in Arab construction employment, which lost 8,300 jobs regionally as a result of the national decline, and less so in agriculture which lost 3,400 jobs. And the national decline in industrial employment was also felt more severely in the Arab region, accounting for a loss of 2,100 jobs. Only in the tertiary sectors was national growth more favourably felt regionally than nationally, with a gain of 5,200 jobs.

The net regional shares effect, by which the Arab region's share of employment in different sectors deviated from the national share is equal to that part of the net relative change (N) not accounted or by the sectoral-mix effect (M). The shares effect (S) shows an increase of 29,700 jobs. This was due to the increase in the region's share of national employment in industry, construction, services and commerce. Only in agriculture did the Arab region's share of national employment decline over the period. Hence the net impact of (M) and (S) added to the national growth effect of +25,600 jobs by +21,100 jobs. The analysis can also be undertaken sectorally. In industry, for example, the difference between the region's actual (R) and potential (N) change, indicates the extent to which the rate of regional industrial growth outstripped national growth (by 9,300 jobs).

This can be explained on the one hand by the effect of the sectoral-mix whereby the relative national decline (lower growth) in industry affected the region more severely than the national average, by a magnitude of 2,100 jobs regionally. However, this is offset by the increase in the regional share of industrial employment of 11,400 jobs. A similar analysis can be applied to other sectors, though the three main productive sectors in the region, agriculture, industry and construction, exhibit an important interdependence in their national relation. They absorb and release labour more rapidly and flexibly than other sectors: industry and construction in the region are 'growth' sectors in terms of their national labour supply role, while agricultural decline feeds this role.

Arab Labour in Israel: The Region Subservient

Location Quotient and Regional Specialisation

We have already encountered location quotient analysis in Chapter Three. In its simplest form, the location quotient (LQ) gauges the relative specialisation of a region in selected sectors. The greater the disaggregation of the variables chosen, the more precise an indicator the LQ can be. When computing the LQ for the Arab region in units of employment, it must be remembered that a large portion of the Arab labour force works in the non-regional sector. Thus, specialisation in one or another sector reflects not only local specialisation but also the role of labour in that sector nationally. The trend in the LQ indicates both the change in sectoral activity within the Arab region and the change in the importance nationally of the region's labour force in different sectors. Calculated in Table 4.11 are the Arab region's LQs for 1974 and 1984, indicating trends and the import/export role of the region in the different sectors (depending on its closeness to 1. 0).

Table 4.11: Location Quotient Analysis of Arab Employment in Israel, 1974-1984

SECTOR	LQ 1974	LQ 1984	TREND	ROLE
* Agriculture	2.2	1.7	Decrease	Export
* Industry, Energy	0.7	0.9	Increase	Local Service
* Construction	2.9	3.5	Increase	Export
* Commerce	1.0	1.0	Constant	Local Service
* Transport	0.9	0.9	Constant	Local Service
* Finance	0.2	0.4	Increase	Import
* Public Services	0.6	0.6	Constant	Import
* Personal Services	1.1	1.1	Constant	Local Service

SOURCE: Calculated from (Israel 1974: 289; 301) and (Israel 1986: 294; 312)

These figures help to elaborate the results of the above mix-and-share analysis. The main exporting sector is construction, showing the region to be highly (over-) specialised in providing the national economy with employment and services. The figures also affirm the extent to which Arab construction activity provides local employment opportunities and dominates regional economic activity. Only in 1984 did industry, commerce, transport and personal services acquire a local service role, indicating regional-national balance in these sectors. Agriculture, despite its decreasing specialisation, still provides a level of export to the national economy, especially in output but also in labour.

The relative balance between regional and national industrial employment indicates that the sector's level of activity in the region is not geared to any crucial role in national industry. However, the Arab region still appears to be a net industrial importer and remains relatively unspecialised in industrial labour. Finance is a sector which is mainly non-Arab, presenting only limited employment local job opportunities. Public services are widely recognised to be deficient in the region, though this sector provides an increasing source of employment for new graduates. Personal services is a sector in which the Arab level of employment is now more or less at the national level of specialisation.

Overall, some of the imbalances in the regional-national relation appear to be easing, though this can be deceptive. The resultant regional sectoral structures could in fact become distorted and underdeveloped, satisfying only the limited local levels of demand for goods and services, if the region's growth continues to be fuelled primarily through its export of cheap and unskilled manual labour.

Economic Base Analysis: the Role of Exogenous Demand

The main assumption of another tool of regional analysis, economic base theory, is that the economic growth of a region depends upon exogenous demand. Its decline or growth depends on its performance as an exporter of goods and services, including labour. The export sectors constitute the economic base of the region. Employment and income in the basic sector are a function of exogenous demand. The additional, supporting activities in the region, such as trade, services and production for local markets, together comprise the non-basic sector. This latter sector depends indirectly on exogenous demand since expansion in the basic sector generates and neccessitates an expansion in the supporting activities. The basic sector can be thought of as the regional exchange economy and the non-basic sector as the regional use economy.

The ratio of basic to non-basic employment or income is called the economic base ratio. If the base ratio is, for example, 1:2, then for every new job (or unit of income) in the basic sector, two new jobs (or units of income) will be created in the non-basic sector. Similarly for every decline of one basic unit, there will occur a decline of two non-basic units. If the base ratio is 1:2, the economic base multiplier is three; when basic employment increases by one, a total of three new jobs, basic and non-basic, will have been created. By multiplying the change in the basic sector by the base multiplier, an estimate of the total impact on the regional economy that results from a change in demand for basic goods can be computed. This form of analysis can be applied to the Arab region in Israel in order to identify those sectors whose position in the national economy is significant and which fuel the growth of the region itself.

One way of identifying the basic sector in the Arab region involves an application of a version of the location quotient method. By this technique, the extent to which actual regional employment distribution by sector (X_{arab}) exceeds the employment distribution by sector that would prevail if the regional employment structure reflected the national structure (X_{reg}) represents regional specialisation aimed at the export market. This extra level of employment constitutes the basic employment in that sector (X_{bas}) and the sum of all positive differences between actual and potential employment is basic sector employment; the remainder is non-basic. Applying this method to 1984 employment figures provides the following results:

Table 4.12: Economic Base Analysis of Arab Employment in Israel, 1984

SECTOR	Xarab	Xreg	Xbas
Agriculture	12.9	7.7	+ 5.2
Industry; Energy	31.7	34.6	- 2.9
Construction	30.0	8.4	+21.6
Commerce	19.1	18.1	+ 1.0
Transport	9.1	9.5	- 0.4
Finance	5.0	13.8	- 8.8
Public Services	25.3	42.5	-17.2
Personal Services	10.8	9.2	+ 1.6

SOURCE: Calculated from (Israel 1986: 294; 312)

The sum of the positive differences, in agriculture, construction, commerce and transport, is 29; the base ratio is calculated as 1:4 and the multiplier is five. Thus, for every new job in the base sector(s), four new jobs are created in the non-basic sector(s). As can be seen, the surplus of almost 22,000 jobs in construction and some 5,000 in agriculture constitute the bulk of the basic sector. In both cases it can be assumed that this excess is due to these sectors' role in exporting labour to the national economy as well as producing exports for the national economy (especially in the case of agriculture, but also in certain construction services). Similarly, the export of Arab commercial and personal services to the national economy indicated by these figures reflects the role of local food markets in Arab towns and services such as car or other repairs and domestic cleaning in catering to the Jewish economy.

A closer examination of Arab agriculture, in terms of the value of its output, reveals the fact that its characterisation as part of the basic sector is probably not primarily due to its supply of labour to the national economy. Through economic base analysis, two of the main branches of production are found to be net exporters to the national economy. Specifically, the basic sector in Arab agriculture is to be found in the vegetables and melons branch and the non-citrus fruit branch. They produced - in 1981/2 value of output figures (Israel 1983a) - a base ratio of 1:3 and a multiplier of four. Consequently, for every unit of value added through the production of these branches, three units of value are added in the non-basic branches (field crops, citrus, and livestock).

Through the preceding analysis, it has been possible to highlight the very specific, and indeed significant, role played by Arab labour in the national economy, the features of which have been dealt with in depth. The discussion of agriculture and labour has been full of data related to differentials and regional handicaps on almost all levels. As such, the present position, and long term prospects for the Arab economy in Israel would appear dim. The next chapter will further examine how these disparities are evident in terms of industrial and business activity in the region. However, for a variety of reasons that will become apparent, the situation in this area gives some hope of a developmental future for the Arab economy, both in terms of that economy's national position, as well as in terms of its internal fabric and interaction. The use of tools of regional economic analysis does not in itself substantiate the argument for a regional understanding of Arab economic development in Israel. As stated at the outset, the concept of the 'Arab region' has been used both for methodological reasons and because it best approximates the economic reality of the situation under investigation. In fact, the 'Arab region' is something of 'still-born' entity.

On the one hand, the Arab economy in Israel exhibits linkages to the national economy which are consistent with that of an economic region. Yet, at another level, since it is not an 'orthodox' region, and as long as it is not officially understood or even dealt with as a region (except in terms of the indirect determinants of policy discussed at the outset), the concept will remain open to criticism by some analysts and anathema to Israeli policy makers and officials. However, as long as regional analysis provides a clearer and more consistent approach to the Arab economy than has been witnessed to date, it stands as a valid, appropriate and the most useful approach available.

NOTES

1. The discussion of trends in this chapter concentrates on data for four years: 1954; 1964; 1974; 1984. This allows for a good trend coverage while the political and other cicumstances affecting labour force development in different years are also accounted for. In 1954, Arab labour had begun to 'reactivate' itself despite military rule. By 1964, conditions had eased, and the effects of the post-1967 boom period had not yet been experienced. The year 1974 was exceptionally good for the Israeli economy, and one in which the impact of labour from the occupied territories had become quite apparent. Data for 1984 allows an examination of the situation after the passage of an additional decade. In cases where 1984 is not representative of the contemporary situation, figures are presented for 1985. Unless otherwise mentioned, figures below for 1954 are calculated from (Israel 1954/5: 7; 116-8); figures for 1964 are from (Israel 1965: 20; 294-7; 306-9; 316-9); figures for 1966 and 1967 are calculated from (Israel 1967: 17; 248-51; 259); figures for 1974 are from (Israel 1975: 19; 289; 301); figures for 1984 are from (Israel 1985: 325; 342); figures for 1985 are from (Israel 1986: 293; 312). Additionally, series figures for 1979-83 are calculated from (Israel 1985a). Comparative sectoral and occupational figures for 1978 and 1983 are from (Israel 1985: 366; 367). Detailed (minor category) figures for 1983 occupational and sectoral distribution are from (Israel 1985c).

2. These are 1954 figures. Here, as elsewhere in the discussion, comparing regional with national figures understates the degree of Jewish-Arab differentials. This is because the national rate includes the high Arab rate and the lower Jewish rate, which combined produce a national rate between the two. While Jewish rates will not be much lower than the national ones quoted because of the greater weight of the Jewish population in the economy, this point should be borne in mind when assessing the extent of differentials in all spheres.

3. The context of this decline was investigated in depth in the previous chapter.

4. The 1983 Census of Population results provide a more detailed sectoral breakdown of the labour force than other annual statistical publications. However, the three sub-branches of construction specified show Arab employment to be concentrated in 'special trade contractors' and to a lesser degree, in 'building contractors'. This is insufficient to indicate where the activity takes place, or within which economy.

5. A detailed analysis of Arab industry is undertaken in Chapter Five.

6. Makhoul argues that the growth in industrial employment is closely integrated with national industrial demand, through the dual "spatial mobility of Arab labour into Jewish-owned urban work-places, and the spatial mobility of Jewish owned work-places into the rural Arab residential places..." (1982: 83). It is by no means clear that a substantial part of Arab industrial employment is thus linked.

7. This classification between 'blue collar' and 'white collar' can be made to differentiate workers engaged in 'mental', mainly office based and not directly productive occupations, from those who work in manual, mainly productive and factory, workshop or open-air (fields, streets, etc) jobs. Classifying standard occupational levels 00 - 49 as 'white collar' and standard levels 50 - 99 as 'blue collar' helps to discern the overall structure of the labour force and trace the broad directions of occupational transformation.

8. In early statistical series, the scientific/academic and professional/technical strata were grouped together.

9. In these three major categories, there are 37 minor categories, of which 12 have 10,000 workers or more. Of the remaining 40 minor categories, 23 have 10,000 or more workers. Though 10,000 employed is an arbitrary cut-off point, it here provides a working definition for the more significant occupations nationally.

10. Data on income distribution is for 1982 and calulated from (Israel 1984a) unless otherwise specified. While most of the discussion here refers to urban employees' households' income, this is representative enough of the Arab population to warrant analysis. As stated above, employees constitute the bulk of the Arab labour force, and areas officially classified as urban in 1983 contained almost 87 percent of the total Arab population. Data on expenditure and savings are 1979/80 data and calculated from (Israel 1982).

11. Data for households' distribution among deciles of annual net money income reveal similar differences.

12. See, e.g. (Lewis 1954) and (Fei and Ranis 1964).

13. The technical methods applied here (mix-and-share, location quotient and economic base analysis) are adapted from the versions advanced in (Bendavid-Val 1983: Chapters Five and Six).

Five

ARAB INDUSTRY AND COMMERCE IN ISRAEL: WORKSHOP ECONOMY AND ENTREPRENEURSHIP

The discussion in the previous chapters established not only a profile of the Arab economy in Israel, but also a framework for understanding its main dynamics. The specific patterns of agricultural activity, and the trends in Arab manpower development have been placed within the wider context of their role in the Israeli economy and its influence on them. The elaboration of the 'regional-national' relationship has clarified these developments as well as systemising and rationalising the analysis of processes which were previously misconstrued, obfuscated or inadequately explained. The use of regional economic analysis, and indeed the affirmation of a 'regional' character to Arab economic activity in Israel, has been a choice of both convenience and necessity.

Equally, the economic significance of Arab industrial experience in Israel since 1948 can be considered, and best understood, within the context of the Arab region's position in the national economy. The pattern of the regional-national industrial/commercial relationship is on the whole similar to those for agriculture and labour, though there are also radical differences. As has already been indicated, the dynamic of regional industrial development shares with Arab labour processes the features of a 'dependent' or subservient position *vis-a-vis* the national economy.

Arab industry in Israel, however, after a generation of 'reconstruction' has re-emerged with a distinct identity which has promising developmental possibilities. A similar dynamic arose in Arab agriculture through the continuation and evolution of established modes of production within the parameters of national agricultural growth. Arab industrial development, however, has resulted in a 'regional synthesis'; a combination of national and traditional influences and creative, indigenous and autonomous elements.

An examination of the local Arab non-agricultural economy reveals a varied and rich range of production processes and linkages, skills development and application, reactive and inventive business enterprises and interests, as well as a significant degree of self-contained and consumed economic activity. Recently, the growing production and market potential of the Arab region has attracted the attention and increasing involvement of state and national economic interests. It is this rather more complex and untapped reservoir of economic growth, within its distinctly Arab (and regional) identity, that poses perhaps the most interesting developmental challenge for both the Arab region and the Israel economy as a whole.

This chapter begins with a review of the main features of Arab industrial and commercial activity before the mid-1970s, the point at which it became possible to discern an 'Arab industrial sector' in Israel. This is followed by an examinination of the determinants and characteristics of contemporary Arab industry, focussing on state and public sector policy and capital involvement in the region and the industrial mix they have produced. The chapter concludes by discussing the significance of the emergence of Arab business and entrepreneurial forms in recent years and its implications for long-term Arab development in Israel.

THE LEGACY OF THE ARAB WORKSHOP ECONOMY

One of the most decisive determinants of the shape of the Arab economy in Israel before the 1970s was the virtual disintegration of the pre-1948 Arab industrial infrastructure. Arab industry had never reached the level of Jewish industrial development in Mandatory Palestine, and much of Arab industry was located in the area which came to be known as the West Bank. The urban Arab economy had by 1948, however, acquired a position for itself in the economy of Palestine. The expulsion of the bulk of Palestine's urban Arab population and Israel's 'inheritance' of their property, land, factories and assets left the remaining Palestinian Arabs in Israel with little to build on. Consequently, until the early-1970s, non-agricultural economic activity was so disparate and weak as to be marginal to the Arab economy as a whole. Since then, however, the dynamic of regional-national relations and the earlier Arab experience have allowed the emergence of a distinct industrial sector.

Industry and Commerce: Workshop Economy & Entrepreneurship

This situation differed from that in Arab agriculture, which, however much reduced and constricted, still had access to the main inputs required for its continued functioning (land, water, labour). Before 1948, Arab industry was primarily located outside the areas in which Arabs remained, and there were virtually no openings for new investment, especially in the early 1950s. The vast majority of Arab industrialists, traders, entrepreneurs and professional elites had gone into exile taking their skills and part of their wealth with them, with which they rebuilt business activity in Arab countries from the 1950s onwards.

The experience and skill levels of the Arab labour force in Israel in this period were most amenable to manual production work in agriculture and construction. The Arab population was mainly rural, newly emergent from subsistence living, with little wealth. There were few opportunities for business enterprises at more than the individual, family or local level. The geographic fragmentation of the Arab population and the degree of control exercised by the military government made it especially difficult for any potential entrepreneur to envisage or plan any serious business venture because of problems such as the absence of credit facilities, marketing openings, access to raw materials and appropriate labour skills, and the competitiveness of subsidised Jewish industry.

Small-Scale Local Enterprises

In this climate it was not surprising that Arab non-agricultural economic activity in the 1950s was small-scale and village-based, geared almost entirely to production for local needs in the spheres of food processing, building, carpentry, blacksmithing, and machine and agricultural implement repair shops.

> Arab workers invested only a very small part of their income in developing independent employment. In an attempt to emulate the Jewish population in the outer manifestations of wealth, the first money went to build new houses. The housing boom led to the establishment of small building trade industries such as carpentry, metalworking shops and cement block factories in the villages themselves (Watad 1966: 30).

The most detailed and careful study dealing with this period estimated that the number of Arabs working in Arab-owned manufacturing enterprises in 1961 was about 3,500, some 1,500 of whom were self-employed and the rest wage labourers (Zarhi and Achziera 1966: 22). They further estimated that there were 1,200 enterprises in the 120 or so Arab localities. It was noted that:

> a) industry under Arab ownership employs only 1.8 percent of the total number of workers employed in industry in Israel; and b) the Arab enterprises are in general very small and underdeveloped. The average number of workers per enterprise under Arab ownership is three, while the average number for the whole of Israeli industry is 10 *(Ibid)*.

Limited Opportunities for Business Initiation

Despite the predominance of these small, village-based enterprises in the Arab non-agricultural economy, there were some individual cases where significant wealth was accumulated. Though the phenonomon was rare, a few Arab businessmen succeeded in 'intermediary', mainly commercial, functions in this period. In some cases, wealth had been accumulated before 1948, either from trade in the larger towns or cities, or through inherited land or commercial capital. In isolated, but significant cases, investment capital was acquired through land sales by larger landowners (to family, neighbours, or Jewish and state interests). Land sales by smaller owners were equally the exception to the rule. The real value of the land to the Arab owner could rarely be realised in a market where the main potential buyer, i.e. the state or affiliated Jewish institutions, had the option of recourse to expropriation.

Otherwise, in this period at least, there were few alternative sources of wealth. The vast majority of the Arab population was either destitute and landless, dependant on limited income from migrant labour, or struggling to remain within the narrow non-agricultural productive sector. Even the middle-man functions of trade, personal services and other 'entrepreurial' activities that might have been open to the Arab population were effectively ruled out for those who might have taken initiatives in different circumstances. Quite simply, there was only a very small amount of real or potential investment capital in the Arab region.

Nevertheless, in the 1950s a few Arabs were able to initiate industrial ventures, either with family or Jewish private sector support and joint finance. Most of these efforts failed. They were either too weak or ill-conceived from the outset, or effectively overwhelmed by powerful Israeli economic (and political) interests which saw them as potentially threatening. One of the

Industry and Commerce: Workshop Economy & Entrepreneurship

best known of these projects was in Baqa al Gharbieh where,

> ... a preserves factory was built in the late 1950s. This was the first attempt at a joint venture of Jewish and Arab capital and it aroused great interest in its time. Yet, in spite of encouragement by the Government, the hopes were not fulfilled. Some time later, it was again tried to open it with fresh investment of capital, but the result was another failure (Harari 1974: 49).

Another disappointment for Arab industrialists, workers and farmers in this period was the closure of the once prominent 'Arab Cigarette and Tobacco Factory Ltd.', which left the market for Arab tobacco to the monopolistic Jewish-owned cigarette industry (almost all of the local supply was Arab). In this case, "the inability of the last large Arab-owned company in Israel... to secure loans on the same terms as its Jewish competitors was a major factor in the decision of its owners to liquidate their assets" (Lustick 1980: 164). A contemporary Arab businessman pointed out that "despite the fact that it was the only one of its kind in Nazareth and in the Arab sector as a whole, it had not won the attention of economic or government circles" (in Watad 1966: 30).

Inadequate State Planning and Aid

The general neglect of Arab industrial development by state policy makers and Israeli investors was hardly compensated for by the half-hearted proposals contained in the two five year plans for the Arab areas, discussed in Chapters Two and Three. The successful connection of a number of villages to national electricity, water, and road networks, in the 1960s was achieved by local efforts and resources to the same, if not greater, degree as state encouragement or funding: it is more accurate to see the state as 'having permitted' such developments, rather than being responsible for them. The first plan's provision of industrial credit facilities for the "development of light industry and craft workshops" only envisaged government providing one-third of the projected investment (*New Outlook* 1962). Furthermore, it predicted its own failure from the outset, attributing lack of success to Arab traditionalism: "Little has been achieved in this field... the implementation of this section of the Plan requires industrial initiative from among the minority population, but to date there has not been enough such initiative forthcoming" *(Ibid)*.

Industry and Commerce: Workshop Economy & Entrepreneurship

In light of our earlier analysis of the development of state policy from the strict confines of the post-1948 period to the more 'liberalised' climate of the 1960s, it should be expected that in this latter period an Arab industrial infrastructure began to emerge. Yet, in fact, no major transformation took place. Rather, this latter period, and until the early-1970s, saw a growth in the number of small Arab manufacturing units, their diversification and first significant linkages to Jewish capital, and the success of the first large scale Arab industrial enterprises established since 1948. Other business oriented formations (cooperatives, professional and personal services and commercial ventures) also began to appear as certain sectors of the Arab population attained a new degree of material and economic security.

Emergent Arab Industries in the 1970s

Most Israeli accounts of the 'encouraging factors' behind these developments stress the 'modernising' effects of the migrant labour process and contact with Israeli society. "Western influence is being felt in Arab villages and the atmosphere for accepting industrial enterprises is now much better" (Harari 1974: 49) - as if there was some innate Arab (non-Western) aversion to machines and industry. There is no doubt, however, that other, more influential factors helped to change Arab industrial patterns by the early 1970s. These included the fact that the requisite infrastructure of water, electricity and communications networks had finally become widely available in Arab areas. Also important to the process was the emergence of a more qualified Arab industrial labour force and the difficulties of expanding job opportunities in the Jewish economy, especially from the mid-1960s (because of the recession in the mid-1960s and the post-1967 influx of Palestinian labour from the occupied West Bank and Gaza Strip).

However, as shall be discussed below, this period also witnessed the beginning of the search by Jewish capital for new and more profitable outlets for investment in productive processes. From the early-1970s, subsidiaries and sub-contractors to Israeli private or public sector firms were established in Arab areas. Coupled with the growth of private Arab capital ready for investment in local ventures and the growing linkages between the sub-areas of the Arab region, the stage was set for a new type and degree of Arab industrialisation.

By the early 1970s, Arab industry had developed in two different sectors. The first was that of the so-called 'workshop economy', consisting of small carpentry, metal-working, machine and car repair shops and garages, seasonal olive presses, and building material manufacturing. In 1972, it was reported that there were some 2,300 such workshops (in Harari 1972: 59), employing between two and four workers each. These figures appear somewhat exaggerated, as data for the early 1980s, discussed below, indicate a much smaller figure then. It is doubtful that the number of workshops decreased between the 1970s and 1980s, or that over 1000 workshops were established in the 10 years from 1961 (see figures above). Whatever their precise number, these workshops were the main manifestation of independent but small-scale Arab capital accumulation and were mainly geared to local (Arab) marketing, though a certain market existed in the national economy for their output, especially in building materials and car repair garages.

Slightly more reliable figures are available for the other sector of Arab industry, that sponsored by larger-scale Arab capitalists and supported (for various political and business reasons) by state or private Jewish capital. These larger enterprises, employing between 20 and 200 workers, numbered between 30 and 60 in 1972/3, were located in 22 different Arab towns and villages, and employed a total of between 2,700 and 4,000 people (*Ibid;* Harari 1974: 50). They included such establishments as the Bulous brothers' marble plant in Bi'neh, the Kadamani metal works in Yirka, three textile factories owned by the Israeli *Gibor* company in Yirka, Daliet al-Karmel and Jish, a diamond-grinding plant in Isifiyeh and an electronic components plant in Daliet al-Karmel.

These few cases of 'large scale' industry in Arab areas in this period, all represent forms of penetration of Jewish/state capital and Arab collaboration with state interests. The Bulous family established their marble factories with capital amassed through (forced) sale of land (i.e. compensation) to allow the establishment of the Jewish town of Carmi'el. The Kadamani metal works was established with the aid of government grants and loans and contracts, among others, to the Israeli military industries. The other plants mentioned were either established as subsidiaries of Jewish firms (e.g. textile factories) to take advantage of low-cost Arab female labour, or in Druze villages, where the alliance of community leaderships with the state and Zionist interests was deemed deserving of 'reward'.

By and large, however, the Arab economy either remained 'underdeveloped' or was only selectively developed by Jewish/national capital and 'suitable' local allies. This is not to say that such efforts, regardless of their motivations and origins, did not have some beneficial developmental effects for the local economy. The potential benefits in providing sources of

Industry and Commerce: Workshop Economy & Entrepreneurship

employment and subsistence of the 'workshop economy' should not be underestimated. Yet, it remains the case that any industrialisation experienced by the Arab economy in the 1970s was either an extension of national economic activity, directly serving and controlled by it, or was at a level which could not really be considered as 'industrialisation'. Nevertheless, the experience accumulated by the end of the period helped to shape the base for the formation of a distinctly Arab non-agricultural economy in Israel in the 1980s.

ISRAELI INDUSTRIAL DEVELOPMENT POLICY
Despite the effective absence of Israeli development efforts in the Arab region, state industrial and business development policy has an important influence in defining the scope for Arab economic activity. This is so not only because of the inhibiting effects of policy, but is also manifested in the specific Arab industrial and business forms that have emerged in response to the absence of state involvement in the region. The relatively high profile of private Jewish capital in the region is a significant part of the resultant structure. Here, however it will be sufficient to outline the way in which state policy promotes an urban Arab productive and service structure with its particular rigidities and flexibilities.

National Industrial Development Laws and Policies

A main element of state industrial/business development policy is the 'Law for the Encouragement of Capital Investment', most recently revised in 1976. The Law emphasises increasing employment in development areas and foreign currency earnings through exports, tourism, etc (see, Bank Leumi Ltd. 1979; *Israel Economist* March 1981; U.S. Department of Commerce 1980). There are three development zones of different priority in which projects can receive benefits depending on their content and aims (e.g. high export potential or science-based industry). An approved project can obtain the status of any of the following: Approved Enterprise; Recognised Enterprise; Approved Investment; Approved Loan; Approved Property. The approved project may be in various areas including industry, tourism, construction, and real estate.

There are four types of benefits available through this law. Investment grants are provided at up to 35 percent of fixed assets in addition to required infrastructural development. Substantial medium-term, low interest loans are available, usually for financing new equipment and construction. Company tax

Industry and Commerce: Workshop Economy & Entrepreneurship

concessions are available as are accelerated capital depreciation, exchange rate guarantees for foreign investors, property tax reduction and waiving customs duty on imported capital equipment. It is also possible to benefit from support such as vocational training cost assistance, profit repatriation arrangements for foreign investors and reduced rental rates. Theoretically, investors in an approved project in the top priority zone need to provide only 25 percent of the fixed asset investment to start out, can obtain a soft loan on 40 percent of the investment and a government grant on the rest, with several years subsidised operations to follow.

There is nothing in this law and overall industrial investment policy that explicitly or otherwise excludes Arabs from the benefits. Yet this can occur as a result of a conscious policy decison to refuse approval to even the most eligible Arab project if deemed politically necessary. The Investment Centre, which approves all projects, has complete discretion in the matter. The 'A Development Zone' comprises some 28 Arab localities with a population of 66,000 and the 'B Zone' 47 localities with 141,000 inhabitants (calculated from Israel 1983a and Bank Leumi Ltd., 1979; see listing in Appendix 2). Together, these 75 localities in top priority zones contain almost 60 percent of the (rural) Arab population (i.e. excluding the Negev, mixed cities, Jerusalem and the four largest Arab towns). The Arab region, though disfavoured in development policy, is not *a priori* excluded from its scope. There is little evidence, however, of benefits accruing to Arab enterprises through this Law.

State Interests in Regional Industry and Business

The fact that state funds are not invested in Arab industrial development has been confirmed at the highest levels, most recently by Prime Minister Shimon Peres (*Jerusalem Post International Edition*, 11 January, 1986). The state, however, does not to see this exclusion as a principle reason for the low rate of Arab industrialisation. Rather, government officials claim Arab businessmen face only one obstacle - 'lack of initiative'.[1]

Speaking to a group of Arab businessmen, the Minister of Trade and Industry expressed his disappointment that "only two new investments were reported in your sector's industries last year, one for establishing a new enterprise and the other for expanding an existing one", despite the fact that Israeli Arabs are "people who like to work and adapt to many trades" (*Jerusalem Post*, 16 January 1986). At the same time he outlined some intriguing options for Arab business expansion which tend to confirm the state's view that Arab industry should not look for - or hope to find - significant business opportunities within the national economy, except when they advance state interests.

In this context, the Minister said that Israel's peace treaty with Egypt had opened new doors for Israeli products,

> and especially the output of the Arab sector... after all, you speak their language.[2] And my office will spare no effort at supporting you all the way... In addition, there are also the indirect avenues of trade - in which your products can be sold to Jordan, Saudi Arabia and the Gulf States *(Ibid)*.

He further urged Arab businessmen to produce mainly for export, recommending food processing plants, since Israel's present level of exports of processed foods "hardly even scratches the surface of this vast market opportunity". Echoing this approach, Shimon Peres told the same group that:

> Our problem is not land, water or good farmers. It is just that we cannot find outlets for our surplus agricultural output. Therefore, it is up to you to take the initiative and lead Arab workers away from the farm in the direction of the factory *(Ibid)*.

It is significant that official policy towards the Arab economy in Israel, as expressed by government leaders in the mid-1980s, included not only a role for the Arab productive sector, but one serving a special function in Israel's Middle Eastern strategic aims and interests. This constitutes a significant appreciation in state awareness of the economic problems posed by the 'Arab question', as well as the need to find effective solutions that provide for some change, yet which are designed with national priorities in mind. Indeed, its elaboration was accompanied by an accelerated public sector involvement in the regional non-agricultural economy, as discussed in the following section.[3]

New Initiatives by the Histadrut

An important aspect of state and public sector industrial/business policy is that espoused by the Israeli labour federation, the *Histadrut,* which has since 1948 assumed for itself a certain degree of moral responsibility for the encouragement of Arab development. Its 1982 Congress passed a lengthy resolution highlighting the importance of the Arab regional activities of *Histadrut* affiliated banking and marketing agencies and the need for intensification of the activity of the *Histadrut* holding company, *Hevrat Ovdim*, in the region. The resolution proposed the "establishment of industrial plants in Arab and Druze villages... and expansion of services provided by *Hevrat Ovdim* companies in the Arab sector" (*Hevrat Ovdim* 1983).

The *Hevrat Ovdim* Council, meeting in early 1983, observing that, "the Arab and Druze villages... do lack an industrial base and services", decided to:

> ...attempt to influence the government to provide development status to industrial zones in the Arab and Druze villages and to prepare an industrial base inside these villages... such ventures to be carried out along with the search for joint efforts, in various forms, among Arab and Druze workers, and investors (initiators)... In order to prepare the needed cadre for industrial plants and services in the Arab sector and in order to bring forward the idea of *Hevrat Ovdim* to the educated in the Arab sector, it will also work to absorb - inside its factories and others' - a group of academics and skilled Arab and Druze workers and elaborate a plan for administration and social training of this group to qualify them to play a role in the industrialisation of the Arab and Druze villages *(Ibid)*.

The initial results of this aggressive new strategy were given prominence by *Hevrat Ovdim* sources in 1984 (see below). These included the implementation of a field survey of existing Arab industrial potential, the cooptation of sympathetic Arab elements, initiation of the first of its Arab-region based joint industrial ventures, discrete efforts at establishing partnerships with Arab businessmen and the encouragment of private Jewish capital towards similar links.

In an economy such as Israel's, where state incentives and regulatory powers are significant and where the public sector controls a substantial part of industry, the exclusion of any region or section of the population from the benefits of such policy is sure to have a negative effect. This will be true at least as regards the scope for regional or communal industrial development.

This has been the case in the Arab experience in Israel. Arab industry and business has been structurally handicapped for over 30 years; starting almost from scratch after 1948 and with only cursory attention paid by the state to its special needs subsequently. The introduction of, for instance, capital intensive or technologically advanced industry was therefore impossible for the Arab region. Meanwhile, those forms of business activity that did emerge were partially conditioned by regional needs and

Industry and Commerce: Workshop Economy & Entrepreneurship

the indigenous capacity in capital and skills to respond.

'Shifts' in state policy towards Arab economic development have also influenced the shape of Arab business activity. These have further served the special interests of national (Jewish) capital in expanding into the Arab region to exploit its established comparative advantage, namely low labour costs. This, in turn, has helped to spawn new forms and directions for Arab industrial and business activity, some of which appear promising, limited though they are. These are dealt with in the following sections.

NATIONAL CAPITAL PENETRATION OF THE REGION

Private Capital Spearheads National Thrust

Israeli public sector finance is by and large only directed to the Arab region on a limited basis and within the framework of central government subsidies and aid to local government. However, there has been an increasing level of Jewish private capital deployment in the region, alongside the *Histadrut* initiatives mentioned above. This private involvement exploits the substantial supply of cheap labour, an opportunity encouraged by the absence of comprehensive state development policy for the region and a consequently underutilised and flexible regional labour market. It is also common to find traditional private sector industries such as textiles and publicly-owned industry such as construction trying to maintain profit margins in an era when the highest growth is promised in new capital intensive and science-based industries.

Private capital penetration of the region has mostly taken the form of sub-contracting, transferring the labour-intensive stages of the production process to areas where abundant and cheap (mainly female) labour can easily be mobilised. It has involved either the establishment of wholly Jewish-owned and managed subsidiaries or joint ventures with local sub-contractors. It is difficult to establish a clear picture of the extent of non-Arab ownership of industrial and commercial enterprises in the region, both because of inaccurate available data and the somewhat ambiguous nature of ownership of some enterprises.

Given the different possible vehicles for external investment - provision of start-up capital, equipment or raw material supply, management and technical supervision, sub-contracting stages of the production/finishing process, marketing facilities - any data on ownership will be at best approximate. For example, of the total of Arab industrial plants identified in a *Hevrat Ovdim* sponsored survey in 1983, 16 percent were 'non-locally owned' (see, Czamanski *et al.* 1984). In itself, this is not an especially high proportion of external control, though this figure only refers to those enterprises which are either subsidiaries of national companies or businesses owned by (mainly Jewish) non-local residents.

There are no figures showing which branches of industries are non-Arab owned, nor the proportion of the region's industrial labour force therein employed. It is safe to assume, however, that the relevant branches are those with direct linkages within the Jewish economy, primarily textiles and clothing, and certain sections of the construction industry, food processing, chemical and plastics, and possibly some jewellery/ornamental plant. It is doubtful that private Jewish investment would be made in small-scale units in any of these branches, so it is likely that most of the non-locally owned factories are 'larger-scale' (in this context, employing more than 10 workers). Given the predominantly small-scale nature of Arab regional industry, a substantial part of the larger units are therefore likely to be non-locally owned.

Direct Jewish control and extraction of value added was the predominant mode of national involvement in regional industrial activity until the early-1980s. Recently, however, a new pattern has emerged. Existing local capital is being coopted into new private Jewish investment on investment- or profit-sharing bases (Jobran 1984: 9). The format for this investment appears to reflect increasing Jewish hesitation about substantial new commitments in the region without concomitant Arab involvement, especially in the mid-1980s recessionary climate. It is also a function of the need of Arab commercial capital to expand into continuously profitable spheres. There is no doubt that the expressed and increasingly manifested intent of *Hevrat Ovdim*, through a new affiliate of its *Koor Industries* corporation, to coordinate joint ventures of Arab and Jewish capitalists and entrepreneurs, has also played an important role in encouraging this process.

The Histadrut Takes the Lead

Histadrut sponsored projects in industry, banking and marketing have complemented and subsequently overshadowed the private sector thrust into the region. The new *Koor* affiliate, the 'Arab-Druze Sector Development Corporation', launched in late-1983 with joint Jewish-Arab management, has initiated "a number of projects based on joint *Hevrat Ovdim* and Arab funding... among them a *tehina* (sesame paste) factory in Umm al-Fahm at a

Industry and Commerce: Workshop Economy & Entrepreneurship

cost of $300,000" *(Ibid)*. This is a 50-50 joint venture between local investors and *Koor* Foods Ltd., which is also likely to market its output, and has established the pattern for future investment in the region. This much heralded factory employs 20 workers under local Arab management and was reported in 1986 to be expanding annual production to $300,000, part of which is for export *(Jerusalem Post,* 7 July 1986).

By 1986, a number of similar investments were reported *(Ibid)*. In Nazareth, the Bulous family, owners of a marble and stone factory since the 1960s, established a $3 million partnership with *Koor's Yuval Gad Ltd.,* to produce prefabricated buildings for Arab localities. Another $4 million joint venture, between a Nazareth investor and *Koor Metals Ltd.,* due to commence operation in 1986, will produce forged iron for building and decorative purposes and employ more than 30 workers. Other planned projects, funded partially by *Koor Chemicals Ltd.,* include two factories for industrial rubber products, one of them a $1.5 million project in a Galilee village exclusively for export and the other, a $500,000 project in the Triangle village of Jatt. Not all attempted joint ventures were successful, however. For example, "a scheme to manufacture electronic heat sensors in a Galilee village for export fell through at the last moment after the British concern that was to buy them found they could get the sensors at a quarter of the price from Taiwan" *(Ibid)*.

Meanwhile, five supermarkets were due to open in the region by 1986, serving a population of over 130,000 and providing 300 new jobs (Jobran 1984: 9). These include both joint Arab-Jewish private sector initiatives, such as the $750,000 centre outside Sakhnin in the Galilee, and other ventures between Arab investors and the *Histadrut* consumer cooperative in Umm al-Fahm (also with an investment of $750,000), Shefa'amr, Rahat (in the Negev) and Nazareth *(Jerusalem Post,* 7 July 1986). This latter project is to be a $3 million 'hypermarket', and the terms of the joint venture indicate the type of future arrangements that can be expected:

> A Nazareth Arab put up the 2,300 square meter building and the *Histadrut's Hamashbir Lezarkhan* consumer cooperative is leasing the building from him and operating the store. The Arab investor will get a share of the profits. It will employ a staff of 70 and, at the request of the Nazareth Labour Council secretary, Mohammed Abu-Ahmed, 10 percent of the jobs wil be given to Jewish workers in recognition of the many Arab workers in Jewish enterprises in Upper Nazareth *(Ibid)*.

Industry and Commerce: Workshop Economy & Entrepreneurship

In addition to the absence of profitable markets, other problems encountered by these new initiatives included the delays in persuading Arab investors to fund new ventures, the development of skilled manpower, obstacles from Israeli Jews, and delays in getting approval from the appropriate authorities *(Ibid)*. However, some of these problems appear to have been overcome under the influence of the 'general philosophy' guiding the corporation's activities, as expressed by its Jewish co-manager, Uri Thon: "We have to live together and we should do business together" *(Ibid)*.

Arab Industrialisation for the Development of the Jewish State?

There is no doubt that the government is backing these developments. In addition to encouragement of specific Arab production and marketing patterns as indicated by government officials' statements quoted earlier, officials have also counselled that Jewish capital be directed towards the Arab region. The Minister of Agriculture, visiting a trade-fair held in Nazareth by an Israeli company (the first ever organised for the Arab market), stated that Israeli firms do not fully appreciate the size and potential of the Israeli Arab market 'right on their doorstep' *(Jerusalem Post International Edition,* 19 July 1986). With recent changes in Arab purchasing habits, the traditional 'corner-shop' mentality has given way to a "large and potentially lucrative market whose buying power had increased recently". Echoing Thon's approach, he held that "...there is nothing better than trade to help relations and establish new connections between Arabs and Jews. Trade is even better than politics" *(Ibid)*.

The penetration of the Arab region by Jewish public and private capital has positive and negative consequences. On the one hand, this is the first time that the Arab region has received such a degree of financial attention and actual business investment. Further, this is not being undertaken in a haphazard or piece-meal fashion; rather, a company has been specially designed to organise and direct investment in a more or less coordinated and comprehensive manner. There now exists a definite 'reference point' or 'investment channel' through which Jewish public and private capital can identify suitable areas for productive investment, with an option for Arab capital mobilisation in the process.

On the other hand, these new investments appear to be primarily a function of the requirements of public sector capital to identify new and more profitable locations for expansion. In this regard, the Arab region offers relatively low labour, land, utilities, and taxation costs. The establishment of supermarkets also manifests a perception by national economic interests of the hitherto insufficiently exploited consumption capacities in the Arab region. In this respect, therefore, the pattern of investment tends to reflect the financial and technological concerns of interests 'external' to the region, despite Arab participation in the projects and some enjoyment of their benefits in terms of profits, employment, and a greater local availability of consumer goods. This new approach, despite its potential for furthering forms of dependent Arab integration into the national economy, should also be viewed in relation to the degree of *Histadrut* activity in the Jewish sector (*Hevrat Ovdim* 1982). Of the 14 large supermarkets in the Galilee region in 1982, one was in an Arab locality; of the 20 *Hapoalim* banks in the Galilee in that year, only three were in Arab towns (see Table 5.1). And while *Hevrat Ovdim* had established 73 industrial projects in the region by 1982, none were in Arab localities. The investment required to drastically alter the present situation is certainly too great to expect any substantial change in the near future.

Table 5.1: Histadrut Economic Projects in Galilee, Arab and Jewish Sectors, 1982

	Marketing			Banking			Industry			Recreation		
	Jewish	Arab	Tot	Jewish	Arab	Tot	Jewish	Arab	Tot	Jewish	Arab	Tot
Total	13	1	14	17	3	20	73	0	73	15	0	15
Percent	93	7	100	85	15	100	73	0	100	15	0	100

SOURCE: From (Hevrat Ovdim Council, 1982: 32).

Recent developments are likely to strengthen a pattern of enforced dependent integration of Arab capital and production into national goals when and if short-term profits are probable. 'Development' *per se* does not appear to be a priority. On another level, the expansion of large-scale Jewish marketing enterprises will threaten the livelihood of an entire small Arab commercial sector without offering any alternative source of work and security (except perhaps as supermarket employees for a few small shopkeepers). Furthermore, the establishment of partially Jewish-financed medium- to large-scale enterprises in traditional Arab production branches (e.g. the factories producing *tehina* and forged iron) will compete against the remaining smaller-scale Arab producers in those fields. Meanwhile, the

Industry and Commerce: Workshop Economy & Entrepreneurship

possibilities for Arab industrialisation along lines similar to, and integrated on an equitable basis within, the diversified structure of Israeli industry, including capital intensive and technologically advanced industry, will continue to be ignored. Instead, the traditional 'comparative advantage' of the region (mass consumption, unexploited industrial space and cheap labour) will benefit primarily national/Jewish capital concerns.

INDUSTRIAL STRUCTURE: SCALE, MIX, EMPLOYMENT, LOCATION

Regional Industry in the 1980s

The most accurate published data on Arab industrial structure indicate that in 1983 there were 410 industrial units in Arab villages and towns in Israel (Czamanski *et al.* 1984; see Table 5.2). Of these, 29 percent (118) employed less than four workers, 31 percent (129) employed between five and nine workers, and 40 percent (163) employed 10 or more workers. In 41 percent of Arab localities there are no industrial enterprises. Most plants were established after 1976: 26 percent were established before 1976, 43 percent between 1976 and 1979 and 31 percent from 1980 to 1983. Two branches are predominant: textile/clothing and construction material manufacture, constituting a total of 148 (36 percent) and 129 (31 percent) units respectively. The two other branches in which there is a large number of generally smaller, and often self-employed, units are those in food production, paper and printing, woodworking and metalworking, constituting 9 percent, 3 percent, 3 percent and 11 percent of all units respectively.

There is a problem in grouping within the same figures self-employed production units (e.g. carpentry and blacksmith workshops) and larger-scale production processes which involve greater application of fixed and variable capital (such as clothes factories, cement or tile factories and heavy metal works). Since the 1983 figures used here do not include the numerous self-employed carpenters and blacksmiths, the number of all wood and metal production units is probably much larger. When these smaller units are included in industrial figures, they render woodworking and metalworking branches as widespread as clothing and construction production.

A 1982 survey (APEF 1983) indicated a total of almost 700 Arab workshops, including some 130 carpentry workshops (compared to only 13 in the 1983 figures) and over 100 car maintenance garages (not included in the 1983 survey). This survey's figures for most branches diverged significantly from those for 1983: 130 clothing/textile (248 in the 1983 figures); 115 stone/brick (130 for 1983); 24 metalworking (46 for 1983). These and other discrepancies appear to arise from surveying errors in the two studies as well as different definitions of industrial units (as compared to the 1983 survey which applied stricter scale and production criteria).

However, looking at the 1982 and 1983 surveys together, we can differentiate between the two predominant scale groups of industrial plant - between those with only one self-employed worker and those with one or more employee - and the picture becomes clearer. The first group includes some 200 units (estimating roughly from the data in the two surveys), almost all in the carpentry and blacksmithing branches, producing primarily for local, individual customers but also undertaking sub-contracts for larger Arab or Jewish concerns in the same or complementary branches (especially construction). The second group is dominated by clothing and construction material manufacture, but also contains some larger metal and wood working plants, as well as units from branches such as food, plastics and chemicals, paper and printing and jewellery and ornaments.

The larger-scale group of industries (which constitutes the main 'population' for the 1983 survey) employed in 1983 over 8,100 workers, constituting 30 percent of the Arab industrial labour force of 28,000 (Israel 1984: 350). Distributed among the 410 surveyed plants, this implies an average scale size of 20 persons employed per plant. The national average industrial scale in 1983 (excluding the region) was somewhat larger, at over 27 employed per industrial unit (Israel 1983: 451). The relatively high Arab average despite the proliferation of smaller units is due to the polarised distribution, with a few large factories, many small workshops, and very few medium-sized industrial units.

Of those locally employed, 71 percent were women, indicating the predominance of textile and clothing manufacture, the branch with the highest level of private Jewish capital penetration. Accordingly, it can be assumed that up to the same proportion of the regional industrial labour force is employed either directly or indirectly by Jewish capital. In national terms, this means that just over 10 percent (some 3000) of the total Arab industrial labour force is employed in exclusively Arab-owned concerns. This is unusually low compared to the situation in other sectors, especially considering that around half of the Arab labour force works in its locality of residence, probably mostly in Arab-owned enterprises or farms. It also implies a high and unbalanced degree of integration of Arab industry nationally.

Table 5.2: Features of Industrial Enterprises in Arab Localities in Israel, 1983

CHARACTERISTIC	TOTAL	PERCENT
Arab localities in Israel	106	100.0
Localities with enterprises	62	58.5
Industrial enterprises	**410**	***100.0***
Branch		
Sewing and textiles	148	36.1
Food products	36	8.8
Bricks, stones, tiles	129	31.5
Metal products	46	11.2
Soap, detergents, chemicals	7	1.7
Plastics	5	1.2
Carton, paper, printing	11	2.7
Wood products	13	3.2
Jewellery, ornaments	3	0.7
Miscellaneous	12	2.9
Ownership		
Locally owned	346	84.4
Not locally owned	64	15.6
Period established		
Established before 1975	109	26.6
Established 1975-79	174	42.4
Established since 1980	127	31.0
Scale		
Employs < 5	118	28.8
Employs 5-9	129	31.5
Employs 10 +	163	39.7
Employment		
Total	8188	100.0
Thereof: female	5850	71.4

SOURCE: From (Czamanski *et. al.* 1984)

A broad description of the functioning of certain Arab industrial branches can be arrived at from an examination of the various groups and types of available data on Arab industrial/business development in Israel.[4] Arab clothing and textile plants appear to be well integrated within the national production process, in one form or another of sub-contracting. One sort of plant prepares garments, another sews together ready-made textiles, while yet another can be engaged in finishing articles of clothing. In some cases all these stages are grouped in one enterprise/space, depending upon a variety of factors. The most prominent of these is the availability of low-cost Arab (almost wholly female) labour. The branch's managerial functions are mostly fulfilled by Israeli Jewish managers or owners, Arab sub-contractors and independent businessmen and, in a few cases, foreign parent company control.

Regional construction units are characterised by a greater degree of Arab ownership, while a similarly wide range of functions are performed. Arab construction activity in fact amalgamates three branches of the workshop economy - stone/tile/brick production, metalsmithing and carpentry. Whereas the former is wholly dedicated to construction activity, the latter two maintain their own alternative markets outside construction, including furniture, household and heating equipment, agricultural implements/equipment etc. The managers and construction bosses include a range of the more classical 'entrepreneurial' types, newer entrants and venture capitalists, active in building in both Arab and Jewish localities.

The construction-related workshops produce a variety of goods and services in addition to those already indicated: iron and aluminium cross-sections and rods, purchased in bulk and cut and joined in the workshop for bolstering cement foundations as well as window and door frames and fittings; ready-mixed cement prepared to order, including delivery and pouring; brick and breeze-block manufacture; marble/tile cutting and polishing; stone quarrying (though this branch has been heavily restricted by state control since the 1950s); equipment and vehicle use or leasing. The two most successful and best established Arab industrial enterprises engage in construction (the Boulos stone and marble enterprises, which recently expanded into pre-fabricated housing for Arab areas) and metal-working (the Kadamani factories based in Yirka, producing middle to heavy industrial equipment), producing for local markets and export.

More than any other branch, indigenous Arab food processing is geared to regional demand and tastes. Small- to medium- scale family or wage-labour based workshops process *tehina*-related products, pickled vegetables, cold-pressed olive oil, ice-cream, ground wheat and pulses, Arab bread and confectionary, a range of dairy products, including yoghurt, *labneh* (yoghurt based cheese), and various other cheeses, and roast/ground coffee and nuts. This branch has its own unique production processes and supplies the Arab market direct, though, as indicated above, capitalisation could radically transform existing processes.

Other branches enjoying less prominence in the Arab industrial sector include leather processing (footwear, bags), paper and carton production, printing (books, magazines, stationary) and chemicals and plastics (household goods, soap and other cleaning materials). There is, in addition, one Arab diamond polishing plant. A few localities boast jewellery, ornament or traditional handicraft workshops, though these crafts are historically linked to central Palestine, especially around Jerusalem. However, in light of recent intiatives, new industries are likely to appear, others expand, and yet others diminish in significance, along with moves towards larger regional industrial investment and scale.

Another perspective from which to view the structure (branch distribution) of regional industry is in comparison with nation industrial structure. Through location quotient (LQ) analysis, already encountered in our discussion of Arab agriculture, it is possible to highlight the relative specialisation of (and imbalances in) regional industrial activity. Thus, a comparison of available data for 1983[5] (in terms of number of establishments per branch) reveals a high LQ for Arab stone/brick/tile production, at over seven, indicating 'over-specialisation'. Similarly, the LQ for Arab clothing/textile worshops is high, at over two; only in food processing is the degree of Arab activity balanced with national industry, at just under one. The LQ for metal-workshops is low, at under 0.5, and all other branches are heavily under-represented in the region, with LQs below 0.01.

The prevailing industry mix therefore appears to be determined by two factors: the extent of public and private Jewish capital penetration of the region and the remaining scope for individual business initiation in labour processes and products which Arab skill levels, capital ownership and, to a lesser extent, local demand permit. In a few individual cases, Arab entrepreneurs have succeeded in combining these two factors to their best advantage and expanded their industries through links with Jewish capital or markets. The main market for Arab industries remains Jewish, except for the smallest and relatively minor producers whose output is locally consumed, and plants producing construction materials which serve both the regional and national markets.

There is nothing in the actual distribution of capital investment between branches that is in itself an obstacle to growth. Despite much fascination with capital intensiveness and advanced technological processes in Israel and elsewhere, there is no clear evidence that more traditional labour intensive processes have less value adding capacity. On the contrary, an analysis of the workshop economy in the occupied West Bank and Gaza Strip indicates just the opposite (Mattin 1985).

The Workshop Sector in Nazareth and Umm al-Fahm

Recently available field survey data from a sample of 59 industrial units in the two largest Arab urban centres of Nazareth and Umm al-Fahm (Khalidi and Sabbagh 1985; see Table 5.3),[6] allow for further definition of the overall profile of the existing Arab workshop economy. The evidence on scale of establishments shows a clear trend until 1984 towards a preponderance of smaller production units, as measured by size of workforce. Whereas in 1982, 76 percent of the surveyed units employed 10 or less workers, by 1984 this figure had risen to 97 percent. In that year, from a total surveyed workforce of 290, the average size workforce per unit was under five workers, within a range of two to 45. Evidence on size of industrial premises further demonstrates the small-scale of Arab industry, with 86 percent of units utilising less than 500 square meters.

Table 5.3: Industry in Nazareth and Umm al-Fahm, 1983 and 1984

	NAZARETH				UMM AL-FAHM			
	1983 DATA		1984 DATA		1983 DATA		1984 DATA	
BRANCH	UNITS	%	UNITS	%	UNITS	%	UNITS	%
Clothing	12	35	8	7	6	31	7	11
Blocks/Stone	6	17	6	5	7	37	19	30
Metal products	6	17	39	36	2	11	15	23
Wood products	-	-	26	24	-	-	18	28
Chemicals	2	7	7	6	1	5	2	3
Paper/Printing	3	9	8	7	-	-	-	-
Food products	5	15	7	6	3	16	3	5
Miscellaneous	-	-	10	9	-	-	-	-
TOTAL	34	100	111	100	19	100	64	100

NOTE: Percentage figures are rounded.
SOURCES: For 1983 data, from (Czamanski *et. al.* 1984). For 1984 data, from (Khalidi and Sabbagh 1985).

In Nazareth, of the total of 1,230 industrial and commercial licenses issued by the municipality by 1984, only 111 were for manufacturing enterprises. There were 130 car repair garages and 989 cover the range of small commercial, professional, public and private services that flourish in the Arab region, and in

Industry and Commerce: Workshop Economy & Entrepreneurship

Nazareth in particular. For Umm al-Fahm, figures compiled locally (by the *Histadrut* office) are not as complete, and only indicate 15 car repair garages and 22 restaurants and food establishments (i.e. excluding food production) in addition to 64 other industrial establishments.

Strictly speaking (in terms of international classifications), there is no such thing as a service industry, rather only services and manufacturing industry. Within these terms, we can see that the economy of Nazareth is dominated by service establishments (91 percent of the total). The situation in Umm al-Fahm appears to be similar with the two service activities for which data exists (food and car repair establishments) accounting for 37 percent of known establishments.

However, service industries can also be defined as those manufacturing activities that directly serve other productive activities, i.e., those industries whose finished product is a raw material for other productive or transformation activity. Within this definition, survey data exists for those three production branches which supply raw materials to the construction industry: blocks/stone; metal; wood. In these terms, results show that the main productive activity in the surveyed towns is definitely service oriented, accounting for over 64 percent of establishments. These so-called service industries are more prevalent in Umm al-Fahm, while Nazareth has a greater variety and proportion of other manufacturing industries.

The available data on ownership of surveyed units indicate that the great majority (95 percent) is locally and individually owned. There are three other variables which provide some indication of the extent of dependence of Arab industry upon external Israeli Jewish sources: source of original investment, source of initiative for establishment and source of raw materials. Only 5 percent of surveyed units (all in Umm al-Fahm) were originally financed by private or public Israeli Jewish capital, with most initial investment coming from the owner himself. The role of family, friends or partners is also considerable, confirming that small-scale Arab industry is largely based on informal and local resources. Outside sources play a small role in initiation of industrial activity, and present owners are the main agents of business initiation in both surveyed localities.

The sphere in which local industry has more links to the national economy is that of raw material supply, though even these are not as extensive as might be expected from an integrated regional economy. Of the specified sources of different raw materials, 99 were either local or other Arab while 94 were Israeli Jewish or import sources outside the region. This reinforces the picture of a relatively self-contained regional economy with specific and limited external linkages. A further investigation of the correlation between scale and ownership reveals that the small proportion of non-locally owned enterprises are among enterprises with few employees, though they appear to be large in terms of area, possibly indicating greater use of machinery and thus requiring more space. This helps to further define earlier impressions about scale and ownership, whereby non-Arab-owned industry is seen to be more capital intensive than Arab-owned industry.

Survey results pertaining to changes in the level of capitalisation show that there has been no significant growth in investment in machines and tools, either in the short-term (the previous two years) or over a longer period; in a few cases there has been a certain degree of disinvestment. Overall, there has been a more or less constant level in capital investment. Of the 64 percent of surveyed units which answered questions regarding investment, some 80 percent valued their industrial equipment at less than $20,000. This holds equally for both localities. The average value of plant in 38 units was $15,600, while the total value in all these establishments was only $592,000. This indicates a level of investment which can by no means be termed 'capital-intensive', especially compared to Israeli industry as a whole.

Though not directly indicating capital intensivity, the value of raw materials, energy and other running costs provides a general picture of the (value) scale of activity, indirectly reflecting the financial level on which Arab industry operates. In all cases, the majority of units (which answered) are found at the bottom of the scale. Accordingly, 56 percent of units spent under $50,000 per annum on raw materials at an average of $22,100; 69 percent of units spent less than $10,000 on energy, at an average level of $1,460. Only with running costs, (including rent, local and other taxes, insurance, maintainence) is there a greater spread among expense brackets, though over 50 percent pay under $5,000, and the average level is $4,340. These results confirm the picture of an industrial sector which operates on a relatively low level of capital and financial outlay, and the observation that Arab industry is overwhelmingly small-scale.

Furthermore, in 71 percent of specified cases, labour skills were estimated by the plant owner/manager to be 'high' or 'medium'. This would indicate that, at least for those who know the work processes best, existing labour is relatively highly skilled. As regards the question of labour supply, the only data available in this survey are the estimates made by interviewees of the main problems facing their businesses. Of the cases in which problems were mentioned, only six percent specified finding appropriate labour. This is not too surprising in light of the increasing availability of skilled Arab workers, unemployed as a result of the economic crisis in Israel.

The marketing of Arab industrial output in these towns appears to follow a fairly clear pattern. Production is in almost all cases of finished goods, marketed equally in wholesale and retail, direct to customers, and in many cases, through a third party. Output is destined both for the local and national markets, (40 percent and 54 percent respectively) with a degree of penetration of the West Bank and Gaza Strip market (7 percent). Non-local marketing is handled by a significant proportion of non-Arab agents (37 percent), though Arab merchants handle output in 43 percent of cases. An interesting result is that direct sub-contracting and production by subsidiaries for a parent company does not figure very prominently (only 6 percent of surveyed units). According to these results, the local industrial base would seem to have a distinct local/Arab market, though with a significant and selective orientation to the national market.

A final set of results of interest are the answers to questions regarding the major problems facing interviewees. The most frequently mentioned problem was taxation, cited by over 75 percent of respondents. Securing finance was considered a problem by almost 60 percent of interviewees, with marketing problems, licensing and other legal issues quoted by 50 percent and 39 percent of respondents respectively. Other important problem areas included availability of raw materials, labour, energy and equipment.

ARAB INDUSTRIAL AND BUSINESS OUTLOOK AND PRACTICE

The level of Arab entrepreneurial activity is determined by various factors, including local infrastructural weaknesses, the constraints imposed by Jewish capital penetration, the market and resource options for business initiation and existing patterns of capital accumulation. These barriers operate on all levels, from the smallest workshop to the largest factory or business. Their perpetuation is primarily a function of the segmentation of Arab society, the isolation and individualisation of enterprises and the generally limited business experience.[7]

On their particular levels and within their different horizons, the strata of self-employed craftsmen or artisans, industrialists, traders and other Arab entrepreneurs naturally have their own goals and strategies. However, in most economies, these different economic initiators have an overall common interest and even a common consciousness. The existence of professional associations, chambers of commerce and specific sectorally-oriented business services testifies to this. In addition to sharing a common interest, the components of the business sector in any country have at different stages and in different ways, a common strategy in regard to relations with consumers, government, labour, financial sources, trading partners and so forth.

Israel is no exception to this pattern, but its Arab business sector is. It might be argued by apologists for state policy that small-scale businesses, Arab or Jewish, have common goals while the larger concerns have theirs. But this is essentially fallacious since all elements of the Arab business sector, even to an extent the coopted ones, are dealt with by Jewish public and private capital as the 'Arab sector' - though constraints are not universally harsh.

Furthermore, the preceding discussion has revealed a distinctly Arab pattern of industrial and business formation, which, with only a few exceptions, has much in common with existing Jewish patterns. The metal and woodworking, sewing, building materials and even car maintenance garages (strictly the latter are services, not industries) of the Arab region in Israel find their counterparts in the West Bank and Gaza Strip much more than in the Jewish sector (see, e.g. UNECWA 1981; UNIDO 1984). The consequent absence of any elaborated or perceived mutual interest and strategy within this sector plays an important role in perpetuating its distortions and dependencies on all levels of scale and capital intensity.

This problem in turn encompasses two more specific weaknesses in the pattern of industrial activity. On the one hand, it is only very recently that the possibilities of intra-entrepreneurial integration have been raised. So far, this has been on the level of horizontal links between wealthy capitalists and businessmen, with an eye to establishing a joint venture Arab commercial or industrial projects. It is possible that this move will be coordinated with Jewish capital and resources, but this is to be expected from such a group.

The first such attempts at breaking out of established patterns and realising a degree of intra-entrepreneurial solidarity cannot immediately make radical departures from well-tried links and methods. Also, this group's interests do not necessarily differ so sharply from the Jewish sector; but the fact that they do enough to give rise to such a development is in itself significant. There is, however, no evidence of similar initiatives occurring between smaller enterprises, so there does not appear to be any general phenomenon of the emergence of an Arab business/industrial 'class consciousness'.

Industry and Commerce: Workshop Economy & Entrepreneurship

This leads to a second consequence of the absence of a sectoral strategy. There have been no attempts to date within the Arab region to mount, identify and mobilise potential intra-sectoral or inter-sectoral linkages, an important characteristic of Israeli economic structure and activity. The whole sphere of sub-contracting within the clothing industry, and to a lesser extent, woodworking and blacksmithing trades is a practice essential to the dynamic of Jewish involvement in the region. While examples may exist of such methods (e.g. within the construction industry where Arab contractors sub-contract to blacksmiths or carpenters for door and window frames), this has not been the result of a clear strategy to most efficiently cut costs and raise profit margins. Nor has there been any significant attempt to invest in food processing industries (except in the case of olive oil and some dairy products) which could have an assured Arab source of supply (if not market).

The absence of intra- and inter-sectoral linkages helps to maintain the fragmentation of Arab producing power nationally. It also restricts entrepreneurial contact and mutual learning and accumulation of comprehensive experience in production and marketing techniques. Most importantly, it slows the expansion of the sector as a whole which remains dependent on existing established sources of materials and lines of marketing.

There are other weaknesses apparent in the path of Arab industrial growth. These include the low level of management and administrative expertise, insufficient absorbtion and utilisation of new technologies (even simple ones), a reluctance to invest and tie up liquid commercial capital in productive spheres, and the absence of any substantial attempts to export or benefit from Israeli strength in the science-based industrial sector. None of these are necessarily the right things for the Arab industrial sector to be doing. However, the very process of considering such options and issues is an essential stage in 'normal' economic development. Though the Arab 'region' is hardly perceived as such by policy makers, external economic agents, or even its inhabitants, the fact that the 'Arab producing and consuming sector' effectively acts nationally as a regional economy does imply the need for such planning processes.

The Arab industrial and business sector does not lack the potential, experience, capital, technical expertise, labour or social structure to ameliorate these conditions of business activity. It has, however, until now lacked the coordination and institutionalisation of its accumulated resources and experience that could more efficiently and successfully mobilise those potentials to the benefit of entrepreneurs and labour alike. Here, the choice of a 'regional' strategy *per se* is of secondary importance to the elaboration of any local (Arab) strategy, prioritisation of needs and choice of options for development.

ARAB FINANCIAL RESOURCES

Of crucial importance is the pattern of savings and the financial resources that could fuel such a strategy. Without such a mobilisation of local resources, the region will most likely remain subservient to the interests and capacities of national capital, a path which has not always been in the best interests of the Arab population. Traditionally, private Arab savings have been directed to conspicuous consumption, residential building, real estate and sometimes small commercial business ventures. The relatively low level of private savings which characterises Arab living conditions dictates a small regional level of savings to start with. An intial directing of existing savings into improving basic living standards (e.g. as measured in possession of consumer durables) is not perverse behaviour. Nor is the need to compensate for the absence of state subsidies on land and residential construction by investing in home building.

Any remaining savings are not deployed in business ventures either because of traditional fear of risk among the older generation which largely possesses this capital or simply because of the serious lack of opportunities, within the Arab business sector at least. The general manager of the Arab-Israeli Bank (a subsidiary of the major Israeli *Bank Leumi)* [8] confirmed that "there is a great amount of money in the Arab sector and some of it is looking for industrial investment opportunities" (in Arnon and Raviv 1980: 223). For the average Arab saver, it is safer and easier to leave savings in a bank in long-term deposits, to lend it locally, or engage in stock market speculation than to invest it in a weak, informal and disorganised Arab industrial or business sector. There is scant information available on aggregate Arab savings and investment potential, though the commercial banking system does not appear to be a significant or active source of credit and investment, whatever might be the level of Arab deposits at its disposal.

One indication of the level of Arab savings and utilisation of the banking system is found in an examination of the activity of the Arab-Israeli Bank which, though not necessarily the repository of the bulk of Arab savings, is the only bank dealing exclusively with the Arab financial sector. In 1984, this bank employed 232 persons in a total of 33 branches, of which 30 were in Arab localities, and three in Haifa and Acre (Arab-Israeli Bank 1985). Most were to be found in the central, and western Galilee, especially in the better off towns and villages, with only

Industry and Commerce: Workshop Economy & Entrepreneurship

four in the Triangle. Even the *Histadrut's* banking affiliate, *Hapoalim,* had a minimal presence in Arab areas; this indicates a low level of Arab utilisation of formal channels of financial intermediation.

Total deposits grew from $43 million in 1979, of which $37 were in fixed term accounts, to some $66 million in 1982, at the height of the Israeli economic boom, with over $60 million in fixed term savings (calculated, according to U.S. dollar exchange rates, from *Ibid*). As the recession began in 1983, depositors began to withdraw their savings, bringing total deposits down to $55 million by 1984; most of this was taken out of long-term savings, which fell to under $53 million. The bank's role as a minor source of credit is indicated by figures on loans which grew from some $5 million in 1979, peaked at $9 million in 1982, and fell back to $7 million by 1984. Data is not available on the number of bank customers.

Data on Arab household savings patterns were discussed in Chapter Four. While the 'average' Arab household will not be the usual industrial or business investor, the significant levels of Arab consumption expenditure, the lack of resources for investment and the preceding figures from the Arab-Israeli Bank indicate a narrow capital base in the Arab region. The main examples of substantial Arab capital accumulation are not to be found in private family savings patterns, but in the instances of individual entrepreneurs and commercial traders who amassed wealth through inheritance, capital originating in land or collaboration with Jewish production and marketing interests in intermediary roles. Other Arab entrepreneurial activities have concentrated in small, often family-based professional or commercial services to the region, such as accounting offices, wholesaling, building material supplies, and agencies for national or imported products such as household appliances, car spares, and consumer goods.

The major area, therefore, for the emergence of new financial patterns has been in linking to Jewish capital and performing the service of deploying it through the region, either through commercial or industrial sub-contracting activities. As has been seen, the successful examples of an independent path of Arab industrial investment and production are few and far between: they too either benefited from a specific Israeli market (e.g. Kadamani metal work contracts with the Ministry of Defence) or else through an advantage in raw material, export market potential or skills (e.g. Bulous marble and granite works). The more recent examples of investment exhibit a departure from the pattern of national policy towards the region, but not of local investment practices. Those Arabs undertaking the new investments are mainly new 'versions' of the few traditional Arab businessmen in Israel and represent a quantative, and not a qualitative change. The bulk of Arab financial resources are either not deployed productively or find their way into small, often short-term enterprise, with little hope for substantial reproduction or agglomeration.

ARAB PRIVATE ENTREPRENEURIAL FORMATION

Without recourse to the extensive theoretical literature on entrepreneurship, and with the limited data on the subject at hand, an initial profile of Arab entrepreneurial types in Israel can be drawn. It serves the purpose of better classifying existing groups which have undertaken economic initiatives of some sort. The specific nature of Arab entrepreneurship in Israel, not even common to West Bank or Gaza experience, is rooted in the historical circumstances of its evolution. In fact, it is significant that it is even possible to talk of Arab entrepreneurs in Israel in light of the fact that they almost all started their businesses from scratch.

The expulsion of the bulk of Palestine's Arab population and the division of the country in 1948 isolated those Arabs who remained in Israel from their industrial and commercial elite and had a devastating effect on their social and economic structure. Though a hard path, the work process as mobile labourers within the Israeli economy laid the foundations for the emergence of individual entrepreneurial experiences. Increasingly, Arab contractors and sub-contractors developed their own contacts, directly initiated employment, became equipped to finance and compete, refused to accept cut-rate work, and developed their own means of production and long experience in produce handling and holding market concessions. Rosenfeld has described the process thus:

> If we accept that the level of the local economic-occupational diversification is not impressive... we see that nevertheless it has meaning in developmental terms. The villagers are clearly not the same lot of unskilled, semi-skilled manual labourers. The village economy is still underdeveloped, not a diversified economic unit of interdependent branches, groups or trades, yet its labour power was not, and is not, solely conditioned by it. What is present now in the village in regard to experience, skills, money for investment in tools, equipment and transport facilities is the villagers' own accumulation, the outcome of the work process, the achievement and human capacity of

those who were the most vulnerable, most exploited workers in the country. Not that there is employment for them in the village, nor can the village answer their problems of livelihood; nor is a self-employed group a sign of local economic independence. But a potential in this direction has begun to accumulate in the village (1976: 399).

Arab Entrepreneurial Types

The most obvious, and now somewhat classic, form of Arab entrepreneurship is that of the few large capitalists and businessmen. This group is active in commerce, industry and agriculture, and includes wholesalers, commercial agents, concession-holders, large-scale industrialists, and modern capitalist farmers or landowners (especially in the Triangle). It is defined primarily by the combination of its own inherited or accumulated wealth with a working relationship with the state and Jewish capitalist concerns. This relationship usually involves some investment by the latter in the form of capital, management or technical expertise or distribution networks; otherwise, legal and political facilties or cover is provided in return for political collaboration and support. The relation of this group to its capital is individual and personal; rarely is it through the intermediary of a large limited share company or other institutional arrangement. Even when these exist (as with Bulous), the personal stake in the concern is considerable.

These are not western-style corporate executives but are more in the mould of the European industrial and financial pioneers of the late-19th and early-20th centuries. The relation of their capital to labour is the classical one of extraction of labour value added through the impersonalised process typical of all capitalist systems (even though Bulous, for example, is known for his close, paternalistic relation with his employees, similar to that of some early capitalists in Europe). The business outlook of this type is progressive, open to modernisation and technological application, but reluctant to enter spheres where a safe minimum return is not guaranteed.

A second entrepreneurial strata can be discerned in the widespread practices of smaller scale intermediation between Jewish (and sometimes big Arab) capital and Arab region consumers and labour. This group is active primarily in commerce and transport, wholesaling on a small scale and retailing, trying to fill in the gaps in distribution linkages within the region and between it and the Jewish economy. It engages as

Industry and Commerce: Workshop Economy & Entrepreneurship

well in regional sub-contracting in industry, through own-production, others' production or providing labour for Jewish capital. This group of entrepreneurs also works in providing labour for export from the region to Jewish concerns outside, alongside Jewish labour contractors and enters financial spheres, engaging in illicit and exploitative usury, drawing on its readily available liquidity.

This strata is defined by the initial absence of its own wealth and its ability to accumulate wealth primarily through exploiting to its advantage the prevailing national-regional relation. Its relation to capital is essentially that of the commission on a certain job or wage. Its relation to labour is one of exploitation on behalf of Jewish capital or facilitating the exploitation of Arab labour's value adding capacity. It might have links with the first entrepreneurial group, in a mediatory role with other entrepreneurs. This group has an aggressive and ambitious view of its potentials, always seeking new ways to make a quick and substantial profit with minimal risk. This is arguably the most parasitic and dependent form of entrepreneurs in the region.

The final typology is that of the smallest scale, usually self-employed (but not necessarily without additional employed labour) entrepreneur in agriculture, industry, construction or commerce. This group includes the individual craftsmen and artisans, small construction contractors, small consumer goods retailers, the constituents of the 'workshop economy', as well as providers of professional, community or private services and the majority of farmers who rely mainly on family and limited wage labour. It is likely that of the 32,000 self-employed members of the Arab labour force in 1984, the bulk (including self-employed farmers) are of this strata.

This type is defined by its minimal initial and subsequent wealth, limited working links with the national economy (except for farmers) and Jewish capital and a consequent dependence on the Arab regional market. Its relation to capital is personal, reproducing it primarily through its own labour, with a minimal extraction of value added by others. Its link with other entrepreneurs is primarily with the second type who occasionally make use of their services or production. The outlook of this group is limited, with little confidence of being able to seriously expand or break out of established production routines, though it is not averse to that possibility were the means to become apparent. It is capable of initiative and development of new skills and techniques but operates under too many constraints to be able to afford the time and financial expense.

Industry and Commerce: Workshop Economy & Entrepreneurship

An Arab Bourgeoisie in Israel?

In a unique field survey of the rise of the 'Arab bourgeoisie' in Israel (see Chapter One), A. Hayder concluded that

> through necessity, family companies were formed which grouped capital that permitted them to enter investment spheres in different sectors. They succeeded in this aspiration to a point whereby the Jewish bourgeoisie attempted, through its desire to absorb this strata, to obtain their participation in different projects, especially in the Arab environment (1986: 5).

Hayder's research points to a number of important results of this process, including the state's success in coopting a section of these strata and the Arab bourgeoisie's ability to use acquired privelages to build its economic base. According to his data, this has been manifested in the emergence of some 300 Arab families into the ranks of Israel's 'large-scale investors', the appearance of another 2,000 Arab families among 'middle-level investors' in Israel, and the existence of some 4,000 Arab academics with 'clear bourgeois aspirations' and who provide an 'ideological cover' for those families *(Ibid)*.

The implications of such results are most interesting, pointing to the rise of a new class of Arab 'economic initiators' (entrepreneurs, family capitalists, bourgeoisie) with a unique position in Israeli society.[9] Though a group with significant links (of differential strength) with Israeli capitalist (and state) interests, their potential for reaping increasing benefits from that system are constrained by extra-economic factors. The extent to which state policy towards the 'Arab question' is capable of effectively integrating such groups will ultimately be a major determinant of the direction of development of this strata's status. Specifically, what is important is whether such a class becomes more a part of the 'Israeli bourgeoisie', with its interests anchored and identified with those of the Jewish state, than as a part of an 'Arab national bourgeoisie' with its own local (and regional) interests and ambitions.

LOCAL AND REGIONAL INSTITUTIONAL INITIATIVE
There also exist three types of local institutions which play a role in regional economic activity. These are cooperative societies, local authorities and various local associations and interest groups. Each suffers from its own problems and weaknesses, and none have explicit strategies for their own development,

much less for that of the region as a whole. Both local authorities and cooperatives are legally and institutionally bound to state and affiliated interests, the Ministry of the Interior and the *Histadrut* respectively. Their sphere of interest is, on the whole, immediate and local, though local authorities do have a coordinating body, the Union of Arab Local Authorities, which attempts to represent its members' interests, though it is not officially recognised by the state as such.

Cooperatives

The local institutions with the greatest interest in economic development are probably the various Arab cooperative societies, though the scope of that interest is very localised. Cooperative societies are all registered with the national cooperative body which is *Histadrut*- affiliated (see, Harari 1974; Harari 1972; Daniel, 1976). Whereas these societies are common in the Jewish sector, they are not as widespread in the Arab region and concentrate on very specific purposes. The wider cooperative structure of commercial, productive and financial services that is taken for granted in the Jewish economy is non-existent in the Arab region. And the regional or sectoral cooperative groupings in the Jewish sector that give these institutions such an influential lobbying power has not been witnessed among Arab cooperatives.

Though accurate up-to-date figures are not available, cross-checking between different sources indicates that there are presently some 200 Arab cooperatives (Weigart 1977; APEF 1983). The vast majority (some 65 percent) provide either drinking or irrigation water to more remote localities. Some 10 percent provide electricity and other infrastructure services account for most of the rest - housing, 7 percent, and transport, 12 percent. There are only a handful of consumer and credit cooperatives and there is a small number of general agricultural and marketing coops. There are few significant examples of successful production cooperatives, in agriculture or elsewhere.

The path of Arab cooperation over the years has been unsure and irregular. A main lesson has been that single purpose coops are more suited to rural Arab communities; the multi-purpose ones almost invariably failed. Factors for success appear to include a minimal degree of mutual confidence among founding members, an urgent local need which only a coop can solve, and the existence of enthusiastic and trained cooperative initiators.

As in most other spheres, state and *Histadrut* aid for coops has been inadequate: the *Histadrut* 'Arab Workers and Farmers

Fund' has never been an effective tool for cooperative finance. Decade after decade, the *Histadrut* and the national cooperative authority pay lip service to the need to develop the Arab region. The Registrar of Cooperatives in 1962 said that Arab coops, "must be fully integrated into the existing appropriate *Histadrut* and financial bodies, centres and funds... Unless this principle is well understood, there is little hope for proper expansion of this movement" (*Ibid:* 32).

In 1977, the Registrar's report was still affirming the need, "to industrialise the Arab village - the order of the day - which should be achieved by pressure exercised by the Arab cooperators on the Government and the *Histadrut,* so that the Arab village will be included in general Israeli industrialisation plans..." (*Ibid:* 33). The *Histadrut* sponsored trends noted above come as a much delayed implementation of these guidelines, motivated much more by national economic prerequisites than the expressed altruistic and enlightened concerns. The minimal success of Arab cooperative efforts to date is essentially the result of local perception of needs and efforts to respond to them, rather than of any significant external encouragement.

Local Authorities

Arab local authorities, though deprived of the resources to cater for the basic infrastructural needs of their inhabitants in education, sanitation, and road building, for example, have a degree of jurisdiction in economic developmental areas. The problems faced by local authorities are considerable and reveal the glaring discrimination against them by the state. These are most pressing in the lack of sufficient infrastructure and the inability to meet the growing demand for water and electricity.

There is a marked lack of school buildings, a shortage estimated in the early-1970s of approximately 3,000 classrooms (Bayadsi 1975). At that time, the investment required to solve the problem amounted to more than the total budgets of all Arab local authorities. The conditions of the old system of unplanned development of Arab towns makes it difficult to convert to modern planning needs. As one commentator has noticed, "a Jewish local authority undertakes the administration of a preplanned settlement, while an Arab local authority administers a community whose development must be begun from scratch" (*Ibid:* 59). The severe crisis in local authorities' capacity to raise local and state finance for such essential services is indicative of their continuing inability to alleviate the pressing demand for

Local authorities' budgets are raised through land and property taxation and rates, taxes on professionals and businessmen, fees for garbage collection, education and services taxation, refunds of part of central government taxes (e.g. property and participation in road maintenance), and statutory grants from various ministries (e.g. Education and Social Welfare). Taxation in Arab communities is almost as high as in Jewish ones, but there is discrimination in the allocation of discretionary government grants. These grants constitute 30 percent of the ordinary budgets of Jewish authorities, but only three percent for Arab ones; local taxes constitute some 14 percent of usual budgets of Jewish local councils and 30 percent of the Arab ones *(Ibid)*.

Clearly, the social and infrastructural problems that are the main concern and jurisdiction of local authorities will remain at the top of their list of priorities for a while to come. This has prompted the establishment of the Union of Arab Local Authorities, (distinct fom the Union of Druze Local Authorites), which between 1985 and 1986 waged a relatively successful campaign for enhanced state aid. This included several strikes, demonstrations and numerous meetings with government officials, followed by promises by the state and a gradual redressing of some grievances. However, most of the points of contention were still outstanding at the end of 1986, revolving around the central issue of differential per-capita state aid to Arab localities, as compared to Jewish towns and settlements.

Despite their representative status, local authorities have only a limited role in regulation of economic affairs (e.g. licensing local business, facilitating industrial zoning). Their inability to raise sufficient funding for adequate social services underlines the doubt that they will ever be able to offer substantial material or technical support for industrial or business activity. However, despite internal weaknesses and central government neglect, Arab local government has developed a role and potential of its own. Arab local authorities continue to have much more in common with each other, in terms of problems, means and outlook, than they do with neighbouring Jewish councils or regional councils which some Arab localities are members of. This indicates both the uniqueness of these institutions (nationally) and their broad 'developmental' potential and role (regionally).

Industry and Commerce: Workshop Economy & Entrepreneurship

Popular Institutions

The final category of institutions involved in the region's development is the range of more informal local or regional interest groups which bring together people of similar professions, areas, religions, or interests. These groups usually together arise in response to a perceived need for popular action in furtherance of a particular cause, be it political, social, economic or other. This category includes groups formed to campaign against land expropriation, for improved living conditions for urban Arabs, for increased employment opportunities for engineering and science graduates, for better health or educational services, for cultural advancement and revitalisation and so forth. It also includes the non-profit societies (formerly Ottoman Associations) which often allow political groups to mobilise support through campaigns on social and economic problems.

These and other bodies (it is difficult in most cases to term them 'institutions') such as the Chamber of Commerce in Nazareth, youth and sports clubs, voluntary work committees and religious committees all play a role in the broader social/institutional building process that cannot be strictly divorced from economic development. They are mostly voluntary bodies with small material resources and organisational capacities. Their primary strength lies in their ability to highlight a serious public need and their success in mobilising popular pressure. In some cases, they embark on economic development projects when the absence of individual entrepreneurship has required broader-based action. In that sense, these collective forms of economic activity also have a certain entrepreneurial element.

THE NEW ARAB BUSINESS SECTOR IN ISRAEL
A field survey of Arab businesses, industries and development projects in 1985 (Khalidi, 1985),[10] covering some 20 existing and planned projects and schemes, sheds further light on the 'entrepreneurial potential' of the Arab economy. The results point to a considerable level of business activity, interest and capability in the Arab areas. Equally significant is the fact that the results highlight the Arab specificity of aspirations and processes that characterise Arab economic activity in Israel.

This supports the argument regarding the Arab areas' 'homogeneity', separateness in certain aspects from the Jewish/national economy and its autonomous economic potential. The micro-level insights these results provide make it important

Industry and Commerce: Workshop Economy & Entrepreneurship

to examine them in greater detail and thereby complete the profile that has so far emerged of Arab business agents and activity in Israel. Overall, the results consolidate and further clarify the analysis undertaken throughout this book, while appearing to indicate a challenging 'way forward' for the Arab economy, issues which are discussed in greater detail in Chapter Six.

Sectoral Links

Several interesting sectoral linkages and overlaps (Industry/Commerce; Commerce/Services) are apparent from the survey results. There is also found to be a larger proportion of new projects than existing or expanding ones. This indicates both an existing sectoral mix as well as the potential for, and interest in, expansion. Though influenced by the method of sample choice and the effect of the geographic parameter in that choice, the geographic distribution of projects highlights the centrality of the 'urban' localities in the region. This is manifested in the prominence of certain towns and centres in the areas of Central and Western Galilee, the north and south Triangle as well as the particular case of the mixed urban localities. These can be seen to constitute the 'poles' of business activity in the region.

The range of types and variety of specialisations and products in the surveyed population is impressive. It indicates both the continuation of more traditional branches and production processes and the presence of innovative and 'progressive' ideas. A most significant aspect is the interest shown in expanding into new fields outside what has thus far characterised Arab economic activity. New projects cited by entrepreneurs include financial consultancy services, valley water drainage, an experimental crop station, low-cost prefabricated housing for Arab urban localities, a sheep cross-breeding station, a houseplant and shrub nursery, commercial/business service centres, a large-scale Arab bread bakery and a tourist hotel/youth hostel venture.

Business Aims and Motivations

Five general types of business aims are apparent from the data, with often more than one applicable to each case. One type is that of practicality, feasibility and a simple 'economic sense' point of view (specified by one entrepreneur in terms of 'investment, high demand, low competititon'). Other aims are characterised by a concern with local and community development and services (e.g. provision of 'local jobs and services'). A third grouping goes a step further and envisages more developmental and integrative or self-sufficiency goals (e.g. 'Arab supply of meat and milk to the region' or, 'advice to Arab investors').

Some proposers are propelled by a type of innovativeness that has a dynamic of its own (e.g. the house plant nursery). And, of course, there is clear strands of values and aims related to profits and income or business achievment (the 'executive' model exemplified by the Kadamani metal works). This trend of diversity and depth in economic aspirations supports the view of the region as a dynamic and yet self-contained unit characterised by many of the usual elements of economic 'viability'.

The range of project sponsors encountered includes individuals, academics, professionals, small and some larger capitalists, community figures, farmers and workers, in addition to state-affiliated individuals and groups. Generational, family and other social bonds also help to encourage various associations. Previous similar experience and an accumulated resource base for expansion also feature as prominent elements characterising Arab business ventures. In most cases, the executor is the same as the proposer. This is not surprising since private motivations and limited experience in such spheres helps determine the range of potential initiators.

Important insights can be gained through examining the motives that proposers ascribe to themselves and their proposed projects. The range of beneficiaries is wide, as has been the case with some other categories. Benefits cover consumers and clients, local communities and workforces, family, partners and investors themselves, in addition to Arab society and its economy as a whole. In some cases the aims are elaborated simply as a way of trying to legitimise or rationalise personal gain, though for most respondants the local service aspect is quite strong and apparently genuine. Respondents' awareness of the significance of stimulating local business and economic activity (linkages to other producers and/or consumers) also implies an appreciation of the need for a fresh and more comprehensive Arab business approach.

Institutional Form, Time Horizon and Finance

Through external participation, family-based enterprises included in the survey are able to obtain further resources and access to facilities, permits, etc., while also making it possible for individual agents to attempt to gain the cooperation of needed and relevant technical and financial sources. It can be seen from this that a significant degree of state and private sector capital linkage (and patronage) is envisaged and considered desirable though not necessarily a prerequisite for implementation (some respondents mention the need to obtain commercial loans, Ministry of Housing or Ministry of Agriculture involvement, agricultural research advice, etc.).

As regards the potential legal status of projects, there are a variety of institutional forms envisaged. Limited or other private companies predominate, with only a small proportion of other associations (such as partnerships, commercial licenses or cooperatives envisaged). This implies both an acquaintance with, and appreciation of, the norms of business activity as well as the existence of the nucleus of a private capitalist sector with possible 'developmental' perspectives.

The time-scale envisaged for the establishment of most projects spans only several years. This allows for a number of implementory stages, from obtaining land, plant, finance, legalisation and permits, to training, establishing marketing frameworks and expansion plans. Some of the projects have recently commenced or are well established enterprises. A number feature assessments and plans that are still fluid and general since finance or other prerequisites are not yet available. There appears, however, to be a good understanding of the steps that any new venture or expansion will require.

Potential sources of personal finance figure prominently in respondents' project planning. In most, the proposer and immediate family or partners are the sources for this type of finance, putting up between 20 percent - 100 percent of total investment. Private finance can also be in the form of cost-sharing schemes or making land available. The central role of informal social relations within the region is clearly apparent here. A number of projects consider state finance to be desirable and possible and mention specific state or public sector sources. These include grants and loans from ministries or banks and other financial facilities such as tax relief. Most of the project proposers who envisage state participation estimate that they might receive less than 50 percent finance from such sources. There is a degree of awareness that obtaining such support is by no means certain.

As with personal finance, the possible role of the wider family is not insignificant, but is actually one of the least mentioned sources of finance. Here also, the range of expected participation is between 10 percent and 50 percent. Non-family based Arab financial sources, while not specified, are considered as a possibility in some cases. This includes those projects which look for a certain level of joint Jewish-Arab private sector involvement. Company and cooperative shares are mentioned in

Industry and Commerce: Workshop Economy & Entrepreneurship

very few cases, while other projects are interested in some form of direct investment.

Only in one case is Jewish finance alone considered a possibility, while in the other cases it figures alongside Arab capital. On the whole, projects which include some level of Jewish (or Arab) private sector involvement also envisage state or family finance. This seems to indicate a general uncertainty both about the possibility of ensuring finance for proposed projects as well as a lack of clarity of the feasibility of obtaining it from the different potential sources.

Capital Investment and Expenses

The survey also provides some information on the cost and variety of plant, including furnishing and facilities, machines and other equipment, land, building costs, start-up raw materials, and in some cases external consultancy. The amount quoted by respondents per project ranges from $25,000 for the most modest project to almost $1.5 million. A degree of caution is needed in assessing the financial data, as estimates involving finance and money are often subject to exaggeration or underestimation. However, checking of figures given against other sources and examinination of the items listed as necessary for various projects, reveals most figures provided to be realistic and more or less accurate. The total minimum sum of required investment for 16 ventures is $8.6 million, a hypothetical average of some $500,000 per project. In most cases, much of the finance is already in place or assured, providing other aspects of project formulation and/or implementation can be ensured.

As regards labour costs (wages, salaries, or consultancy fees), the number of staff actually or potentially employed in surveyed projects ranges from 10 to 170 with the monthly wage per employee ranging from $200 for the lowest paid workers to $1,000 for professionals or consultants. For the 12 projects for which there exists data, the total annual amount required for labour costs comes to $1.9 million or a hypothetical average labour cost of $250 per person employed. In light of data discussed in Chapter Four, this appears to be a realistic reflection of present average wage levels in the region.

Social Benefits and Costs

All proposers hope that their projects will create direct and indirect employment. This covers not only providing work for local inhabitants, Arab professionals and university graduates, but also the improvement of income generation and employment opportunities outside the project itself. The level of awareness, and even concern, in regard to the importance of this benefit, not only reflects the magnitude of the employment problem faced in the region as a whole, but also a sort of 'community or group' identity and spirit. This can also be noticed through several respondents' contention that their projects will provide new skills and production techniques.

In addition to the employment service/benefit, more widespread local services are prominent in almost all projects. An important characteristic is the role of projects in stimulating Arab economic growth, locally and regionally, on both the demand and supply sides. The 'service' to consumers, through making new or improved quality products more easily available, is also mentioned frequently. Economic linkages, inter- and intra-sectoral, are viewed as equally important. Other interesting benefits cited are housing for young couples and providing opportunities for local female employment.

As would be expected, profits are mentioned in almost all cases, though the level and use to which they could be put are not similar. In most situations, profits are hoped for, but it is clear that respondents are aware that profit levels are dependent on performance and success in business. The uncertainty of this, and the restrictions on obtaining finance mean that projects cannot expect profits to be high or available for immediate reinvestment.

The implicit value of introducing new or improved products is most noticeable. From projects producing new economic services, to new agricultural varieties, and to a range of new consumer goods, Arab economic initiators exhibit traits that could loosely be termed 'entrepreneurship'. While not all the products mentioned are necessarily feasible or well market surveyed, most appear upon examination to be promising as innovative ideas and to make simple business sense. The importance of providing the Arab population with certain needs or outputs only available in the national/Jewish sector is highlighted by several respondents. As mentioned above in relation to employment, most projects can also be examined from the perspective of the creation and expansion of the range of skills available to the community and the provision of opportunities for new vocational school graduates. As well, the absorbtion of unskilled workers at a first stage and providing on-site training is mentioned several times.

Other 'positive' aspects mentioned by interviewees add to the general economic and social services role of such projects. In two cases relatively sophisticated developmental goals, such as 'local centralisation of supply points' and even the more general 'local development pole', are among respondents' concerns and aspirations. Data on respondents' awareness of possible negative aspects and effects of their projects is most interesting. The concern, for example, about the possibility of squeezing smaller individual farmers, owners or businesses is explicit in a number of projects. This sense of 'social responsibility' is natural in the relatively close and traditional family environment of the region. It also exhibits a degree of thought and evaluation on the part of respondents regarding the complexities and calculations that must necessarily surround the implementation of a serious business venture.

The answers to questions regarding possible technical problems, group together both obvious and more specific problems. These include the technical problems of ensuring land or location, finance, and market penetration, as well as state or political harassment. Most of these problems do not, in themselves, constitute a sufficient obstacle to actually prevent project implementation. But their solution is in most cases not directly in the hands of the project proposers. As with the previous category, the data on this subject indicates a high level of understanding by those most concerned with the real and potential problems they face in trying to grow.

There are several problems mentioned that can be directly ascribed to the local or regional level. The problems mentioned are a low level of popular appreciation of the need for specific projects, possible objections to the placement of another project and the possibility in another case of local political hostility. The sphere which constitutes the greatest potential obstacle to initiation of most projects and is most regularly referred to is the complicated one of obtaining approval and legalisation. Industrial zone planning, licenses, ministry approval and political harassment are all areas where Arab development efforts can easily founder. The room for manouevre here is extremely limited, and the best that initiators can hope for is that safeguards and contingency plans can be well-elaborated to help ensure the successful implementation of projects.

These results bring us back to the general theme that has run through much of our analysis of the Arab economy, namely, that a central determinant of the scope and nature of activity has been official policy and the local leverage for counteracting it. It is true that recent years have witnessed the emergence and consolidation of a variety of dynamic forms of Arab business and commercial activity. These, however, are increasingly facing the hard choice of whether to allow further expansion of their capital in a subservient 'integrated' pattern with national interests, or stagnate within the limited boundaries of the local eonomy and, at best, achieve marginal improvements.

Given the structural limits to regional economic growth, the traditional role of intermediation by Arab venture capital between the national and regional economies is no longer as attractive or lucrative an option as it was in the past. The barriers inherent to Israeli Jewish official and public attitudes towards the Arab economy have constrained Arab capital's 'natural' expansion into the national economy (as argued in Hayder, 1986). Notwithstanding the strong endogenous potential for development exhibited in most sectors, as shall be discussed in Chapter Six, the continued operation of state policy towards the region appear as the major factor shaping its future growth prospects.

NOTES

1. This is a more obvious and recent example of the political interpretation of Zionist political economy's thesis of the 'modernisation process'. This viewpoint also exhibits features of underlying Zionist attitudes to Palestinian Arabs and their 'underdevelopment', as discussed in Chapter One.

2. It should perhaps be mentioned that this especially blatant view was expressed by a somewhat controversial figure, namely Ariel Sharon, in his capacity as Minister of Trade and Industry during the period of Shimon Peres' leadership of the National Unity coalition government. Nevertheless, it constitutes a fairly accurate representation of much official attitude.

3. It remains to be seen, however, whether these and similar developments witnessed in the mid-1980s will go down in history as a 'golden era' of enlightened rule, under Ezer Weizmann, minister with special responsibility for Arab affairs and his aide, Yosef Ginat, working with the blessings of the then Prime Minister, Shimon Peres.

4. These include the two mentioned surveys, historical accounts, statistical data and other evaluations. However, the overall weight of this sector of the Arab economy within the national economy is not such as to merit any separate mention or reference in standard official statistical series produced by the Israel Central Bureau of Statistics. Their inclusion in the future, perhaps as a result of further developments in that sector, would provide a valuable source of further information.

5. The *Histadrut* sponsored survey (in Czamanski *et al.* 1984) and national statistics (in Israel 1984).

6. See Appendix 1 for a summary of survey coverage and methodology.

7. It has not been possible to benefit from the most interesting work recently concluded on industrialisation and entrepreneurship in the Arab region by D. Czamanski and M. Meyer Brodnitz (1984). In their contribution to a forthcoming book on rural industrialisation in Israel, they have analysed the *Hevrat Ovdim* data on industrialisation, in light of past state development efforts and relevant theories of entrepreneurship. As an initial comment on this work, I draw readers attention to the discussion of Zionist political economy in Chapter One. A published analysis of the significance of the

Industry and Commerce: Workshop Economy & Entrepreneurship

results of this research, from an interesting Arab viewpoint, is that in (Khmaysi 1985).

8. It is interesting to note that the seven-man Board of Directors of this bank has three Arab members, and the Chairman of the Board is always a Jewish nominee of the parent bank.

9. As Hayder's research has only been available in summary form, a fair evaluation of his results is not possible. There are clear differences between his work and the present study in terms of methodology and survey scope, though his results point in a similar direction as my own. However, Hayder seems to have resorted to a 'class analysis', and his quantitative results and their implications for the degree of Arab 'bourgeoisification' in Israel differ somewhat from those reached here. Hayder's work also focusses on the political manifestations of the rise of the Arab bourgeoisie, linking its rise to that of the Progressive National List, an Arab-Jewish movement that recently challenged both traditional Zionist and Israeli Communist Party hegemony over Arab society and political life. He also argues that this movement has 'mediated' between the Arab bourgeoisie and the state, something that is by no means self-evident.

10. As will be noticed below, results are not reported here in strict quantative terms, as the survey was aimed more at discerning broad trends on the basis of a structured sample of case studies. It does not seem necessary in most discussions of the results to indicate totals and percentages, as statistical accuracy was not a central concern of this survey. For details of the coverage and methodology of this survey, see Appendix 1.

Six

REGIONAL GROWTH PATTERNS AND THE FUTURE OF THE ARAB ECONOMY IN ISRAEL

DEVELOPMENT, IMPROVEMENT OR STAGNATION OF THE ARAB ECONOMY?

Ultimately, the validity of a regional development theory and the success of any regional planning strategy depends on the assumptions about the development process which informs it. *If the developmental assumptions are weak, the regional theory will be weak* (Gore 1984: 171).

As relevant as is Gore's observation to any application of regional economic analysis, it holds special importance in the context of our study of the Arab economy in Israel. Because of the particularly complex nature of the parameters which have been seen to define and characterise that economy, the 'regional identity' of the Arab economy remains an elusive and indefinite feature. This is not only due to the unconventional nature of the Arab region - arising from the geo-demographic, administrative and functional aspects of the Arab economy which are defined officially and otherwise in non-regional terms by observers and policy makers alike.

A greater obstacle to the emergence and acceptance of a regional definition of the Arab economy, to a regional path for Arab development, and to any Arab development for that matter, is the maintenance of official policy which explicitly or actively mitigates against 'Arab development' in Israel. It is perhaps self-evident that without serious political change in Israeli attitudes towards, and measures in dealing with, Palestinian Arabs in Israel, any discussion of the development prospects of the Arab economy becomes spurious and irrelevant. The preceding chapters have exhibited how state policy blocks Arab development, both consciously and through the exclusionary arrangements which characterise the institutional framework of economic activity.

This not only constitutes a barrier to the elaboration of the form and content of the Arab region, but also appears to render hypothetical any serious discussion of regional growth patterns with reference to the Arab economy in Israel. Thus, while regional theory suffers from its own internal conflicts and deficiences, doubt is also cast on its applicability in the present case. This is especially problematic when it comes to employing regional development theory in trying to structure the crucial discussion of the prospects for the Arab economy in Israel. The usual models of regional growth, potential strategies for local/regional development, and mechanisms for economic growth promotion which might be desirable, or apparently feasible in a case such as this, seem to be ruled out *a priori* by the operation of Zionist policy towards the Arab economy.

It is true, as was observed (in Chapter Two), that Zionism's attitudes towards the 'Arab question' have evolved over time, and that government policy has shown a growing, though clearly insufficient, appreciation of the need to address the issues of Arab development. Yet, such positive developments, however necessary and welcome, remain essentially palliative and incapable of structurally transforming and developing, the conditions and dynamics of Arab economic activity in Israel. Indeed, it might be argued that in light of past policy and given the limited potential for future change, the best that can be hoped and planned for with regard to the Arab economy is an *amelioration* of existing conditions, perhaps along the lines of the 'improvement in the quality of life' policies advocated by some for the West Bank and Gaza Strip under Israeli occupation.[1]

WHAT ROLE FOR REGIONAL ANALYSIS?

Such a dead-end to our analysis need not, however, be the only result of a realistic appraisal of the political climate which has characterised the national-regional relation to date and which is likely to continue to prevail (barring radical transformations of Zionism and within Israeli Jewish society). Just as Zionist colonisation in Palestine before 1948 and the occupied West Bank and Gaza Strip since 1967, created 'facts' which forced themselves onto the geo-political map of the Middle East as a whole, so is Arab demographic growth, Palestinian political mobilisation and the continuing consolidation and expansion of a distinctly Arab economy in Israel, creating a very different set of 'facts' in Israel that remain to be addressed. These phenomena have been recognised by more extreme Zionist forces as a 'threat', by pragmatic Israelis as a cause for renewed efforts to 'coopt' the Arab population and its elites within the Zionist establishment, by sympathetic liberal or non-Zionist circles as encouraging signs, and by the Arab population itself as a source of increasing identity, strength and self-confidence.

The present approach recognises the emergence of the Arab region in Israel as all of these and more. Specifically, it aims to institute and systemise a frame of reference for future analysis and action, namely that of an Arab regional economy. This is not simply a function of the analysis itself: the acceptance of the usefulness of regional analysis in diagnosing the operation of the Arab economy is not, *per se*, a reason for exploring future prospects in the same terms. Here, however, the regional approach serves two functions, on two different levels.

On the one hand, charting potential paths and tools for Arab regional development in Israel provides a guide, a reference point, against which to evaluate actual policies and pinpoint their deficiencies. The aim is not to provide a 'blueprint' for a 'model' development path that is anyhow unlikely to emerge in existing political circumstances. However, given the validity of the concept of the Arab region, it is necessary and useful to examine how *prescriptive* regional development analysis can contribute to marginal *improvements* and/or overall *development* of the Arab economy. On this level, an Arab regional development policy can constitute a technically (developmentally) feasible and desirable programme for those liberal or non-Zionist Israelis who have recognised the need for radical change in the position of Arabs in Israel. It can also act as a focal point for those Palestinian Arabs in positions of local economic or political power who believe that change can be achieved and demands met within the present environment.

At the same time, an awareness of the political contradiction inherent in the very idea of *Arab economic development* in a *Jewish state* leads to the derivation of a different benefit from an examination of regional development theory in the present case. On this level, models, strategies and mechanisms are of interest and use to the extent that they can be adopted and absorbed, partially and not comprehensively, by a population whose developmental prospects are dim. Accordingly, some of the underpinnings of a regional analysis can be understood and advocated in terms of a method towards the survival (or 'steadfastness' - *sumud*) of an Arab economy (regional or other) in an essentially hostile environment. Regional development thus becomes a plank of 'struggle' (along the lines proposed by

Rosenfeld, Makhoul or Zureik) for Arab-Jewish equality in Israel. In both this and the preceding case, narrowing differentials, improving the overall position of Arabs in Israel, and establishing a base for future development are feasible, realistic and operative concepts for action to be deduced from regional analysis.

ALTERNATIVE DIRECTIONS
The Arab regional economy has been seen to have a dynamic relationship with the national economy. Despite the particular political circumstances operative here, and the technical arguments (geographic, administrative, economic) against considering it so, it has been argued that the Arab region in Israel is a reality - born of utility and necessity - which should be dealt with as such in economic analysis of Arabs in Israel.

Yet the future prospects of the Arab region in Israel cannot be clearly distinguished. The region has a range of features which have been seen to act as barriers and incentives to growth. This was noticed, for example, in the manner that policies which have hindered agricultural or industrial enterprise, have often led to increased attachment to the land and agriculture or to innovative and fruitful forms of business activity. Similarly, though certain aspects of Arab society have been the source of divisions and rivalries, their exploitation and crude manipulation by the state has also led to consolidation of a distinctly Arab social structure. The situation is fluid both regionally and nationally, and the dichotomous operation of these barriers and incentives has contributed over the years to the establishment of an unbalanced and unequal regional-national relation. Consequently, their dissolution or weakening can reverse existing patterns and trends.

There are a number of specific developments which could decrease regional/national divergences: a change in state resource distribution; an alleviation of political grievances that have provided a focus for crystallisation of a Palestinian Arab identity; continued convergence of demographic trends; or the breakdown of patterns of geographic and residential segregation, either through the Arab population spilling over into Jewish areas, or through successful 'Judaisation of the Galilee'. Most of these, admittedly, are not immediate prospects.

On another level, increased Arab agricultural innovation, more aggressive and innovative entrepreneurship, or the beginnings of significant Arab private capital accumulation and investment would lead to a more pronounced Arab regional profile, regardless of any political change (or lack thereof). This would encourage a greater homogeneity of sources and modes of production, consumption and income, greater localisation of economic activity and a consistent, systematic and institutionalised pattern of response to external factors, especially state policy. Such factors could combine, even in the absence of policy changes, to provide a basis for an internally generated dynamic of a regional economic development pattern.

As already noted, a radical legal and political transformation of Israel is not likely; and without it the liberal economic policy necessary for the region to flourish is impossible. The effect of the various barriers to an autonomous development of the region remain formidable and the degree to which patterns of integration and subservience are entrenched is a measure of the success of national policy towards the region. Under these conditions, the Arab region is likely to maintain its present path - a distorted reflection of national patterns and prerequisites - a sort of 'growth without development'.

Regional analysis offers several paradigms for examining patterns of development and planning for the future. Of course, their use as planning guidelines is predicated on the adoption by the central national authorities of some premise of the existence, functioning and special requirements of a region. Three notional models are discussed below, not to see to what degree they approximate the realities of the Arab region in Israel, but to examine whether the dynamics they represent could provide a framework for a future more equitable and efficient development of the Arab region. That is to say, we are interested in whether the conceptualisation of the Arab economy in regional terms, and an exploration of regional growth models can help in the elaboration of effective solutions to very real problems.

While the requisite political transformations for such solutions might be a concern of economic analysis, such transformation cannot be its aim *per se*. The main task here remains that of further clarifying and exposing a specific situation, thereby helping to 'clear the way' for future solutions. The issue of how this might be achieved is ultimately a matter which will be most deeply influenced by the course of macro-economic developments in Israel. Yet, the inhabitants of the region can also have a role in consciously determining that path. As long as the complicated process of elaborating a regional (or even Arab) development policy remains the prerequisite of the state, it is unlikely that the Arab population of Israel will be able to exercise a concerted or determining influence upon such policy.

On the other hand, in recent years regional (Arab) institutions have been created, weak local economic power centres have emerged and alongside them capitalists with a minimal 'regional outlook'. This in itself constitutes a basis for the generation of low-level policy formulation and planning (the process of *development from below).* Additionally, the 'integrative' influence of relations with the national economy and state is by no means the sole, or dominant, one operative in the modern Arab economy. Greater homogenisation of certain modes of production and consumption, specialisation, isolation and self-subsistent economic activity can be seen throughout the regional economy.

The demonstrated validity of the methodological and theoretical underpinnings of regional analysis, and certain relevant political and economic developments outlined above, render a discussion of regional growth patterns worthwhile and timely. The following characterisations are advanced in order to provide an initial idea of the form of growth in the Arab region and certain future directions it could take. From this starting point it is possible to better evaluate the roles and influences of different Arab socio-economic and business strata in the elaboration of an Arab development strategy in Israel. Ultimately, whether this is a 'regional' or other pattern of growth is not of great importance. What counts above all is that the need for encouraging, or at least laying the bases for, some measure of development be clearly recognised by those concerned, Palestinian Arabs and Jewish Israelis alike, so as to propel the issue from the realm of analysis and discussion into the arena of development.

GROWTH MODELS FOR ARAB REGIONAL DEVELOPMENT

There is a rich regional economic literature and the debate within the discipline is often fierce, as the theories surrounding regional economics undergo continuous transformation. This is an outcome of an interplay of spatial, political, and of course economic, factors which is inherent in the very idea of regional development, and intrinsic to the debate itself. The issues thus raised constitute a potential minefield for researchers whose interest in regional theory is motivated overwhelmingly by methodological considerations. Our analysis focussed upon the regional concept as a way of crystallising otherwise disjointed observations and empirical findings into a coherent and systematic understanding of a controversial issue.

This neither means that such an approach is exclusive of others, nor that it should constitute the optimal basis for envisaging the future of the Arab economy in Israel. Accordingly, we do not need to be bound by regional theory's prescriptions nor need we be overly concerned with its intricacies and the problems surrounding its viability in general and in the present application.[2] Its utility, as well as the limits of its relevance in the case of the Arab economy in Israel have already been sufficiently expounded.

Thus, a representative, though by no means definitive, characterisation of the major trends in regional growth theory can be adopted here suitable to the specific illustrative purposes with which we are concerned.[3]

Growth pole oriented models envisage a region constituted by a major town with a loosely defined hinterland. With a concentration of economic activity and population, the town is linked to a metropolitan centre outside the region. It is characterised by economies of scale and agglomeration rooted in centralised production-distribution-production linkages. These make the growth pole the focus for self-reinforcing growth and the most efficient location for regional non-farm investment.

Development is achieved mainly through production for trade outside the region (the exchange economy). A thriving new industry in the growth pole spreads benefits throughout the region via market mechanisms which link the pole to the hinterland. Ultimately, regional development is seen to depend on the prosperity of growth pole located enterprises. The planning that is needed to ensure regional development is that which ensures a favourable infrastructure and the location of growth industries in the pole.

Functional integration models see the region as a network of different sub-regional poles: farms clustered around villages, villages around market towns and so forth. Different economic activities are located optimally in the region according to regional efficiency considerations. This encourages an integration of different sub-areas' absolute and comparative advantages in such a way as to maximise overall regional prosperity. As with growth poles, development comes through production for the exchange economy, while benefits also accrue from production for local use.

Such models view the *de facto* distribution of population and economic activities as the rationale for making that distribution work for the benefit of the region as a whole through a functional intra-regional integration. Investment priorities may therefore be different from those which would prevail if micro-profitability was the sole concern. Planning is disaggregative, from the regional to sub-regional levels, with a high level of intra-regional coordination.

Decentralised territorrial integration models consider the region as a loosely connected collection of sub-areas. The use economy of each area and the region are emphasised. Development is defined in terms of self-sufficiency rather than trade. Investment encourages small scale production for local markets and selective linkages to the other sub-areas and the national economy. Local participation in investment is desirable and regional planning is decentralised and aggregative - regional goals arise through aggregating sub-regional goals. In order to maintain the self-sufficiency implied in this model, investment to develop local planning and manpower capacity should proceed at the same pace as direct local productive investment. The regional economy should have a degree of leverage nationally so as to be able to establish trade preferences and/or barriers.

As with most models, these assume some pattern of explicit and rational economic development, planning, and organisation of production and distribution. Quite simply, this situation does not prevail in the Arab region. It is not recognised nationally as a region *per se;* nor has any local or national initiative been taken to plan or organise development in or for the region. Even an assumption of 'economic growth of the Arab region', measured in terms of capital/output ratios, productivity rates or domestic or regional product, is not altogether tenable. Conventional economic analysis does not always easily adapt to this economy. Nevertheless, the Arab region today can be seen to resemble a somewhat haphazard synthesis of these models. It combines functional integration without a rational pattern of integration, the growth pole pattern without significant growth (except perhaps in terms of private consumption), and a decentralised territorial pattern without special emphasis on local use or self-sufficency.

The four towns of Nazareth, Shefa'amr, Umm al-Fahm and Taibeh are the major regional locations of concentrated economic activity and population, with a relatively advanced infrastructure (electricity, water, roads) and regional production and marketing centres. The region produces mainly for exchange, partially through these towns, but with a degree of local use and direct regional-national trade. Investment is dispersed geographically, with a certain concentration in these poles - however, considerations of efficiency or profitability often draw local and national investment to other points in the region, if not altogether outside it. External and internal linkages are active and diverse, though not with a definitive function, except perhaps in response to external (national) determinants or to exploit the advantages of geographic proximity and family or other social relations.

Any further attempt at this point at defining the Arab region in terms of the above models is unnecessary. Suffice it to say that the deviations of the actual picture from that implied by the notional models exhibits more than anything else how the peculiar position of the Arab region results in a distortion of more standard patterns of economic development.[4] The reference point of other development experience is useful and necessary in the present analysis. It enables us to turn economic analysis into developmental analysis, and identify the aims, components, and mechanisms necessary for advancing a regional Arab strategy in Israel. Understanding the deviations from 'normal' development patterns which arise from the particular operation of policy and ideology in the Jewish state is a first step to elaborating methods for effectively confronting that policy and its debilitating effects on the Arab region.

This is done in the following sections through examining how different policies, socio-economic goals, and economic and agents and business initiators can combine within an Arab regional development effort in Israel. Specifically, we investigate the prerequisites of integrating the principles of self-reliant development, small business (and/or entrepreneurial) promotion, 'participatory development' projects into Arab regional programmes. This helps to broaden the horizons for conceptualisation of a future for the Arab economy in Israel, while offering positive, relevant and feasible propositions to stimulate thought and action.

HARNESSING ARAB PRIVATE BUSINESS GOALS TO REGIONAL DEVELOPMENT

Chapter Five highlighted an important series of events and trends related to multi-sectoral Arab small business development. The recent emergence of new forms of Arab entrepreneurism embodies important experiences and local economic achievements, which cannot be ignored by any development/growth promotion efforts for the Arab region. How, therefore, can entrepreneurial encouragement and a policy for growth of (and at least protection for) small business can fit into a regional development strategy?[5]

Different economic systems hinder or encourage entrepreneurship to differing degrees, and in some it is redundant (see, Kirzner 1980: 17-25). For example, it is not possible to assume that in a centrally planned economy (where the private entrepreneurial function is absent and prices are a fixed parameter), the function of price can be simulated. This function depends greatly on entrepreneurial discovery of new openings for pure profit. A free market, on the other hand, is characterised by freedom of entrepreneurial entry. The unexploited opportunities for reallocation of resources from a low market valued use to another of higher value offer the opportunity for entrepreneurial gain. A misallocation of resources is assumed to occur when market participants do not notice the opportunity of a price discrepancy. This tendency is one of the most impressive aspects of the market system.

In a regulated market economy, well exemplified by Israel, and especially by the Arab economy, there remains genuine, but inhibited, entrepreneur incentive: government regulation of prices and resource allocation tends to be a process in which knowledge and discovery are absent. Much of regulation consists in creating barriers to entry. Such barriers may, by removing the personal gain which entrepreneurs might have reaped by their discoveries, mean that some opportunities are not discovered by anyone.

It is in this direction that the Israeli economy has dealt with Arab entrepreneurship; it is not therefore surprising that barriers have resulted, mostly devised specifically to restrict free Arab economic activity, with unfettered 'entrepreneurial discovery' remaining basically the prerogative of the Jewish sector. However, it is equally likely that with the flourishing Israeli black market economy and the informal sector in which Arabs are very active, regulations and barriers might paradoxically be an incentive to 'entrepreneurial discovery'. Their continued operation could encourage an even greater degree of the 'resourcefulness' that has characterised much of recent Arab experience in agriculture and small industry and business.

One observer (Watkins 1976) has noticed that the aim from the regional standpoint is not simply to encourage entrepreneurship, but to encourage it in those sectors which can expect above average growth. The problem that emerges is that when such a sector has been identified, concentrations of enterprises have already been built on a localised basis. These develop strong linkages on both the input and output sides and with the providers of professional services to the emergent industries. In addition, new firms are likely to develop in that locality through 'spin-off' or emulation. Firms which can be mobile consider moving to that area to take advantage of the developing linkages, thereby reinforcing them.

This 'natural' market mechanism has been one of the problems encountered by Israeli (Jewish) regional development programmes and can also be seen in patterns of Arab business initiation (see, Czamanski and Meyer Brodnitz 1984; Khmaysi 1985). Similarly, in a relevant non-Israeli case-study (Watkins 1976: 27), almost all entrepreneurs located their businesses within close commuting distance of their homes. It appeared in fact that most new businesses were formed within the industry in which the entrepreneur was previously employed, or utilising the skills for which he was employed.

Though a regional development effort's task is usually to strengthen local enterprise and attract external entrepreneurs, this latter course is one that would have to be handled very carefully in planning for the Arab region. From a simplistic 'autonomist' or populist developmental viewpoint, it would seem preferable to encourage indigenous entrepreneurship rather than attempt to attract firms from outside the region. But Israeli public and private capital is already deployed within the Arab region, and this is not likely to diminish. The only recent discouragement to that deployment has been the effects of the present economic crisis on national firms with regional subsidiaries. Therefore, if only in light of existing conditions, any Arab development effort would have to accomodate Israeli public and private capital. At the same time mechanisms are needed to ensure that external capital is directed to locally based/initiated investments which are not harmful to local resources and growth potential.

Whatever the source of investment, and within whichever context it is deployed, an Arab regional agency is vital to the successful implementation of a development strategy. As elsewhere (including Israel), it would have to undertake several specific roles (*Ibid*). At the first stages of the business initiation process it would identify and publicise skill deficits within the region and link up successful regional entrepreneurs possessing complementary skills. At a later point, the specific product/market or service/market analysis must be elaborated as the prospective entrepreneur becomes less mobile with the growth of linkages. Indigenous entrepreneurs need to be further bound to the region through the creation of 'instant' linkages - introductions to banks, accountants, customers, suppliers, etc. At a later stage, time and money need to be invested in evaluating and testing the market.

There are no indications that the Israeli state will provide such an agency for the benefit of the Arab region or of its entrepreneurs. Nevertheless, it is worth understanding the functions that should exist so that it can be seen that the task is neither very daunting, costly or even subversive. Indeed, an effort of this sort, especially if involving official resources, would probably go further than anything else has towards dealing with the 'Arab problem in Israel', at least as conceived by the state. However, the inhabitants of the Arab region also have interests which they are increasingly recognising as vital, and are thus responding to the continued absence of centrally guided efforts in various ways. This in itself is an encouraging sign of a potential for 'self-development'; here also, regional strategies can contribute.

In addition to basic capitalist motives, Arab responses and initiatives arise from strands of more broadly based, communal and/or cooperative aims and forms. Aspects of these reflect two well-established components of third world development experience and theory, namely *self reliant development* and *participatory development*. Both easily adapt to a regional framework and have been pronounced aspects of Arab rural and agricultural survival in Israel, as noticed in Chapter Three, as well as other sectors of the economy. When integrated with business promotion policies, they can constitute a viable and relevant component of efforts to ameliorate conditions experienced by the Arab economy, especially those which might be undertaken in present circumstances.

FROM SELF RELIANCE TO PARTICIPATORY DEVELOPMENT

The preceding discussion highlighted private, if not individualist, levels of economic growth promotion. It raised the possibility that a private sector capitalist path could be desirable for the Arab region. It might appear that somehow, the aims and content of 'development' became lost in the emphasis upon growth and economic intiative. However, it should not be forgotten that we are discussing first and foremost the development of the Arab region as a whole. None of its component areas, its constituent population groups, or its diverse economic or social formations has more rights than another to the benefits of its growth.

Just how resources and benefits might be evenly or fairly distributed is another issue, more the object of political activity than economic analysis. This is not to say that economic progress cannot or should not be channelled in such a direction that increases the chances for the widest possible spread of its benefits, especially to those who 'create wealth'. However, it must be realised as well that if there is no economic growth at all, there will be no benefits, or at least they will be so narrowly available that only one small section of society will be able to receive them, somewhat as the situation has been until now. In the present circumstances, the question that arises is just how growth and its agents can be encouraged so as to include among its beneficiaries a wider population than only those who devise or take initiatives.

Given the constraints that have been analysed in this book, a development effort cannot afford to exclude those elements that have to date proven their economic and business abilities. Thus our interest in entrepreneurship covers both its specific and broader contexts. Nor can the wider population, the prime intended beneficiaries of Arab regional growth, be excluded from action and determination of the course of development - therefore the following discussion of participatory development projects. Economic growth promotion cannot determine the nature of any consequent political, or even economic, configuration. But it can give those without the resources greater ability to obtain them, while directing those with the resources into their more beneficial deployment.[6]

A strategic framework applicable here and which can further these aims is that of so-called 'self reliant development'. Though usually elaborated as a national strategy, its potential relevance as a set of principles for a regional strategy is not difficult to perceive. It is interesting to examine in detail a representative statement of what is meant by 'self reliance'.[7] Simply substitute 'regional' for 'national' and 'national' for 'international', and self reliance acquires an interesting correspondence to the sort of path aimed at here:

> Self reliance often takes the form of an exhortation, to be understood in light of the harsh realities which prompt it. It indicates the strong motivation of developing countries to use the concept of 'liberation' to provide at least a part of the emotional force to bring about needed socio-economic and political change while also reflecting a determination to eliminate poverty and oppression. Operationally, self reliance has been defined at the national level as the will to build up the capacity for autonomous decision-making and implementation on all aspects of the development process. The content, direction and pace of social and economic change has to be defined and executed with reference to national needs and aspirations.
>
> This approach to self reliance is reflected internationally as opposition to dependence and changing the mode of incorporation of the developing countries in the international system. Developing countries have to recapture and internalise the centres of decision making on their destiny. Self reliance is not to be equated with economic nationalism, autarky or self-sufficiency. It does not imply a lessening of interest in international economic relations but a desire to instill them with a sense of interdependence and economic justice. Further, self reliance is a component of alternative strategies or modes of development which are directed at satisfaction of basic needs of the entire population as the primary development objective.

Balanced progress towards desired development objectives may call for trade-offs between the extent of self reliance attainable in each field. It is important to ensure that these are made in such a way as the content and direction of development remains under national control. Self reliance cannot be achieved within monolithic structures, but involves choices and decisions at different levels - individual, village, district, province and country, leading to the 'collective self reliance' of developing countries as a whole.

Participatory institutions and social processes at all these levels are essential for self reliant development. Self reliant strategies emphasise the need to evolve technological styles suited to local environment, resource endowment and basic needs. This is the so-called 'walking on many legs' - the rural and the urban, the small scale and the large scale, labour intensive and capital intensive, technically sophisticated and unsophisticated. This leads us to the next link in our chain of Arab regional development in Israel, namely participatory development efforts.

PARTICIPATORY DEVELOPMENT IN REGIONAL STRATEGIES

It should again be emphasised that there is not necessarily a sole *correct* development strategy for the Arab region, if indeed any *strategy* can be considered feasible in a politically hostile, and at best indifferent, environment. However, if popular participation is assumed to enhance the quality of development, can its encouragement then provide a basis for efforts and projects destined to bolster the position of the Arab region and lay bases for its future development?

The range of regional development theory is much wider than even that: from the original growth pole strategy to those of polarised development, the dualist models, the centre-periphery 'development of underdevelopment' and the variety of neo-populist strategies. Naturally, there are sharp disagreements about how the geographical pattern of development in the poorer countries of the world may be explained and about how a more desirable pattern may be engineered through planning intervention.[8] The same could be said about the case of the Arab region, except that the analysis of why conditions are as they are is clearer and simpler; and effectively, the options for intervention are so limited, that there is not much room for disagreement.

However, there is an interesting strand of regional development thought which combines regional development objectives with possibilities for popular participation. 'Territorial regional planning' and 'development from below' are the alternatives to the approaches referred to as 'functional regional planning' and 'development from above'.[9] Functional planning is concerned with the location of economic activities and the spatial organisation of an urban system. It relies heavily on mathematical models such as input-output analysis and emphasises efficiency, while policy decisions are usually made outside the regions which are affected by them, in a few centres of power. The urban industrial growth pole policy is an example of the functional approach.

The alternative, 'territorial regional planning', is argued to offer a better approach to the task of promoting regional development and aims for an integrated mobilisation of human and natural resources of specifically defined regions. It is an 'endogenous' activity conducted within the regions where its decisions take effect. It engages the people of that region within the planning process, which necessarily becomes a political process, emphasising equity through seeking an improvement of the quality of living for all the people in the area.

Another description of this paradigm is between 'development from above' and 'development from below'. The former conforms to functional planning, following what is described as a 'top-down centre-outwards' approach. This equates development with economic growth, emphasises urban and industrial capital-intensive investment, maximum use of internal and external economies of scale, large scale projects and the latest technologies. Here, the trickledown effects of growth pole strategies originating in a few sectoral or geographic clusters generate development.

'Development from below', in contrast, rests upon what is described as a 'bottom-up periphery-inward' approach. Here, development is defined as an integral process of widening opportunities for individuals, social groups, and territorial communities at small and intermediate scale, mobilising the full range of their capabilities and resources for the common benefit. Economic efficiency criteria are not ruled out. But, instead of maximising the return of selected production factors, the objective is to increase the overall efficiency of all production factors of the region in an integrated manner, such that the population of the region broadly benefits.

This approach envisages a greater degree of self determination for regions such that they are free to decide their own development path, to the extent of instituting selective spatial closure of the region as a means of enhancing the possibility of self-reliant development. Both territorial regional planning and development from below draw their strength from a perceived failure of strategies of accelerated industrialisation. They both attempt to apply 'neo-populist' ideas within a regional context: reversing 'urban bias', promoting greater equality, satisfying 'basic needs' of the majority of the population, re-establishing local communities and avoiding centralisation of decision making.

The two alternatives to functional planning outlined here could fit well into the sort of path needed for the promotion of Arab economic growth and development in Israel. By broadening the concept of popular participation to include community institutions and entrepreneurs, a working link can be established between self-reliance, participation and regional development strategies. It must re-emphasised that the real possibilities for the elaboration of such an integrated approach remain largely dependent upon the likelihood of official Israeli political acquiescence towards such measures. However, as crucial a factor is the local need and willingness to embark upon those challenging initiatives that must emanate from within the regional economy if growth and development are to occur. It is this activation of the Arab economy's internal dynamics which can open horizons - create facts - that in themselves transform the perspectives, the realm of the possible, of that economy.

COMBINING POLICIES AND MECHANISMS TO BRIDGE THE ARAB-JEWISH DEVELOPMENT GAP IN ISRAEL

Clearly, the policies set out above require local mechanisms to achieve them. The nature of these aims to a great extent determines the appropriate institutional forms for their implementation: individual small or large scale forms of business association and services, integrated elements of an industrial and agro-industrial production process, and broader based cooperation efforts between farmers or other producers.

This interdependence and integration of aims and means is not coincidental. In fact, it is our contention that only such an approach can maximise the possibilities for desirable results. Otherwise, the potential benefits of development funding could be misinformed or misdirected, easily dissipated, reach too few or even unworthy recipients, and fail to lead to significant development. A favourable return upon an investment does not in itself have any intrinsic developmental content. If *growth* in one sectoror region is not part of an interdependent *process* that includes a qualitative *change*, there is no basis for considering it to be developmental. These three terms together are essential.

Once this interdependence of established goals, private sector entrepreneurship and popular participation in projects is accepted, then the question arises as to the degree of compatability between the encouragement of individual entrepreneurs and popular based, cooperative associations. After all, in trying to suggest ways of alleviating obstacles to Arab development, new ones should not be created. There are a number of ways in which these two potential economic initiators could be perceived to be opposed.

To begin with, lines of social fragmentation could become more pronounced if the two formations were to correspond with such divisions. Also, the principles and economic ideology underpinning these mechanisms are opposed: collectivism and egalitarian distribution of benefits *versus* individualism and the private profit motive. There are complex practical problems inherent in combining the resources of entrepreneurial elements (characterised by a degree of integration and identity of interests with the state and/or Jewish capital) with those of popular, communally oriented bodies (non-state affiliated, and often politically opposed to official policy). Furthermore, whereas entrepreneurship is a reality in contemporary Arab society in Israel, experience of participatory projects is not.[10] Finally, the administrative difficulties of integrating such diverse forms of economic activity into policies for the implementation of a regional strategy opens up a whole new aspect of programme management.

There are two levels on which such issues may be accomodated. On the one hand, the differentiations which characterise Arab society are not so clearly evolved nor polarised that enmity will necessarily arise between these two forms of economic/business association. In fact, society is fragmented in such a way that such forms could coexist and even cooperate without being aware of any necessary contradiction between them. On another level, if the understanding of participatory development is broadened so as to accomodate entrepreneurial groups, then the contradiction is internalised in one of the institutional forms and the scope for its divisive influence is limited. Indeed, given the wide variety of Arab economic and business agents and formations noted in this study, an Arab regional development effort needs to aim at mobilising the widest possible range of elements for the broad benefit of the region. Participatory projects are a natural reponse by a deprived and dispossesed community to official neglect and hostility, while also providing a workable and effective formula for engineering Arab developmental efforts in Israel.

Whatever might be the eventual content, aims and form of Arab development in Israel, it is certain that the issue itself deserves a position of recognition it has not so far received. On the analytical and diagnostic levels at least, this study has highlighted the need for such recognition and the options for future treatment of the issues. Our examination took a step further forward, into the realm of development planning, on the assumption of the economic and political desirability, if not feasibility, of some *developmental future* for the Arab economy in Israel. Whether it be as the Arab region, areas, sector or minority is really immaterial at this stage. What counts above all is that a viable and valid framework has been elaborated, thus opening the door for further contributions and efforts.

This is not only a challenge for Palestinian Arabs in Israel and a potentially constructive path for other Palestinians to contemplate. As has been seen, the overriding interest of establishing a Jewish state in Palestine wrought havoc upon its indigenous Arab inhabitants, including those who remained behind. During the forty years of destruction and neglect witnessed by the Arab economy, Israeli and international public opinion was practically silent. Now more than ever, there is a crucial role that many Israelis - academics, political activists, policy makers and citizens - can and must assume in actively advocating radical changes in policy and attitudes to the Palestinian Arab population of Israel. Given that some of these elements contributed to exposing and analysing the realities of Arab economic deprivation in Israel, they now have a responsibility to mobilise for effective change.

There exists perhaps an even more crucial challenge for government policy, which has for too long ignored, or at best tried half-heartedly to tackle, the pressing issues of the Arab-Jewish development gap in Israel. Even in terms of Israel's strict definitions of its best interests (especially those related to security), the now chronic and worsening contradictions between the state and the Arab (and Druze) population demand urgent treatment. Further neglect, inaction and apathy will only produce greater differentials and discontent, thus perpetuating Arab 'underdevelopment' and giving rise to a host of perils for the future of the Jewish state.

NOTES

1. See, e.g. (UNCTAD 1986).

2. In this context, the reader is referred to the stimulating and comprehensive review and critique of contemporary regional economic theory contained in (Gore 1984). An important conclusion reached, and one which is as serious a critique of regional theory in general as it is of the way that it can be applied in practice, centres upon the need to view regional development theory in terms of

> how the theory is used in practice. No abstract generalisations may be made about whose particular interests the theory supports and damages.

> But the characteristic which gives the theory its ideological flexibility and potency is clear. It is that characteristic which...I have termed 'spatial separatism' - that is, the structuring of the theory in a way which separates space from social processes. The working method at present used in the field gives rise to insoluble logical problems. But the logical problems of the theory are at the same time ideological opportunities. The conflation of social problems located in cities and regions with problems of those cities and regions, the commitment of ecological fallacies and confusion of 'place prosperity' with 'people prosperity', and the displacement of analysis from an examination of social relationships to an examination of spatial relationships, have all stymied adequate theorisation, and all stem from the conceptualisation of space. Yet with this conceptualisation, it is possible to formulate metonymical regional policies which serve diverse social interests in the name of developing an area, and appear to be technically rational. The conceptualisation of space on which regional development theory rests is not only the source of its ideological weaknesses. It is also the source of its ideological power. (Gore 1984: 263-4).

This might be construed as valid a criticism of the application of regional analysis in this book as it is, though from a different angle, of Israeli policy towards the Arab region itself. It is also an eloquent statement of the importance of not exaggerating the scientific and/or political necessity/desirability of regional analysis in the present case.

3. The following exposition of three regional development models is adapted from the characterisations elaborated in greater detail and precision in (Ben-David Val 1983: 10-15).

4. If my arguments for the Arab region are considered valid, then there is an economic and political basis for differentiating study of the Arab economy with that of the Israeli economy as a whole along regional/national lines. This could encourage a new approach to the study of the economic development of the occupied territories within the same framework. Not only are the West Bank and Gaza Strip administratively, politically and geographically distinct regions (though admittedly distinct from Israel), but they also exhibit a complex and interdependent network of internal economic relationships. Furthermore, their economic relation to the Israeli economy proceeds along clearly differentiated lines. Though their links to the Arab hinterland (and particularly the Jordanian economy) imply a regional relation, these territories need not be considered a region of the Israeli economy *per se*.

Rather, they could be considered as regional (because non-national) economies existing under the influence of a powerful national economy and maintaining links to other national economies. It might be argued that such economic analysis reinforces and legitimises the political *status quo* in permanently linking the territories' economy to the Israeli economy. On the contrary, I believe that regional economic analysis of the situation would reveal that there is a clear basis for arguing that these areas constitute a region with sufficient autonomous growth potential and prerequisites to allow (or necessitate) their separation, if not isolation, from the domination of the Israeli economy.

5. There is a wide range of interesting theoretical and empirical studies relevant to the issues of entrepreneurism, small business and minority and ethnic business initiative. Some useful examples for our purposes are: (Casson 1982); (Bruce 1976); (Kirzner 1980); (Marris and Somerset 1971); (Ward and Jenkins 1984); (Watkins 1976).

6. Without idealistically believing that such agents could be expected to accept losing them in the process.

7. The following statement on self reliant development is adapted from the report of the 24th Pugwash Symposium of 1975 in (Pugwash 1977: 257-65).

8. The curious reader is referred to the excellent bibliography of regional development literature in (Gore 1984).

9. The following characterisations are borrowed from (Gore 1984: 159-64), but (Ben-David Val 1983) also covers some of this area. Some of the more recent and very instructive literature on participatory development can be found in: (Dumas 1983); (Gerry 1980); (Jobert 1983); (Reboul 1981).

10. Unlike the occupied West Bank and Gaza Strip where, since 1967, a diverse range of local and international private voluntary organisations have stimulated a much greater degree of local project formulation, implementation and funding.

APPENDIX 1
FIELD SURVEY METHODOLOGY

I. (Khalidi and Sabbagh 1985) *Survey of Industrial Enterprises in Nazareth and Umm al-Fahm.*

AIMS.

The survey of Arab industry in Nazareth and Umm al-Fahm aimed at investigating six main hypotheses about Arab industry in Israel, arrived at through observations based on earlier published work. The hypotheses investigated were:
1. that Arab industry was primarily small-scale;
2. that Arab industry was primarily service oriented;
3. that larger-scale industry is non-Arab owned and/or financed;
4. that investment is minimal and production processes labour intensive;
5. that labour skills are not high or especially abundant;
6. that marketing is mainly local or subcontracting nationally.

The survey aimed, through sampling industrial units in the two largest Arab localities, at establishing a more precise and detailed profile of Arab industry than previously available.

DESIGN

The choice of the two survey towns was deliberate: a survey of all localities was impossible; the two towns contained 13% of all Arab industrial units according to one major statistical source (Czamanski *et al.*, 1984), and substantially more according to field observations; they are geographically dispersed (Nazareth in the Galilee and Umm al-Fahm in the northern part of the Triangle); they are characterised by a good sectoral spread of industries.

Appendix 1. Field Survey Methodology

The first stage of surveying involved establishing a population frame from which an appropriate sample could be chosen. There were several sources from which to choose, from different years, using different criteria and definitions, and of varying quality and disparate accuracy. The frame was eventually established through a process of comparison and adjustment, supplemented by direct field observations and enumeration of units through access to Nazareth municipality records of currently valid commercial and industrial licenses and Histadrut (Umm al-Fahm branch) records of all industrial units.

A final sample was arrived at through adhering to five main parameters:
* a definition of industrial unit as 'producing and marketing a specific output in a specific place, with 2 or more employed' - i.e., excluding one-person owner/operator establishments';
* including a minimum sample from each of the seven major branches of manufacturing industry;
* including a minimum sample from each branch, also taking into consideration the scale range in each;
* obtaining an overall 30%-35% sample from the total population, which was considered a safe margin for statistical accuracy;
* a random selection of survey units to compose each sub-sample, with no demographic, geographic or other bias in selection. The final sample size totalled 59 units (39 in Nazareth and 20 in Umm al-Fahm), distributed as shown in the following table:

BRANCH	NAZARETH Field Observations		NAZARETH Sample		UMM EL-FAHM Field Observations		UMM EL-FAHM Sample	
	UNITS	%	UNITS	%	UNITS	%	UNITS	%
Clothing	8	7	5	13	7	11	3	16
Blocks/Stone	6	5	4	10	19	30	5	25
Metal products	39	36	7	18	15	23	5	25
Wood products	26	24	12	31	18	28	5	25
Chemicals	7	6	2	5	2	3	2	9
Paper/Printing	8	7	4	10	-	-	-	-
Food products	7	6	5	13	3	5	-	-
Miscellaneous	10	9	-	-	-	-	-	-
TOTAL	111	100	39	100	64	100	20	100

NOTE: Percentage figures are rounded.
SOURCES: Nazareth field observations from Nazareth municipality files, 1985; Umm al-Fahm field observations from Histadrut Umm al-Fahm branch files, 1985.

Appendix 1. Field Survey Methodology

IMPLEMENTATION

Partly due to its greater urban character and function, Nazareth was the more difficult locality in terms of both organisation of surveying and degree and accuracy of responses. These problems were overcome at the field level and through subsequent statistical treatment. Umm al-Fahm's smaller size and a greater degree of local cooperation rendered the results obtained there more consistent and detailed.

Enumeration of units, establishing the frame and sample in Nazareth began in December 1984 and lasted until the end of January 1985. The same process was undertaken in February 1985 in Umm al-Fahm while pilot surveys were run in Nazareth. Interviewing took place in late February and March in both localities. Interviewing conditions were sometimes difficult, though the field staff were able to overcome most problems: in all cases, interviews were carried out on-site and to the greatest extent possible, efforts were made to verify responses with direct observations and through the presence of two enumerators at each interview.

Subsequent statistical analysis involved coding of answers, classification, and computerised generation of bivariate tables. The original questionnaire contained over 175 questions with possible answers and up to ten classifications of answers for each. Due to non-reponse on a number of questions, especially those covering income and costs, and through statistical analysis, this was reduced to 75 questions. Subsequent data tabulation and stratification further reduced the useable data to approximately 40 bivariate tables of locality by variable$_n$ with a maximum of 7 coding groups.

LIMITATIONS

There are several factors which can cause inaccuracies and bias with regard to generalisation of results. These involve statistical sampling error, or human error in interviewing, registering responses, and data manipulation. These are not of great significance in this survey. However, limitations can arise from the following factors:

<u>Inaccurate Data</u>: Most inaccuracies are noticed in questions directly or indirectly referring to income; those which deal with costs of raw material and other expenses; questions demanding historical figures to gauge growth of plant, costs or workforce; questions to which respondents provided data in different units.

Appendix 1. Field Survey Methodology

Low Response Level: In some cases, especially with quantative questions, a high number of 'non-specified' answers effectively reduce the sample size and distort the sample structure. Initial questionnaire design, however, avoided most of these problems.

The Frame as 'Untypical': This concerns the extent to which the surveyed towns provide valid 'representative' cases. In this survey, there are three possible aspects of distortion: urban originating bias, whereby the more urban character of the chosen towns can be argued to have an unknown determining effect on the specific structure and nature of local industry; scale bias, whereby a number of the largest Arab industrial establishments are not located in the surveyed town; size bias, whereby the locality's size and population in itself might influence certain industrial patterns and structures.

These three major sources of bias do not appear to seriously affect the overall validity of the results, since there is little evidence of great diversification in the Arab region other than shown in the present sample, and the few exceptions to this are clearly identifiable.

II. (Khalidi and Sabbagh, 1985a) *Survey of Agriculture in Two Arab Villages in Israel.*

AIMS

Despite the existance of a number of Israeli field surveys of Arab agriculture, this survey was designed in order to provide new insights and additional information on certain issues not covered in available sources. It was not expected that such a survey could hope to be comprehensive, or even 'representative', of Arab agriculture in general or in the areas surveyed. Yet, through careful choice of two villages which were relatively 'average' in terms of agriculture in their respective areas, results could be valid enough to confirm, elaborate or contradict existing assumptions. Some of the priority issues aimed for investigation included land utilisation, ownership, labour application, use of inputs, types, quantities and value of output, and marketing arrangements.

DESIGN AND IMPLEMENTATION

For reasons of time and resources, it was only possible to survey two villages. In order to choose the most 'appropriate' villages for the survey, it was necessary to undertake a lengthy process of classification of the three main Arab farming areas, namely the

Appendix 1. Field Survey Methodology

Nazareth, western Galilee and the Hadera areas, according to village data available from the 1972 Census of Agriculture (the most recently available comprehensive source).

The classification procedure involved investigating the distribution of localities according to number of farms, size of farms, size of plots and percentage of irrigated land. Accordingly, it was possible to draw a 'profile' of these areas, from which a village was chosen to be closest to the 'average'. Though statistically unconventional, the procedure produced two villages which overall, exhibited many of the 'usual' features associated with Arab agriculture, in terms of population, climactic conditions, fragmentation, farm organisation, and crop patterns.

The two localities that emerged from this selection procedure were Jatt in the Triangle and Shefa'amr in the Nazareth/Western Galilee region, characterised by the following parameters:

	Cultivated area	Area per holding	Irrigated area	Farm size (dunums) 1-15	16-30	31-100	>100
	Dunums			Percentages			
Triangle (average)	3971	20	20	58	22	18	2
Jatt	5128	14	43	54	30	16	-
Galilee (average)	5822	39	3	36	23	36	5
Shefa'amr	7537	41	19	34	22	36	8

Enumeration of the population frame was undertaken in February and March 1985, using data supplied by local agricultural cooperative societies. After establishing the population frame, and stratifying it according to size of holdings, sampling units were chosen according to a random selection procedure. It was found that there were 199 holdings in Shefa'amr, from which a sample of 16 was chosen (8%); in Jatt, of a total of 66 holdings, a total of 14 units were sampled (21%). Here, the aim was to provide a total sample size of 30, with a large enough proportion chosen from each village to maintain statistical accuracy.

Subsequently, in the period March and April 1985, the chosen units were interviewed, usually at respondents homes, as that was the most appropriate location, or at cooperative societies' offices. Problems encountered included a degree of apprehension by some villagers about the survey's aims (for example, in a few cases interviewees suspected that the survey was related to tax collection), problems in estimating labour application, classifying units and types of inputs and outputs, and provision of data regarding costs and income.

Following the data collection process, information was subjected to a process of manipulation and analysis similar to that used for the above survey of industrial units. Overall, while the

Appendix 1. Field Survey Methodology

survey cannot be considered as useful as the industrial survey in drawing general observations about the sector under investigation, the precision of population and sample choice and close supervision and cross-verification of results ensured that its results provided limited and accurate observations about agriculture in more or less 'representative' villages.

III. (Khalidi, 1985) *Survey of Arab Business Projects and Potential in Israel.*

AIMS

The aim of this survey was to collect data on a range of existing, partially implemented or planned economic and business projects within the Arab region, focussing on motivations, problems, and requirments for successful implementation. It further aimed at gauging the scope and potential for development which were assumed to exist throughout the region but hitherto had not been examined in any consistent fashion.

DESIGN AND IMPLEMENTATION

In devising a methodology for data collection, it was especially important that preconceptions and existing hypotheses regarding Arab business/developmental potential did not influence the surveying. Equally, the survey aimed to avoid bias through establishing broad parameters for choice of interviewees, such that results might reflect the scope of business experience and activity in the region. The main design problem was that of defining a population from which a more or less 'representative' sample might be chosen for surveying through targeted, as opposed to random, sampling. Because of time and material constraints, neither a comprehensive nor statistically representative sample was established; instead, a series of case studies emerged from the survey.

Within the general parameters for choice of project (see below), the choice of interviewees depended on existing contacts/introductions to potential interviewees and satisfaction of preliminary investigations regarding interviewees' serious involvement with the projects involved. A total of 19 interviews were conducted in April 1985 by one researcher, at the place of business, with questionnaires filled out by the researcher according to information supplied by interviewees. Errors, inaccuracy or possible distortion of figures by interviewees were noted, identified and taken into consideration in analysing results.

Appendix 1. Field Survey Methodology

The parameters that were devised to choose interviewees were: geographic location; type of locality; sector and sub-sector; and institutional form. These were further subdivided according to an arbitrary proportionate distribution which was the only level at which research preconceptions of significance of surveyed unit influenced the choice of case studies. Certain of the parameters could not, however, be adhered to: 1.c), 3.i) and 4.a) in the below table. Additionally, the designed proportion of projects from each category was not achieved, though the relative weight of each was more or less ensured. The parameters applied were as exibited in the following table.

Subsequent treatment involved a three level analysis: i) comprehensive, itemised and detailed classification of all data as provided by interviewees; ii) a content analysis summarising the main data from each questionnaire, in standardised database format, according to the main headings of the survey forms, allowing for quick and clear comparison of different projects and further evaluation; iii) An abstract analysis of each heading in general terms, highlighting the main trends which emerge. The discussion of results in this book has drawn on all three levels so as to provide general and specific observations.

Major Parameter	Sub-Group	Proportion for Sampling		Actually Sampled
1. Geographic	a) North-Galilee	60%	12	63%
	b) Centre-Triangle	30%	7	37%
	c) South-Negev	10%	0	0%
2. Locality	a) Arab villages	50%	7	37%
	b) Arab towns	40%	11	58%
	c) Mixed cities	10%	1	5%
3. Sector	a) Agriculture - land improvement	5%	1	5%
	b) Agriculture - water sources	10%	1	5%
	c) Agriculture - improved inputs	10%	2	11%
	d) Agriculture - products/market.	10%	2	11%
	e) Industry - traditional products	10%	1	5%
	f) Industry - labour intensive	10%	4	22%
	g) Industry - large scale	10%	1	5%
	h) Tourism	5%	1	5%
	i) Agriculture/Industry credit	10%	-	0%
	j) Commerce	10%	2	11%
	k) Professional economic services	5%	1	5%
	l) Housing	-	1	5%
	m) Industry - other	-	2	11%
4. Form	a) Local councils	10%	-	0%
	b) Political groups	15%	3	16%
	c) Professional associations	10%	2	11%
	d) Cooperatives	25%	3	16%
	e) Individuals, private sector	40%	11	57%

Appendix 2

ARAB LOCALITIES IN ISRAEL, BY DISTRICT, LOCAL AUTHORITY STATUS AND DEVELOPMENT ZONE

The following table (from Israel 1983a) is a complete listing of all exclusively Arab localities in Israel, according to their sub-district and local authority status as of 1986 (Local councils; municipalities; regional councils grouping several Arab and Jewish localities - RC; those localities whose status is unknown are left blank). The position of each locality within the Israeli development zoning (first priority A, second priority B) has been estimated roughly according to maps in (Bank Leumi Ltd.1979). Those localities with unknown or no development zone status are indicated by (..).

NAME	SUB-DISTRICT	MUNICIPAL STATUS	DEV. ZONE
'ARA	HADERA		..
'ARAMSHA	AKKO	SULLAM ZOR RC	A
'AR'ARA	YIZRE'EL		..
'ARRABE	AKKO	LOCAL COUNCIL	B
'EILABUN	KINNERET	LOCAL COUNCIL	A
'EIN AL-ASAD	AKKO	MEROM HAGALIL RC	A
'EIN AS-SAHLE	HADERA		..
'EIN MAHEL	YIZRE'EL	LOCAL COUNCIL	B
'EIN NAQQUBA	JERUSALEM	MATTE YEHUDA RC	B
'EIN RAFA	JERUSALEM	MATTE YEHUDA RC	B
'ILUT	YIZRE"EL		..
'ISIFIYA	HAIFA		..
'UZEIR	YIZRE'EL		B

227

Appendix 2. Arab Localities in Israel

NAME	SUB-DISTRICT	MUNICIPAL STATUS	DEV. ZONE
ABU GHOSH	JERUSALEM	MATTE YEHUDA RC	B
ABU SINAN	AKKO	LOCAL COUNCIL	B
AKBARA	AKKO		A
AL BAYADA	HADERA		..
AL DAHI	YIZRE'EL		B
BAQA AL GHARBIYE	HADERA	LOCAL COUNCIL	..
BARTAA'	HADERA		..
BASMAT TAB'UN	YIZRE'EL	LOCAL COUNCIL	B
BEIT JANN	AKKO	LOCAL COUNCIL	A
BEIT JIMAL	JERUSALEM	MATTE YEHUDA RC	B
BEIT NAQUBA	JERUSALEM		..
BEIT RAFAT	JERUSALEM		..
BI'NE	AKKO	LOCAL COUNCIL	A
BIR AL MAKSUR	AKKO	BEDUIN SETTLEMENT	..
BIR AL SIKKEH	HASHARON	BEDUIN SETTLEMENT	..
BU'EINE	YIZRE'EL		B
BUQEI'A	AKKO	LOCAL COUNCIL	A
DABBURYE	YIZRE'EL	LOCAL COUNCIL	B
DALIET AL KARMEL	HAIFA	LOCAL COUNCIL	..
DEIR AL ASAD	AKKO	LOCAL COUNCIL	A
DEIR HANNA	AKKO	LOCAL COUNCIL	A
DEIR RAFAT	JERUSALEM	MATTE YEHUDA RC	B
FASSUTA	AKKO	LOCAL COUNCIL	A
FUREIDIS	HADERA		..
GA'AZALIN	YIZRE'EL	BEDUIN SETTLEMENT	..
HAJAJRE	YIZRE'EL	EMEQ YIZRE'EL RC	B
HAWASHLA	YIZRE'EL	EMEQ YIZRE'EL RC	B
HILF (ARAB AL)	HAIFA	BEDUIN SETTLEMENT	..
HUJEIRAT (DAHRA)	AKKO	BEDUIN SETTLEMENT	B
HURFEISH	AKKO	LOCAL COUNCIL	A
I'IBILLIN	AKKO	LOCAL COUNCIL	B
IBTAN	HASHARON		..
IBTIN	HAIFA		..
IKSAL	YIZRE'EL	LOCAL COUNCIL	B
JALJULYA	PETAH TIQWA	LOCAL COUNCIL	..
JATT	HADERA	LOCAL COUNCIL	..
JATT (GALILEE)	AKKO	MERKAZ HAGALIL RC	A
JISH	ZEFAT	LOCAL COUNCIL	A
JISR AL ZARQA'	HADERA	BEDUIN SETTLEMENT	..
JUDEIDE	AKKO	LOCAL COUNCIL	B
JULIS	AKKO	LOCAL COUNCIL	B
KA'ABIYE TABBASH	YIZRE'EL	EMEQ YIZRE'EL RC	B

Appendix 2. Arab Localities in Israel

NAME	SUB-DISTRICT	MUNICIPAL STATUS	DEV. ZONE
KABUL	AKKO	LOCAL COUNCIL	B
KAFAR BARA	PETAH TIQWA		..
KAFAR KAMA	KINNERET	LOCAL COUNCIL	A
KAFAR KANNA	YIZRE'EL	LOCAL COUNCIL	B
KAFAR MANDA	AKKO	LOCAL COUNCIL	B
KAFAR MISR	YIZRE'EL		A
KAFAR QARA	HADERA		..
KAFAR QASEM	PETAH TIQWA		..
KAFAR SUMEI'	AKKO	MERKAZ HAGALIL RC	A
KAFAR YASIF	AKKO	LOCAL COUNCIL	B
KHAWALED	YIZRE'EL	BEDUIN SETTLEMENT	B
KISRA	AKKO	MERKAZ HAGALIL RC	A
KOKAB	AKKO		B
MAJD AL KURUM	AKKO	LOCAL COUNCIL	B
MAKR	AKKO		..
MANSHIYET AL ZIBDA	YIZRE'EL	EMEQ YIZRE'EL RC	B
MARJA	HASHARON		..
MAQURA	HADERA		..
MASHAYIKH SAADIYE	YIZRE'EL	BEDUIN SETTLEMENT	B
MAZRA'A	AKKO		..
MEISAR	HADERA		..
MESHED	YIZRE'EL	LOCAL COUNCIL	B
MI'ELYA	AKKO	LOCAL COUNCIL	A
MU'AWIYA	HADERA		..
MUGHAR	KINNERET	LOCAL COUNCIL	A
MUQEIBLE	YIZRE'EL	GILBOA RC	B
MUSHEIRFA	HADERA		..
MUSMUS	HADERA		..
NA'URA	YIZRE'EL	GILBOA RC	A
NAHEF	AKKO	LOCAL COUNCIL	A
NAZARETH	YIZRE'EL	MUNICIPALITY	B
NEIN	YIZRE'EL		B
NUJEIDAT	YIZRE'EL	BEDUIN SETTLEMENT	B
QALANSAWE	HASHARON		..
RAME	AKKO	LOCAL COUNCIL	A
RAS 'ALI	HAIFA		..
REIHANIYE	ZEFAT	MEROM HAGALIL RC	A
REINE	YIZRE'EL	LOCAL COUNCIL	B
RUMAT HEIB	YIZRE'EL	EMEQ YIZRE'EL RC	B
RUMMANE	YIZRE'EL		B
SALEM	HADERA		..
SAJUR	AKKO	MEROM HAGALIL RC	A
SAKHNIN	AKKO	LOCAL COUNCIL	B
SANDALA	YIZRE'EL	GILBOA RC	B
SAWA'ID (ARAB AL)	AKKO	BEDUIN SETTLEMENT	..

Appendix 2. Arab Localities in Israel

NAME	SUB-DISTRICT	MUNICIPAL STATUS	DEV. ZONE
SHA'AB	AKKO	LOCAL COUNCIL	B
SHIBLI (ARAB AL)	YIZRE'EL	BEDUIN SETTLEMENT	B
SHEF'AMR	AKKO	MUNICIPALITY	B
SHEIKH BUREIK	HADERA	BEDUIN SETTLEMENT	..
SHEIKH DANNUN	AKKO	GA'ATON RC	B
SULAM	YIZRE'EL		B
TAB'UN	HAIFA		..
TAMRA (ZUABIYA)	YIZRE'EL	GILBOA RC	A
TAMRA	AKKO	LOCAL COUNCIL	B
TARSHIHA	AKKO	LOCAL COUNCIL	A
TAYIBE	HASHARON	LOCAL COUNCIL	..
TAYIBE (ZUABIYA)	YIZRE'EL	GILBOA RC	A
TIRE	HASHARON	LOCAL COUNCIL	..
TUBA	ZEFAT		A
TUR'AN	YIZRE'EL	LOCAL COUNCIL	B
UMM AL-FAHM	HADERA	MUNICIPALITY	B
UMM AL GHANEM	YIZRE'EL	BEDUIN SETTLEMENT	..
UMM AL-QUTUF	HADERA	BEDUIN SETTLEMENT	..
WADI AL HAMAM	KINNERET	BEDUIN SETTLEMENT	A
YAFA (NAZARETH)	YIZRE"EL		..
YAMMA	HASHARON		..
YANUH	AKKO	MERKAZ HAGALIL RC	A
YIRKA	AKKO	LOCAL COUNCIL	B
ZALAFE	HADERA		..
ZARZIR	YIZRE'EL	EMEQ YIZRE'EL RC	B
ZUBEIDAT	HAIFA	BEDUIN SETTLEMENT	..

	BEDUIN IN NEGEV		
'AMMUR	BEER SHEVA		B
'ATAWNE	BEER SHEVA		B
'UQBI	BEER SHEVA		B
A'SAM	BEER SHEVA		B
ABU 'ABDUN	BEER SHEVA		B
ABU 'AMM'AR	BEER SHEVA		B
ABU 'AMRE	BEER SHEVA		B
ABU 'ARO'ER	BEER SHEVA		B
ABU BALLAL	BEER SHEVA		B
ABU JUEI'ID	BEER SHEVA		B
ABU QUREINAT	BEER SHEVA		B
ABU RUBEI'A	BEER SHEVA		B
ABU RUQAYYEQ	BEER SHEVA		B
ABU SUREIHAN	BEER SHEVA		B
AFEINISH	BEER SHEVA		B

Appendix 2. Arab Localities in Israel

NAME	SUB-DISTRICT	MUNICIPAL STATUS	DEV. ZONE
ASAD	BEER SHEVA		B
ATRASH	BEER SHEVA		B
AZAZME	BEER SHEVA		B
HUZZAYYEL	BEER SHEVA		B
JUNNABIB	BEER SHEVA		B
KESEIFA	BEER SHEVA		B
LOTEM	BEER SHEVA		B
MASUDIN AL NASASRA	BEER SHEVA		B
QABBO'A	BEER SHEVA		B
QAWA'IN	BEER SHEVA		B
QUDEIRAT AL-SANI	BEER SHEVA		B
RAHAT	BEER SHEVA	LOCAL COUNCIL	B
SAYYID	BEER SHEVA		B
TARABIN AL-SANI	BEER SHEVA		B
TEL SHEVA	BEER SHEVA	BENE SHIM'ON RC	B
ZABARGA	BEER SHEVA		B

REFERENCES

Abdelfattah, K. (1983) "The Geographical Distribution of the Palestinians on Both Sides of the 1949 Armistice Line" in A. Scholch (ed.), *Palestinians Over the Green Line*, Ithaca, London

Abu Kishk, B. (1976) *Land in the Arab Sector: The Aims of its Use and the Problems Blocking its Development*, The Popular Council for Social Renewal, Arab Affairs Department, Nazareth (in Arabic)

- (1981) "Arab Land and Israeli Policy", *Journal of Palestine Studies*, No. 41
- (1981b) *The Industrial and Economic Trends in the West Bank and Gaza Strip*, United Nations Economic Commission for West Asia, Beirut
- (1984) "Arab Agriculture in Occupied Palestine", *Samed al Iqtisadi*, Nos. 50/1 (in Arabic)
- (1985) Interview with the author, London
- (N.D.) "The Concept of Comprehensive Regional Planning and the Arab Reality in Israel", (unpublished), Nazareth (in Arabic)

Abu Lughod, I. (1971) *The Transformation of Palestine*, Northwestern University Press, Evanston Ill.

- (1977) "Palestine Arabs in Israel", *MERIP Reports*, No. 58

American Palestine Educational Fund - APEF (1983) *A Survey of Palestinian Institutions Under Israeli Jurisdiction*, unpublished report, Wash. D.C.

Amiran, D. et al. (1976) *The Process of Sedentarisation and Settlement Among the Beduin of the Negev*, Hebrew University, Department of Geography, Jerusalem

Arab Israeli Bank (1984) *Annual Report 1983*, The Bank, Haifa (in Arabic)

- (1985) *Annual Report 1984*, The Bank, Haifa, (in Arabic)

References

Arnon, Y. and Raviv, M. (1980) *From Fellah to Farmer: a Study on Change in Arab Villages*, Settlement Study Centre, Rehovot

Bank Leumi Ltd., International Consultants Guide (1979) *Trade and Investment in Israel: A Businessman's Guide*, The Bank, Tel Aviv

Bar-Gal, Y. (1980) *Geographical Changes in the Traditional Arab Villages in Northern Israel*, Centre for Middle East and Islamic Studies, Durham

Bayadsi, M. (1975) "The Arab Local Authorities: Achievements and Problems", *New Outlook*, Vol. 18, No. 7

Ben Porath, Y. (1966) *The Arab Labour Force in Israel*, Maurice Falk Institute, Jerusalem

Ben-david Val, A. (1983) *Regional and Local Economic Analysis for Practitioners*, Praeger, N.Y.

Bruce, R. (1976) *The Entrepreneurs: Strategies, Motivations, Successes and Failure*, Libertarian Books, London

Carmi, S. and Rosenfeld, H. (1974) "The Origins of the Process of Proletarianisation and Urbanisation of Arab Peasants in Palestine", *Annals of the N.Y. Academy of Science*, No. 220

Casson., M. (1982) *The Entrepreneur - An Economic Theory*, Martin Robertson, Oxford

Connell, J. et al. (1976) *Migration from Rural Areas: the Evidence from Village Studies*, Oxford University Press, New Delhi

Czamanski, D. et al. (1984) *Employment Potential of University Graduates in the Arab Localities in Israel*, Technion Centre for Research of City and Region, Haifa. (in Hebrew)

Czamanski, D. and Meyer-Brodnitz, M. (1984) "Industrialisation in Arab Villages in Israel", draft for R. Bar-el (ed.), *Industrialisation in Rural Israel* (forthcoming)

Daniel, A. (1976) *Labour Enterprises in Israel*, Jerusalem Academic Press, Jerusalem

Davis, U. (1983) *Comparative Study of Land, Labour and Citizenship Control in Israel and South Africa*, U.N. International Conference on the Question of Palestine, Paris

Dumas, A. (1983) "Participation et Projets de Developpement", *Revue Tiers Monde*, Vol. 24, No. 95, (in French)

Falah, G. (1983) *Patterns of Spontaneous Beduin Settlement in Galilee*, Department of Geography, University of Durham, Durham

- (1985) "How Israel Controls the Beduin", *Journal of Palestine Studies*, No. 54

References

Farjoun, E. (1980) "Palestinian Workers in Israel - A Reserve Army of Labour", *Khamsin*, No. 7

Fei, J. and Ranis, G. (1964) *Development of the Labour Surplus Economy*, Homewood

Flapan, S. (1962) "Integrating the Arab Village", *New Outlook*, Vol. 5, No.3

- (1963) "Planning for the Arab Village", *New Outlook, Vol. 6*, No 8

- (1963a) "Planning Arab Agriculture", *New Outlook, Vol. 6*, No. 10

Gerry, C. (1980) "Petite Production Marchande ou 'Salariat Deguise'?", *Revue Tiers Monde*, Vol. 21, No. 82, (in French)

Godfrey, E. M. (1973) "Economic Variables and Rural-Urban Migration: Some Thoughts on the Todaro Hypothesis", *Journal of Development Studies*, Vol. 14, No. 1

Goering, K. (1979) "Israel and the Beduin of the Negev", *Journal of Palestine Studies*, No. 33

Gore, C. (1984) *Regions in Question: Space, Development Theory and Regional Policy*, Methuen, London

Gottheil, F. (1973) "On the Economic Development of the Arab Region in Israel" in M. Curtis and M. Chertoff (eds.), *Israel: Social Structure and Change*, Transaction Books, New Brunswick

Granott, A. (1952) *The Land System in Palestine*, Eyre and Spottiswoode, London

Hadawi, S. (1970) *Village Statistics 1945: A Classification of Land Area and Ownership in Palestine*, P.L.O. Research Centre, Beirut

Hadawi, S. and Kubursi, A. (forthcoming) *Palestinian Losses in 1948*

Harari, Y. (1972) *The Arabs in Israel: Statistics and Facts*, Centre for Arab and Afro Asian Studies, Tel Aviv

- (1974) *The Arabs in Israel 1973 (Facts and Figures)*, Centre for Arab and Afro Asian Studies, Tel Aviv

Hevrat Ovdim Council (1982) *Resolutions*, The Council, Tel Aviv (in Hebrew)

Heyder, A. (1986) *The Emergence of the Arab Bourgeoisie in Israel*, Arab Thought Forum, Jerusalem (in Arabic)

Hobman, J. B. (1946) *Palestine's Economic Future*, Lund Humphries, London

Hunt, A. R. (1974) *Production and Marketing of Fruits and Vegetables in Israel*, Anglo-Israel Association, London

References

Institut National des Sciences et Etudes Economiques (INSEE) (1948) *Palestine: Memento Economique*, Presses Universitaires de France, Paris (in French)

Israel, Central Bureau of Statistics (1955) *Statistical Abstract of Israel 1954/55*, C.B.S., Jerusalem
- (1961) *Statistical Abstract of Israel 1961*, C.B.S., Jerusalem
- (1964) *Statistical Abstract of Israel 1964*, C.B.S., Jerusalem
- (1965) *Statistical Abstract of Israel 1965*, C.B.S., Jerusalem
- (1966) *Statistical Abstract of Israel 1966*, C.B.S., Jerusalem
- (1967) *Statistical Abstract of Israel 1967*, C.B.S., Jerusalem
- (1970) *Statistical Abstract of Israel 1970*, C.B.S., Jerusalem
- (1971) *Statistical Abstract of Israel 1971*, C.B.S., Jerusalem
- (1974) *Statistical Abstract of Israel 1974*, C.B.S., Jerusalem
- (1975) *Statistical Abstract of Israel 1975*, C.B.S., Jerusalem
- (1976) *Statistical Abstract of Israel 1976*, C.B.S., Jerusalem
- (1979) *Income Elasticities of Demand 1975/76*, C.B.S., Jerusalem
- (1980) *Statistical Abstract of Israel 1980*, C.B.S., Jerusalem
- (1981) *Statistical Abstract of Israel 1981*, C.B.S., Jerusalem
- (1982) *Family Expenditure Survey 1979/80 - Part A, General Survey*, C.B.S., Jerusalem
- (1983a) *Agricultural and Rural Census 1981 - Provisional Results*, C.B.S., Jerusalem
- (1983b) *Statistical Abstract of Israel 1983*, C.B.S., Jerusalem
- (1984) *Statistical Abstract of Israel 1984*, C.B.S., Jerusalem
- (1984a) *Surveys of Income 1982*, C.B.S., Jerusalem
- (1985) *Statistical Abstract of Israel 1985*, C.B.S., Jerusalem
- (1985a) "Labour Force Survey 1984", *Monthly Bulletin of Statistics*, Vol. 36, No. 3, March Supplement
- (1985b) *Agricultural and Rural Census 1981: The Village in Israel*, C.B.S., Jerusalem
- (1985c) "Census of Population and Housing, 1983 - Employed Persons in Annual Labour Force" *Monthly Bulletin of Statistics*, Vol. 36, No. 4, April Supplement

Israel Economist (1981) "Red Carpet for Foreign Investors", *Israel Economist*, March Supplement

Jewish Agency, Rural Settlement Department (1974) *The Mountainous Galilee: Proposed Plan for Accelerated Development*, Jewish Agency, Jerusalem

Jiryis, S. (1973) "The Legal Structure for the Expropriation and Absorbtion of Arab Lands in Israel", *Journal of Palestine Studies*, No. 8
- (1976) *The Arabs in Israel*, Monthly Review Press, N.Y.

References

- (1981) "The Palestinians in Israel: Nationality and Expropriation of Land and its Annexation", *Journal of Palestine Studies*, No. 112
- (1981a) "The Palestinians in Israeli Laws: A Legal and Political Treatment: Security and Ownership Laws Expropriate Property and Liberties", *Journal of Palestine Studies*, No. 113
Jobert, B. (1983) "Clientalisme, Patronage et Participation Populaire" *Revue Tiers Monde*, Vol. 24, No. 95, (in French)
Jobran, R. (1984) "The Arabs in Israel: Their Demographical and Economical Structure and Entrepreneurial Activities", (unpublished monograph)

Katz, S. and Menuhin, N. (1978) *Preliminary Conclusion on the Galilee*, Settlement Study Centre, Rehovot
Katz, S. et al. (1982) *Regional Organisation and Management of Development - Israel and Galilee Case Study*, Settlement Study Centre, Rehovot
Keim, K. (1980) *Marketing in Israel - Overseas Business Reports: No. OBR 80-24*, U.S. Department of Commerce, Wash. D.C.
Khalidi, R. (1981) *The Development of the Arab Labour Force in Israel: Mobility or Migration?*, School of Oriental and African Studies, University of London (M.Sc. Dissertation)
- (1984) "Book Review of Arnon and Raviv, From Fellah to Farmer *Samed al Iqtisadi*, No. 50/1 (in Arabic)
- (1985) *Survey of Arab Business Projects and Potential in Israel*, (unpublished)
Khalidi, R. and Sabbagh, Z. (1985) *Survey of Industrial Enterprises in Nazareth and Umm al-Fahm*, (unpublished)
- (1985a) *Survey of Agriculture in Two Arab Villages in Israel*, (unpublished)
Khalidi, W. (1971) *From Haven to Conquest*, Institute for Palestine Studies, Beirut
Khmaysi, R. (1985) "Self Initiative and Industrialisation of the Arab Village" *Al Mawakeb*, (in Arabic)
Kirzner, I. M. (1980) "The Primacy of Entrepreneurial Discovery", in I.M. Kirzner et al. (eds.),*The Prime Mover of Progress*, The Institute of Economic Affairs, London
Kislev, R. (1976) "Land Expropriations: History of Oppression", *New Outlook*, Vol. 19, No. 6
Kolton, Y. (1932) *Towards the Jewish Question and Its Solution*, Tel Aviv

References

Lewis, W. A. (1954) "Economic Development with Unlimited Supplies of Labour", *Manchester School*

Loftus, P.J. (1946) *National Income of Palestine, 1944*, Government Printer, Palestine

Losch, A. (1964) "The Nature of Economic Regions" in J. Friedmann and W. Alonso (eds.), *Regional Development and Planning: a Reader*, MIT Press, Cambridge, Mass.

Lustick, I. (1980) *Arabs in the Jewish State: Israel's Control of a National Minority*, University of Texas Press, Austin

Makhoul, N. (1982) "Employment Structure of the Arabs in Israel", *Journal of Palestine Studies*, No. 43

Mar'i, S. (1978) *Arab Education in Israel*, Syracuse University Press, Syracuse

Marris, P. and Somerset, A. (1971) *African Businessmen: A Study of Entrepreneurs and Development in Kenya*, Routledge and Kegan Paul, London

Mattin - Centre for Production Development (1984) *Survey of Industrial Manpower in the West Bank and Gaza Strip*, (unpublished), Ramallah

Meyer Brodnitz, M. (1971) "The In-situ Urbanisation of the Arab Villages in Israel", *Plan East Africa - Journal of the Architectural Association of Kenya*, Vol. 2, No. 3

Nakhleh, K. (1977) "Anthropological and Sociological Studies of the Arabs in Israel: A Critique", *Journal of Palestine Studies*, No. 24

- (1979) *Palestinian Dilemma: Nationalist Consciousness and University Education in Israel*, Association of Arab American University Graduates, Detroit, Mich.

- (1982) *The Two Galilees*, Association of Arab American University Graduates, Belmont Mass.

Nathan, R. et al. (1946) *Palestine: Problem and Promise*, Public Affairs Press, Wash. D.C.

New Outlook (1962) "Five Year Program for Arab and Druze Villages", *New Outlook*, Vol. 5, No. 3

Oded, Y. (1964) "Land Losses Among Israel's Arab Villagers", *New Outlook*, Vol. 7, No. 7

Picadou, N. (1982) "La Bourgeoisie Palestinienne et L'Industrie" in A. Bourgey (Ed.),*Industrialisation et Changements Sociaux dans L'Orient Arabe*, Centre d'Etudes et Recherches sur le Moyen Orient Contemporaire, Beirut (in French)

References

Pugwash Society, "The Role of Self Reliance in Alternative Strategies for Development", *World Development*, Vol. 5, No. 3, 1977

Reboul, C. (1981) "Le Lent Apprentisage de l'Autogestion", *Revue Tiers Monde,* Vol 22, No. 88, (in French)

Rosenfeld, H. (1962) "The Arab Village Proletariat",*New Outlook,* Vol. 7, No. 3

- (1964) "From Peasantry to Wage Labour and Residual Peasantry: The Transformation of an Arab Village" in R. Manners (ed.), *Process and Pattern in Culture.*, Aldine Publishing Co., Chicago

- (1978) "The Class Situation of the Arab National Minority in Israel", *Comparative Studies in Society and History,* No. 20, July

Sayigh, R. (1979) *Palestinians: From Peasants to Revolutionaries,* Zed Press, London

Scholch, A. (ed.) (1983) *Palestinians Over the Green Line*, Ithaca Press, London

Segev, T. (1986) *1949: The First Israelis*, The Free Press, N.Y.

Shehory, Y. (1980/1) "Agricultural Marketing for Exports: The Israeli Case of Export of Fresh Produce", *Agriculture in Israel,* Winter

Shemesh, E. (1975) "Israel's Arabs - 1975", *New Outlook,* Vol. 18, No. 7

Smooha, S. (1978) *Israel: Pluralism and Conflict*, Routledge and Kegan Paul, London

Standing, G. (1981) "Migration and Modes of Exploitation: Social Origins of Mobility and Immobility", *Journal of Peasant Studies,* Vol. 8, No. 2

Szeskin, A. (1979) "The Rational Use of Capital in Agriculture: The Israeli Experience", *Agriculture in Israel,* Winter

TEAM International (1983) *The Palestinian Labour Force in Lebanon,* TEAM, Beirut

Tessler, M. (1980) *Arabs in Israel*, American Universities Field Staff Reports, Hanover, N.H.

Todaro, M. P. (1976) "Rural - Urban Migration, Employment and Job Probabilities: Recent Theoretical and Empirical Research" in A. Coale (ed.), *Economic Factors in Population Growth*, Halsted Press, N.Y.

References

United Nations Conciliation Commission on Palestine (1951) *General Progress Report and Supplementary Report, December 11, 1949*, U.N. General Assembly Fifth Session Official Records, N.Y.
- (1951a) *Progress Report, January 23 to November 19, 1951*, U.N. General Assembly Sixth Session Official Records, N.Y.
- (1954) *Thirteenth Progress Report, November 19, 1952 to December 31, 1953*, U.N. General Assembly Ninth Session Official Records, N.Y.
- (1955) *Fourteenth Progress Report, December 31, 1953 to December 31, 1954*, U.N. General Assembly Tenth Session Official Records, N.Y.
- (1956) *Fifteenth Progress Report, January 1 1955 to September 30, 1956*, U.N. General Assembly Eleventh Session Official Records, N.Y.
- (1958) *Sixteenth Progress Report, October 1, 1956 to May 31, 1958*, U.N. General Assembly Thirteenth Session Official Records, N.Y.
- (1959) *Seventeenth Progress Report, June 1, 1958 to August 31, 1959*, U.N. General Assembly Fourteenth Session Official Records, N.Y.
- (1962) *Nineteenth Progress Report, November 12, 1960 to October 13, 1961*, U.N. General Assembly Sixteenth Session Official Records, N.Y.

United Nations Conference on Trade and Development - UNCTAD (1986) *Recent economic developments in the occupied Palestinian territories, TD/B/1102.*, UNCTAD, Geneva

United Nations Economic Commission for West Asia - UNECWA (1983) *Summary of the Final Report on the Economic and Social Situation and Potential of the Palestinian Arab People in the Region of Western Asia*, UNECWA, Baghdad

United Nations Industrial Development Organisation - UNIDO (1984) *A Survey of Manufacturing Industry in the West Bank and Gaza Strip*, UNIDO, Vienna

Ward, R. and Jenkins, R. (eds.) (1984) *Ethnic Communities in Business: Strategies for Economic Survival*, Cambridge University Press, Cambridge

Waschitz, Y. (1975) "Commuters and Entrepreneurs", *New Outlook*, Vol. 18., No. 7

Watad, M. (1966) "Unemployment Haunts the Arab Village", *New Outlook*, Vol 9, No. 7

References

Watkins, D. (1976) "Entry into Independent Entrepreneurship: A Model of the Business Initiation Process", Manchester Business School Working Paper No. 24, Manchester

Weigart, G. (1977) "The Arab Cooperative Movement in Israel", *Kidma,* Vol. 4, No. 3

Weimer, R. (1983) "Zionism and the Arabs after the Establishment of the State of Israel" in A. Scholch (ed.), *Palestinians Over the Green Line,* Ithaca, London

Yalan, E. *et al.* (1972) *The Modernisation of Traditional Agricultural Villages: Minority Villages in Israel,* Settlement Study Centre, Rehovot

Zarhi, S. and Achziera, A. (1966) *The Economic Conditions of the Arab Minority in Israel,* Centre for Arab and Afro-Asian Studies, Tel Aviv

Zureik, E. (1979) *Palestinians in Israel: A Study in Internal Colonialism,* Routledge and Kegan Paul, London

INDEX

Abu Kishk, B. 61n10
accounting services 183
Acre 29n8, 49, 52, 72
agriculture 32-3, 39-40, 43, 45, 65, 157, 185, 188, 203
  almonds 97, 104
  apple area (Golan Heights) 89
  apricots 97
  avocados 97, 101
  bananas 97
  barley 94, 104
  beans 94, 104
  cabbage 95
  capital input 83-4
  cattle 97-8
  cherries 97
  chick-peas 94
  citrus 32, 67, 97, 104-6, 109n9
  cold storage facilities 102
  commercial crops 30, 94, 100
  commercial infrastructure 82
  commoditisation 32, 68, 143
  cotton 95, 104
  credit 82-3
  crop diversification 92-3
  cucumbers 95, 104
  cultivation permits 100
  drainage 78, 82, 192
  eggplants 95
  eggs 105
  export crops 100
  extension service 11, 67, 109n11
  family farming 11, 73-4, 82, 92, 110n13
  family labour 84-5, 115, 129-30

agriculture,
  farm size/scale 68-9, 74-5, 92, 110n13, 110n22
  field crops 70, 72-3, 94-5, 104-6
  fish 105
  fruits 70, 95, 97, 104-6
  goats and sheep 98
  grading 101
  grape vines 104
  groundnuts 94, 104
  industrial crops 94-5
  irrigation, 11, 62n12, 70, 74, 76-8, 80, 83, 110n25, 111n26, 110n27, 144-5
  Jewish 12, 32, 67, 83, 87-91, 143
  labour input 89-91
  labour intensive 84-5, 91-5, 104, 107
  livestock 97-8, 105
  maize 104
  marketing 22, 82, 93, 99-102
  marrows 95, 104
  mechanisation 11-12, 66, 79-83
  melons 95, 104-6
  olives 92, 97, 104, 111n37
  onions 104
  pack-house facilities 101
  peaches 97
  peas 95
  peppers 97
  planting area quotas 101-2
  plums 97
  poultry 97, 105
  pricing 70, 93, 101-2
  production and marketing boards 99-100
  production quotas 93, 100

agriculture,
  quality control 100-2
  rainfed crops 94
  sesame 97, 104
  sharecropping 73
  specialisation 103-8
  strawberries 95, 104
  subsistence 27, 32, 67-9, 71, 85-6, 94
  sugar beets 94
  sunflowers 94-5, 104
  technology 79-84
  tobacco 94-5, 104, 159
  tomatoes 95, 104
  traditional 66-9, 85-6, 92
  value of production 68, 105-6
  vegetables, potatoes and melons 95, 104-6
  wheat 94, 104
Agrexco 100-2
agro-industry 215
aid, government 39, 43, 47, 57, 69-71, 81-3, 93, 138, 159-65, 189-90, 194, 198n3
Approved Projects 162
Arab Cigarette and Tobacco Factory Ltd 159
Arab Workers and Farmers Fund 188
Arab-Druze Sector Development Corporation 167
Arab-Israeli Bank 182
Arens, M. 41, 62n15
Arnon, Y. and Raviv, M. 10-11, 85
autarky 212

Bank Hapoalim 170, 183
Bank Leumi, 182
Bank of Agriculture 82
banking 139, 167, 170, 182
Baqa al Gharbieh 159
Bar Gal, Y. 11
basic needs strategies 213, 215
basic sector 150-2
Battuf valley 73, 77-8
Beduin 40, 49, 57, 62n21, 72, 84, 94, 98, 110n17
Beersheba 52
Ben Porath, Y. 8, 10, 14
Bi'neh 161
boom, economic 115, 118-19, 142, 153n1

bottom-up periphery-inward growth 214
Boulos, family/enterprises 161, 168, 174, 183, 185
bourgeoisie 19, 24, 187, 199n9
business activity 157, 163-6, 169-70, 174, 179-82, 185-7, 191-8, 215-16
  obstacles to 178-9, 197
business, sectoral strategy, 181, 192

capital 81-4, 158-63, 166-7, 169-72, 174-5, 181, 183, 185-6, 193, 195, 197-8, 203, 210-11
capital, Jewish 160-1, 165-7, 169, 177, 179-80, 183, 186
capital-output ratios 83-4, 207
capitalists 170, 174, 180, 185-7, 205, 211
Carmi'el 29n8, 62n11, 66, 161
Carmi, S. and Rosenfeld, H. 31, 61n4
chambers of commerce 180, 191
Circassians 57
cities, Jewish 52
cities, mixed 24, 29n8, 37, 42, 49, 52, 138, 141, 144, 163
citizenship, Israeli 3
class analysis 17, 199n9
class formation 16-18, 21, 130-1, 179-81
commerce 158, 160, 176, 180-3, 188, 192
  agents merchants, middlemen 62, 157-8, 179, 183, 185-6, 210
  professional and personal services 176, 183, 186
  restaurants 177
  retail 168, 170, 179, 185-6
  wholesale 93, 111, 166, 170, 172
communal bodies 215
communal conflict 58
contracting 184, 186-7
control systems 5, 21-3
cooperatives 43, 75, 77, 82-3, 93, 99-100, 110n20, 112n39, 160, 187-9, 215
cooptation/collaboration 21, 38, 40, 45, 58-9, 165, 183, 185, 202
Czamanski, D. 13, 198n7

242

Daliet al-Karmel 161
Dayan Plan 69-70
decentralised territorial growth 207
demand elasticities 139
demographic structure 53-4, 133, 139
demographic trends 33, 54-5, 114-15, 117-18, 201, 203
dependence 21, 170, 212
dependency theory 18
deposits (bank) 182-3
development from above 214
development from below 204, 214-15
development status (towns, zones) 43 162-3, 165
development, autonomist 210
development, barriers and incentives to 10-13, 60, 64, 179, 203-5, 209
 centre-periphery 213
 dualist 5, 11-14, 25, 109n10, 213
 goals and strategies 179-80, 204, 213-17
 promotion 43-6, 162-6, 208-10
development, separate 33
differentials (Arab-Jewish) 14, 24, 26-8, 32-3, 42-3, 68, 77-8, 81-4, 90-1, 105-7, 118-22, 127, 129-30, 133-5, 137-9, 144-5, 153n2, 154n11, 203-4, 217
discrimination 16-18
domestic/regional product 207
Druze 41, 55, 57-8, 69, 161, 217

economic base analysis 146, 150-2,
economic centralisation 207-8, 210, 215
economies of scale 206, 214
economy, (Arab pre-1948) 31-4, 66-7, 156-7
 Arab 9-10, 13-14, 20, 23-6, 47-8, 64-5, 71, 91, 103, 107-8, 152-3, 200-4, 207-8
 exchange 150, 206-7
 Israeli 9, 18, 26, 28, 30-1, 36, 38, 40, 45-8, 62n16, 62n18, 109n3, 114, 118, 153n1, 203-4
 non-agricultural 11, 142-5, 156-7
 use 150, 207
 village 16, 184
 workshop 33-4, 160-2, 171,9, 186
education 55-6, 184

electricity 43-5, 45, 51, 159-60, 188-9
employees (waged labour) 85-90, 111n31, 111n34, 129-30, 134, 137-8, 154n10, 144-5, 195
employment,
 accounting 118, 129
 administrative/managerial 126-7, 129-30, 126-7, 129-32, 143-5, 148, 150, 152
 agricultural 67, 84-90, 103-4, 109, 119-23,
 blue collar 126-7, 131, 154n7
 business and legal services 122
 chemicals/plastics manufacture 121
 clerical workers 126-7, 131
 commerce 121-2-2, 125-6, 131, 148, 150
 construction 120, 122-3, 125-6, 129, 131, 142, 144, 148, 151-2, 153n4
 diamond manufacture 121, 130
 education 121, 129
 electrical/electronic 121, 130
 female 115, 117, 161, 172, 174
 finance 122, 125, 150
 food, beverages and tobacco 120-21
 government administration 121
 health services 121
 hotels, restaurants,cafes, and retail 111, 122-23
 industrial 119-23, 125-6, 147-8, 150, 154, 160, 172, 177
 machinery assemblers, installers, repairers 121, 130-1
 mental categories 130, 154n7
 metal and metal products 120, 129-30
 military industries 121-2, 130-1
 mining and quarrying 126
 occupational characteristics 16-17, 113-14, 125-6
 occupational/sectoral mobility 115, 125, 131
 personal services 121, 123, 125, 130-1, 143, 150, 152
 policemen, watchmen and related 129
 printing/paper 121
 production workers 125-7, 129-31, 134

243

employment,
   professional/technical 126-7, 131, 134, 154n8
   public services 121, 125, 150
   regional-share 146-8
   scientific/academic 126-7, 131, 154n8, 165, 187
   sectoral structure 119-23, 125, 153n4, 154n5
   self-employed 88-90, 129-30, 137, 158, 161, 179, 186
   services 114-5, 119-20
   skill levels 125-31, 134-5, 154n7, 169, 175
   tailors and dressmakers 129
   textile/clothing 120, 129
   transport and communications 121, 125-6, 129, 148, 151
   vehicle and other repairs 123, 131
   white collar 126-7, 131, 154n7
   woodworkers and carpenters 129
energy 179
entrepreneurial activity 174-5, 179-81, 183-6, 191-2, 208-10, 216
entrepreneurs 13, 122, 157, 174-5, 179, 183-7, 192, 198n7, 203, 209-12, 215-6, 218n5
exogenous factors 14, 26, 59, 143-4, 150-2
expenditure, consumption 133, 138-9, 175, 182-3, 207
   luxuries 139

Farmers Union 62n13, 100, 110n20
Fei, J. and Ranis, G. 109n10, 142
finance and credit 47, 69-70, 82-3, 157, 159, 162, 177-9, 182-3, 188, 194-5, 197
financial consultancy services 192
financial resources 182-3, 194-5
functional integration 206-7
functional regional planning 214-15

Galilee 26, 49, 66, 72-3, 75-6, 83, 102, 110n25, 111n26, 111n31, 111n37, 168, 170, 182, 192, 203
geographic and settlement patterns 11, 19, 24-7, 52, 144, 195
Gibor industries 161
Ginat, Y. 37, 198n3
Golan Heights 2, 6, 97, 109n2

Gore, C. 27, 200
Gottheil, F. 27-8
growth (Arab economy) 200-3, 205-8, 211-15
growth pole models 206-7, 213-14
Gulf States 164

Hadera 49, 52, 72, 76, 110n18
Haifa 27n8, 49, 52, 72, 110n18
Hamashbir Lezarkhan 168
Hayder, A. 24, 29n9, 187, 199n9
Hevrat Ovdim 165-7, 170
Histadrut 38, 47, 61n8, 62n13, 99-100, 110n20, 164-6, 168-9, 177, 183, 188-9
homogeneous region 25-6
housing 41-3, 53, 69, 157, 188

identity, (Palestinian Arab) 1, 3, 6, 16, 30, 37-41, 57-60, 65, 201-4
ideology, and motivations of analyses 7-10, 12-19, 22-3
immigration, Jewish 31, 33, 38, 40
income distribution 8, 133-5, 138, 142-3, 145, 154n10
income generation 137-8, 196
industrialisation 2, 13, 22, 39, 46-8, 158-62, 164-71, 180-1, 198n7
industry,
   car maintenance 123, 161, 171, 180
   carpentry 157, 160, 171-2, 174, 181
   chemical/plastics/rubber 167-8, 172, 175
   construction materials 157, 161, 167, 171-2, 174, 177, 181, 184
   diamonds/jewellery 161, 167, 172, 175
   electronic components 161, 168
   family enterprises 177, 187, 193
   food processing 157, 159, 164, 171, 174-5, 177, 181
   geographic distribution 171, 192
   implement repair shops 157
   labour intensive 166, 175, 213
   leather processing 174
   marketing 157, 161, 164, 167, 170, 174, 179, 181, 188

industry,
  metal and blacksmiths 157, 161, 171-2, 174-5, 181
  military 161
  olive presses 161
  ownership 159, 166-7, 177-8
  paper and printing 171-2, 175
  raw materials 177-8, 181, 183, 195
  running costs 178
  scale 160-1, 167, 171-2, 177-8, 213-14
  science-based 181
  service 177
  space 178
  textiles/clothing 161, 167, 171-3, 175, 181
  traditional handicraft 175
inflation 47
informal sector 209
infrastructure 69, 179, 188-9, 206-7
infrastructure, industrial 160
inheritance practices 74, 110n13, 110n21, 158, 183
institutional development 12-13, 21-2, 24, 80, 82, 181, 191, 194, 204, 215
integration, of Arabs in Israel 10-11, 15-16, 37-41, 46, 59, 170, 187, 197, 205
internal colonialism 5, 18-20
investment 39-40, 69-71, 159-60, 162-3, 165-8, 177-8, 181-2, 185-6, 194-5, 203, 206-7, 210
  social costs and benefits 195-7
Investment Centre 163
Isifiyeh 161
Israel, Declaration of Independence 60n1
Israel Land Authority 109n6
Israel Water Commission (Mekorot) 76-7, 110n25
Israel, establishment of 34-5

Jaffa 29n8, 52
Jaffa oranges 97
Jatt 62n12, 77, 168
Jerusalem, East 2, 6, 29n8, 49, 52, 54-5, 79, 89, 109n2, 117, 163
Jewish Agency 44, 61n18, 73
Jewishness 4, 31-2, 41, 45, 202
Jews, oriental 133-4
Jish 161

job opportunities 107, 142-5, 160
job security 118-19, 126
Jordan 164
Judaisation 40, 55, 203

Kadamani metal works 161, 174, 183, 193
Kinneret sub-district 49
Koor Chemicals Ltd. 168
Koor Industries 167-8
Koor Metals Ltd. 168

labour,
  East Jerusalem 117
  de-skilling 131
  demand for 38, 87-9, 114, 119, 122-3
  Jewish 31, 43, 122-3
  market 17, 122-3
  mobility/migration 1, 8-10, 17, 34, 42, 47, 67-8, 86, 107, 141-5, 154n6
  productivity 67, 105-8
  supply 87, 90, 122-3, 188
  surplus 68, 85-8, 113, 142
  unpaid family 84-5, 90, 129, 137
  West Bank and Gaza Strip 87-8, 123, 153n1
labour costs 195
labour exchanges 37, 118,
labour force characteristics 3-4, 34, 40, 42, 47, 113-15, 117-18, 157, 161, 177-9
land,
  arable/cultivated 66, 68, 72-3, 94-7, 103-6, 109n4, 109n5
  area (Palestine) 109n2
  area for town expansion 42
  classification/quality 72-5, 92
  communal *mushaa'* 68, 74
  consolidation 73, 75
  expropriation 2, 12, 37, 41, 61n10, 66, 109n5, 109n6, 111n28, 111n37
  fragmentation 66-8, 70, 74-5, 110n13, 111n28
  geographic distribution 72
  leased 42, 73, 111n21
  marginal 73, 97, 107, 111n37
  ownership 42, 66, 73, 185

245

land,
  reclamation 66, 70, 77-8, 82, 109n4
  sales 73, 158, 161
  shortage 42, 68, 74-5, 86, 109n7, 144-5, 158
Law for the Encouragement of Capital Investment 162
Lebanon, Palestinian refugees 67, 109n9
legal aspects 30, 41-3, 48, 60n1, 61, 82, 93, 99-101, 176, 179, 197
Lewis, W.A. 109n10, 130, 142
local associations 187-91
local authorities 43, 47, 57, 62n17, 188-90
localities, Arab 49, 52-3, 138, 141, 144, 163, 190
location quotient (LQ) analysis 103-5, 112n40, 149-50, 175
Lustick, I. 22-3, 26, 29n3
Lydda 29n8

Maalot/Tarshiha 29n8
Makhoul, N. 17-18, 122-3, 203
management, 167-8, 174, 181, 185
methodology 9, 13-14, 19, 21-2, 24-5, 205
Meyer-Brodnitz, M. 13, 185
migration (population) 52, 57, 61n5, 117
migration theory 142-3
military government 3, 9, 37-8, 66, 86, 118, 141, 153n1, 157
military service 41-2, 57, 137
Ministry of Agriculture 82, 100, 102, 110n15
minority status 9, 15-19, 21, 23, 35-40, 43-44, 66
Mix-and-share analysis 146-8
modern sector 11, 133, 172
modernisation 5, 9-13, 15-17, 42, 45, 58, 63n24, 67-8, 85, 89, 109n11, 198n1
municipalities 49, 52, 57, 62n17, 62n20
Myrdal, G. 27, 29n9, 48

national insurance payments 138
nationalism, economic 212
Nazareth 49, 52-3, 57, 62n20, 72, 76, 118, 168-9, 176-9, 207

Nazareth Labour Council 168
Negev 26, 49, 57, 62n21, 72-4, 84, 94, 98, 109n4, 110n17, 163
neo-populist strategies 210, 213, 215
non-profit societies 181
non-Zionist research 14-15, 17
Northern District 44, 49, 52

Ottoman Associations 191

participatory development 211-16
peasantry 12, 15-16, 19, 109n11
pensions 138
Peres, S. 163-4, 198n3
planning 43-5, 48, 56, 69-71, 181, 204-8, 210, 213-7
  territorial regional 213-14
Plans, Five Year 38, 43-5, 69-70, 110n22
policy,
  liberalisation 16, 38-9, 40-1, 142
  official Israeli 4, 11-14, 16, 19, 21, 24, 30, 35-43, 45, 47, 52-3, 57, 61n6, 61n9, 164-70, 187, 197, 200-2, 204, 208, 210, 217
  regional development 27-8, 29n9, 43-6, 162-3, 200-1, 204, 210-16
population 2-4, 9, 33-5, 49, 52-6, 60n3, 61n5, 117-8, 163
  expulsion 34-6
  rural 12, 33-4, 67-8, 89-90, 156-8, 163
pre-fabricated housing 174, 192
private sector 158, 166, 194, 215
production process 91-3, 130, 157, 172-5, 181, 186
productivity 67-8, 78, 105-8, 144-5, 207
professional associations 180
proletarianisation 15-19, 34, 86, 130-1, 143
protest, (Arab) 17-19, 37-9, 41, 59, 62n17, 69, 178, 190
public utilities 48, 52

Rahat 168
Ramleh 29n8, 52
recession, economic 33, 47, 115, 117-19, 122, 129, 141, 160, 183
Recognised Enterprise 162
refugees 35, 61n5, 65-61
region, Arab 25-8, 43-5, 48-9, 56-8, 60, 156, 197-8, 200-2, 207-8, 216-17
   economic 24-6
   functional 25
   homogenous, 25
   polarised 25-6
   programming 25-6
regional councils 49
regional development analysis 6, 24, 112n40, 146-52, 176, 201-3, 205-7, 213-15, 217n2, 218n4
regional-national relation 9, 15-16, 18-19, 21-3, 26-8, 46, 48, 103-8, 113-14, 122-3, 146-8, 152, 154n6, 155-6, 200-1, 203-5, 210
Registrar of Cooperatives 189
regulation, economic 93, 99-102, 190, 208-9
religious committees 191
religious/ethnic composition 55, 57-60
resource distribution 2, 37, 39-43, 74-8, 186, 213
roads 43, 52, 159, 189
Rosenfeld, H. 15-19, 29n5, 184, 203

Safad 35, 49
Sakhnin 168
sanitation 52, 189
Saudi Arabia 164
savings 67-9, 133, 138-9, 141, 182-4
Sayigh, R. 61n6
sector, Arab 9, 12-15, 19
Segev, T. 61n6
segmentation of Arab society 21, 179
segregation, residential 37-8, 52, 56-7, 61n11, 138, 141, 143-4, 203
self reliant development 212-13, 215
self-sufficiency 12, 193, 207, 212
services, public/personal 52, 145, 189-90, 196
settlements, Jewish 31, 39, 41, 46
Sharon, A. 192n2

Shefa'amr 52-3, 55, 62n12, 62n20, 168, 207
Smooha, S. 27
social aspects, Arab 11, 15-16, 18-19, 21-2, 24, 26, 28, 34, 48, 54-60, 63n22, 63n24, 70, 115, 191, 195-7, 199n9, 203-4, 216, 217n2
sociological model 17
spatial closure 202
spatial separatism 29n6, 217n2
specialisation (Arab) 95-8, 149-50, 175, 205
Standing, G. 143
steadfastness (sumoud) 202
stock market 181
sub-contracting 160, 166-7, 172-4, 179, 181, 183-6
subsidiaries (of non-Arab companies) 160-1, 167-8, 177, 179, 210
Supervised Credit Scheme 82

Taibeh 207
Tamra 53
taxation 70, 133, 138, 162-3, 179, 190
technological aspects 12, 39, 66-7, 79-84, 109n9, 175, 181, 213-14
Thon, U. 169
Tnuva, 99
Todaro, M. 142, 145
tourism 47
trade 2, 150-2, 158, 164, 168-9, 174, 183, 206-7
trade union system 119
traditionalism (Arab) 11-13, 15, 19, 22, 24, 58, 60, 67-9, 110n24, 159
transport and communication 60, 185, 188
Triangle 26, 49, 57, 62n12, 72, 74, 76-7, 79, 83, 90, 102, 109n11, 111n31

Umm al-Fahm 52-3, 57, 62n20, 167-8, 176-7, 207
UN Palestine Conciliation Commission 61n7
UN Palestine partition resoluton 34, 66
unemployment 35, 47, 67-8, 87-9, 118-19, 122, 129, 142
Union of Arab Local Authorities 62n17, 188, 190

Union of Druze Local Authorites 190
unit, economic 16, 23-4
　spatial/geographic 26
Upper Nazareth 26-7, 52, 62n11, 66
urban bias 215
urban pull 142, 145
urbanisation 17, 34, 63n22
usury 47

Village Studies Programme 142-3
voluntary bodies 191

water 70, 76-8, 110n25, 146-7, 175-6
Weimer, R. 36, 38
Weizmann, E. 40, 62n15, 198n3
West Bank and Gaza 2-3, 35, 39, 56, 61n9, 87-8, 123, 153n1, 156, 160, 175, 179-80, 184, 201, 218n4

Yalan E., 10
Yirka 161, 174
Yizre'el (sub-district) 49, 72
Yuval Gad Ltd 168

Zarhi, S. and Achziera, A. 8, 10, 71
Zionist movement 31-2, 35-6, 39-40
Zionist political economy 8-18, 29, 43, 198n1
zoning, industrial 47, 165, 197
　town 22, 42, 52
Zureik, E. 18-20, 33, 203